'A complete guide to dating, from online swiping to starting a relationship. Very handy for seasoned daters or anyone venturing into their Tinder years with trepidation. It's the dating guide I wish I'd had when I was single. Fascinating!'
 — Laura Price, author of *Single Bald Female*

100 Dates

The Psychologist Who Kissed
100 Frogs so You Don't Have To

Dr Angela Ahola

Translation by Johnathan Daily

bluebird
books for life

First published 2021 by Sapiens Publishing, Stockholm
First published in the UK in paperback 2023 by Bluebird
an imprint of Pan Macmillan
The Smithson, 6 Briset Street, London EC1M 5NR
EU representative: Macmillan Publishers Ireland Ltd, 1st Floor,
The Liffey Trust Centre, 117–126 Sheriff Street Upper,
Dublin 1, D01 YC43
Associated companies throughout the world
www.panmacmillan.com

ISBN 978-1-0350-0027-2

1 3 5 7 9 8 6 4 2

A CIP catalogue record for this book is available from the British Library.

Typeset by Palimpsest Book Production Ltd, Falkirk, Stirlingshire
Printed and bound by CPI Group (UK) Ltd, Croydon, CR0 4YY

Visit **www.panmacmillan.com/bluebird** to read more about all our books
and to buy them. You will also find features, author interviews and
news of any author events, and you can sign up for e-newsletters
so that you're always first to hear about our new releases.

To my family.
And all of you who have so generously
shared your experiences with me.
Thank you.

We accept the love we think we deserve.
The Perks of Being a Wallflower
BY STEPHEN CHBOSKY

Contents

Why *one hundred* dates?

Single life can be fantastic. There's no need to compromise, no risk of getting hurt. And yet few human beings ever stop scanning for potential partners – we've evolved with our radar permanently switched on. We check folks out in the bar, at work, and at the gym, and most singles have at least one dating app. The problem these days is that dating can easily turn into a part-time job. According to the stats, 67 per cent of singles say their dating lives aren't going well and 75 per cent think it's difficult to find people to date.[1] We spend more time than we'd like on our dating apps yet, despite our best efforts, our results come up short. Things feel dead in the water, our self-confidence wavers, and we delete the app out of mounting frustration. Then a little time goes by . . . and we download it again.

Dreams of romance, visions of finding a soulmate, linger on. I suspect that most of you probably feel the way I do – that single life should be fun! Whether you're out for intimacy and sex, a relationship, or just a little attention, dating should be exciting, efficient, and give you what you're looking for. It ought to feel like a stroll in the park on a pleasant evening in early summer, when the air is tingling with anticipation.

My name is Angela Ahola. I am a doctor of psychology, an avid researcher and author of *Your Hidden Motives* and *The Art of Making an Impression*. When I found myself single again after a long relationship, I realized that nothing about the contemporary dating world is easy to interpret. There's a slew of unspoken rules, concepts, and expressions to be aware of, and a great deal of psychology to contend with. But since the very first day that I decided to start meeting people, I've been dating. Although every book requires some research, and performing experiments is nothing new to me, this research really took the cake – I've played every role myself in this particular project. I led the experiment but was also its test subject. I've downloaded the dating apps and swiped away countless hours, experimenting with different profile pics and bio texts. I maximized the age range of my potential dates, from 18 to 100, and matched with a wide variety of people. I've gone on genuine dates all over Sweden, from urban Stockholm to the pastoral countryside, from the far north to the far south, and even across the Baltic to Helsinki in Finland. I've texted with thousands of people, testing various opening strategies such as GIFs, emojis, and a zillion forms of 'How's it goin'?', as well as waiting to let the other person initiate the conversation. I've met guys down at the bar, on cruises, in my job and at speed-dating events, and many well-intentioned friends and relatives tried to hook me up with someone too, of course. From matching and chatting, to first dates and post-date contact, I've recorded statistics regarding my experiences, and analysed and tested the entire process from the ground up. I've been in situations that looked good on paper – they were pleasant, and not much else. I've felt everything from anticipation and hope to sadness and even futility as I've navigated the emotional uncertainties that dating entails.

I titled this book *100 Dates* because – combined with extensive scientific research, interviews with other daters, and my 10,000 matches – it is the result of my own series of dates with over one hundred different individuals. Going on those hundred dates was certainly a challenge, but obviously this has also been an exciting and educational adventure.

This book is aimed at everyone. For simplicity's sake, the pronouns *she*, *he*, and *they* have been chosen at random. While my research relates to my own dating experience, I've tried to make sure that the results for any given example are applicable across sexual orientation.

So why 100?

I wanted to ensure that I'd experience a full spectrum of the situations we encounter in the dating game. That being said, I still dismissed individuals to whom I felt no attraction. This was legit, the real deal. I met some of my dates several times, while many I only went on one date with. I've met city dwellers and country fellers, students, the self-employed, career jockeys, and guys still trying to figure out what to be. A few were stuck on auto-speak and others were quiet types. Extroverts, introverts, tell-it-alls, secret-keepers, the compliant, the dominant, the alphas, and the team players. Some greeted me nervously at first. I've met men who I had a great deal in common with, and I've been on dates that nearly finished before they started. I even got catfished, ending up on a date with a guy who had used someone else's photos. Imagine my shock as I stepped through that door to be greeted by a different face! I've been on dates in coffee shops, bars and restaurants, on piers and in people's homes, and have enjoyed picnics and long walks. Some dates went great, some not so great, and I've met people with completely different life goals. I've gone on dates without any expectations which turned out fantastically, and on dates with high expectations that bellyflopped completely. I have, for a very long time, been *living* this dating experiment. I was single, I began dating, and my emotions have been fully engaged – no holds barred. Had I stumbled into true love on my tenth date, it would have ended there.

The factors that affect human attraction – what two people like about each other, for instance, and which psychological mechanisms function as clickbait – have all been researched. I've pulled out all the stops searching for optimal ways of attracting others and will teach you all about it: trigger words, which attributes strike us as charismatic, and how the psychological phenomenon of *mirroring* affects dating.

Single life doesn't have to be a drawn-out, tedious wait for that dream catch; you ought to be out there enjoying yourself! You can't predict when you'll bump into the right one, and what if this is the last time you'll be single for the rest of your life? Shouldn't you make the most of it? Create memories, meet whoever you want, and don't let the fear of disappointment hold you back. Be appreciative of each person you meet and the lessons they have to offer. Enjoy it while it lasts, and know that you're (in one way or another) probably getting one step closer to that Big Love. Have fun with the flirting, and also learn to recognize when it's time to ditch the apps.

One thing I'm sure of is that you'll sense when you've met the right one – no one needs to read a book to figure *that* out. On the other hand, you need to know *how* to get to that first date with a good person in the first place. And you may need a few new tools for improving your odds of scoring a *second* date. We need to know how to respond when asked, 'What are you looking for here?' to avoid friend-zoning our date, despite the fact that we want more out of them. And how do we re-ignite flirtation? There'll be no second date if the chemistry isn't there. Should you or they initiate contact after your first date, and how soon should you meet up again so that it doesn't peter out? Which texts keep that fire alive? Racy photos – what's the best way to manage *that* whole situation? Also, I'll teach you about three categories of daters. (Heads-up! One of these should be avoided.)

One major challenge you face is this: dating apps have distorted our impression of reality – we believe there are endless hordes of potential partners running around out there, just waiting for us to snatch them up. We can swipe and swipe until our fingerprints rub off, enraptured by the illusion of it all. It's like a warehouse of singletons, and those bygone days when you only had three odd villagers to choose from are long gone. ('Better snap up ol' Jonas quick . . . What if Anna grabs him first?') As a result, we've grown shallower and more nitpicky – we objectify more. We're hastier at severing contact with folks over tiny misses, like mixing up the word order in a text, or if they don't ask us the right questions.

The catch-22 here is that you've got a whole lot of other faces clouding your vision. The competition can be overwhelming – we're like snowflakes in a blizzard, or sand in the Sahara. We can't see the wood for the trees and soon enough the lonely nights start piling up. Evenings get ground down chatting and swiping instead of getting our hearts stoked on romantic dates with great people. *This is why you need to take control of the signals that you're sending* – at each and every level of dating. You've got to nail that first impression so that it stands out and sticks around. Dating well is an art. And dating that leads to results? Gear up for the big leagues!

Please allow me to offer you all my best advice, advice that I'm sure will enhance your success. Whether you're looking for your dream partner, a little appreciation, or just a companion for those long winter evenings, keep these words close to your heart:

When nothing is certain, everything is possible.

Introduction

When I first became single, I was churning with mixed emotions: I wanted to date, yet I didn't want to date. I was content being single and not in the market for something new, at least not yet. Still . . . curiosity kept tickling me.

Let's examine why we search for love in the first place.

Why is our radar on?

What is it we're longing for?

To begin with, as a species, human beings have evolved to be social and are naturally drawn to groups. For example, it's said that folks are generally more afraid of speaking in front of large audiences than they are of death. Public speaking feels dangerous because getting rejected by a vast crowd is an intimidating risk. What if everyone judges us as worthless, and all at the same time? That's an intimidating thought because, for our ancestors, exclusion was essentially a death sentence.[1] But for members of a group, life became easier: everyone had greater access to a larger number of potential partners, could share food and child-raising responsibilities, and could help keep the fire going.

A significant portion of our feelings – everything from ecstatic happiness to intense pain and anguish – is linked to our relationships. A relationship can allow us to experience mind-blowing rapture, yet that very same relationship, should it come to an end, can also make life feel utterly devoid of meaning. It hurts, exactly as it's supposed to, because these feelings are hardly an accident. They have aided our survival: we're *supposed* to care about other people, and social pain is *real* pain.[2] We're *supposed* to attach to other people. We should *want* to keep our children safe nearby. We should *want* to have friends and to stay engaged socially.[3] Having people around who are important to us infuses our lives with a sense of meaning, and we relax together with other people. Due to our inherent social nature, our brains enter into a relaxed state when we're spending time with the people we're close to, conserving energy. The closer the relationship, the less energy required; we save the most energy in the company of people we trust. We're unable to achieve this effect if we're constantly meeting new people. Hanging out with an ever-changing roster of different individuals is less rewarding than repeatedly meeting up with the same individual.[4] Who hasn't found themselves feeling drained after a full day at a convention, or after mingling at a drinks party?

Having someone important in our lives who we don't get to meet regularly is also a dissatisfying scenario; we humans have a basic need to belong to one another.[5] Now that human life expectancy has been dramatically extended, is it perhaps time to ask ourselves whether it would suit us to stay with one person until the end of our days, or if a series of partners would perhaps be better? Or even seeing more than one person at the same time?

Will a partner make you happy?

Do we really need a *partner* to satisfy our social needs? What is it about romantic relationships that differentiates them from other relationships?

For starters, most of us seeking romantic relationships are probably doing it for emotional intimacy. Or perhaps you'd like to start a family. We harbour the hope that someone is going to love us in our entirety – warts, scars, flaws, and all; we seek the feeling of total acceptance. We're prepared to face disappointments, boring dates, and those painful break-ups because, if everything works out just right, we'll find that one person who made it all worthwhile. It's as if an invisible force is compelling us to find someone. A romantic relationship is the closest we adults can come to re-experiencing the depth of the relationship we had with our parents as children (in a best-case scenario). Further along in the book, we'll spend some time looking at potential obstacles that can trip us up on our way towards finding these special relationships.

What do we hope a partner will bring to our life?

A dating site asked its members: 'Why are you looking for love? What is your personal reason for wanting a partner?' They received a bunch of different answers. Some folks said they were looking for hope.[6] Another wrote:

My life wouldn't really be happy without love. I just know that I need that kind of romantic intimacy in order to truly feel meaning in it. Love is the missing puzzle piece that makes my life complete.

Others focused on having someone to share experiences with, such as decorating the Christmas tree, cooking food, or just lying around in bed watching a movie together. Someone to send a photo of the sunset to, or maybe to have children with. One response read:

Searching for love is more about finding someone who it's worth sharing all of the wonderful things in life with, on a level that friends don't reach. And don't forget how it feels to come home to an open embrace. Someone to comfort you on those days when nothing seems to go your way. I'm looking for love because life is just too short to waste, and life is best when I get to share it with someone wonderful. Someone who I can share laughter with, but at the same time the heavier moments in life, too. Someone who brings out the warmest feelings in me with only a smile. I want to be someone's.

Another response:

I'm looking for love because it's one of those beautiful things in life that we can't recreate or pretend to have. It has to be for real. We can't force it into existence, and we can't make it all alone. It has to be genuine.

So, searching for love is a deep-seated inner need.

Having a special person in our lives is, generally speaking, different from just having friends. People in positive romantic relationships enjoy better health,[7] recover from illnesses more quickly,[8] and live longer.[9] Close and satisfying relationships are one of the most powerful determinants of our happiness,[10] while loneliness and poor relationships, on the other hand, are linked to an increased risk of depression and illness.[11] Romantic relationships are likewise linked to feelings of euphoria, connection, and inspiration[12] – the feeling that everything is A-OK, all's well with the world. Infatuation affects our neurochemical compounds: studies from China have revealed a unique reaction that occurs in the reward centres in our brains when we're shown pictures of our loved ones.[13]

A new contract

Until relatively recently in the long course of human history, we've been coerced by external circumstances to commit ourselves to long relationships, and intimacy was often more of a pleasant bonus effect. We face a different situation these days: modern society has opened up opportunities for living alone, and it's also become an option to avoid the pain of love. Should we choose, we can pretty much just dismiss intimacy if it's associated with too many heavy and painful emotions.

Proportionally, there are more single households today than there have ever been. For thousands of years it was taken for granted that people would live together, but in the western world single households became more common during the middle of the last century due to numerous political and cultural shifts, and that trend can now be witnessed globally. In Sweden, single households have established themselves as the most common form of habitation.[14]

So how did we end up like this? In a nutshell, because we *can*. Most of us can easily make our way through life without a partner. Many of us no longer struggle with the same logistic or economic dependencies that previously 'forced' us together. It's expensive to live alone, so a society requires minimum levels of prosperity and security before this option becomes reasonably viable on a large scale. Birth control helps us to prevent the unwanted pregnancies that have otherwise denied women their independence, and romantic relationships are a voluntary union – we *choose* whether or not we want to get in the game. We can choose temporary hook-ups too, or just go on pleasant dates without any heightened expectations. This increase in single households has been one of the most significant societal shifts in modern times, according to Eric Klinenberg, Professor of Sociology at New York University. Now let's get this straight: not everyone who lives alone is single. But the trend seems pretty obvious, and those who choose to live alone give many reasons for doing so, such as freedom, control over their own lives, the opportunity for self-realization, and voluntary isolation. Many people would like to find their feet in a new life after they've come out of a relationship, to find their way back to themselves. Gender equality is another contributing factor – when women are politically and economically free, the statistics reveal it: people marry later and divorce more often, which results in more people living alone. At the same time, most of us don't live alone throughout our lives – it's often contingent on which phase of life we find ourselves in. And, as opinions about living alone have grown more positive, so many people now live alone that it's become commonplace. Perhaps this signals greater freedom and individual strength? In precisely the same way that internet dating went mainstream, there's no longer anything shameful about being single.

Since we increasingly live alone these days, how is it affecting us? For a long time we believed that loneliness, as a condition, primarily affects the human psyche, but today we know that it also leads to physical illness. Loneliness can even lead to death.[15] That being said, it's important to distinguish *voluntary* isolation from *forced* isolation. Many singles with the means to do so live alone voluntarily, enjoying life on their own terms. They're most likely far from lonely: many have children, friends, and family – just not a partner (a fact they might see as a relief). Isolation can have negative consequences, it's true, but it's *forced* isolation that carries with it an increased risk for cardiovascular disease and premature death. We experience pain more intensely when we're alone than when we're not, and the stress hormones that activate the brain's pain system can harm us. Simply put, it was *togetherness* that became humankind's secret for success. We experience things that benefit our survival as positive, so when having a bit of company around caused our ancestors' brains to release neurochemical substances providing them with a sense of well-being, they naturally repeated the behaviour. This *conditioning* explains why we feel motivated to seek out contact with others – from the day we're born till the day we die.

Does love find us once we stop looking for it?

Several studies have shown that very little is necessary for a human relationship to form. (Which almost sounds like an insult to anyone who's spent years dating and still hasn't landed someone, right?) Allow me to explain: the mere fact of living close to one another is often all that's required for human beings to form social bonds. Other research has shown that we tend to like just about anybody we spend enough time with – even in situations with people we didn't like previously.[16] When two individuals have experienced a difficult situation together, it often leads to increased emotional ties between them. This might seem a bit contradictory, considering that the fundamental idea behind conditioning is that positive associations promote attraction. The researchers Latande, Eckman, and Joy found instead that those study participants who experienced electrical shocks together tended to like each other more than those who had been shocked individually.[17] This same phenomenon can be seen in military personnel who have faced heavy combat together. The fact that two people can develop a bond with one another in connection to frightening circumstances carries two explanations: 1) a kind of emotional mix-up occurs (*misattribution*) that causes us to experience the exhilaration of fear as a form of attraction, and 2) the presence of another person reduces our level of discomfort – in which case the positive emotional relief becomes associated with whoever happens to be in close proximity.[18] (Do we really want to take on challenging activities on that first date, if this is the case?)

And that thing about love suddenly popping up out of nowhere like an unexpected postcard, does that work? Here I'm afraid I'll have to answer both yes and no. The reason for my ambivalence is this: when we really desire something, we send out vibes of desperation – that we *need* the other person. And that isn't attractive; in fact, it signals poor self-esteem. So it's important that we don't view every date as 'The One'. Relaxed vibes that say 'I'm pretty happy with the way things are' are far more enticing. When you focus on your own goals, needs, interests, and personal development, you radiate self-confidence, and self-confidence is attractive! That being said, behaving complacently when it comes to dating (just sitting around at home) is the number one way for nothing to happen. We'll never get the ball if we don't even step onto the pitch.

Dating as an experiment

Dating is an experiment in its own right, and arranging dates with romantic candidates is a process of trial and error. We hang out a bit, get to know each other a little, and then decide whether this person seems appropriate for us: are we a match? Certain traits are visible, such as physical attractiveness. Others are not, unfortunately, and a person's character can take more time to figure out. However, having insight into these issues can determine whether you get out of a bad situation in time, before you're paying for mortgages, cars, and puppies together. Or ensure that you don't miss a good one.

What factors are important to consider when judging potential dates? Obviously, it's important to us to find ourselves reasonably equal to our partner in certain aspects. These might be attractiveness,[19] intelligence, economic views, or our values or life goals – we seek out similarities. Other aspects of our personalities, however, pair better when they're *dissimilar*. In those instances, we complement one another (you'll learn more about this later on in the book). Many people also contend that we all have a 'soulmate' out there, but that concept brings drawbacks with it, which again I'll discuss later.

The most common way to find a partner these days is over the internet (23 per cent).[20] The next most common ways are through friends (21 per cent), the workplace (14 per cent), in bars (13 per cent), and at dinner events or parties (8 per cent). Of course, there are other situations in which we meet people, for example at university, on a dance course, or through some other pastime, but the internet has now taken pole position as a meeting point (even if these statistics vary from country to country). And once we finally started dating online, we were ready to invest a whole lot of time in it. We check the popular dating app Tinder between 9 and 11 times per day[21] – 62 per cent of users are men; 38 per cent are women.[22] Now, a more surprising stat: 54 per cent of the users on Tinder are single, 12–30 per cent are *already* in a relationship (!), and 3 per cent are divorced singles. (These numbers are likely to vary from country to country.) There are even niche dating apps designed for 'cheaters' – participants who often book their dates during working hours and manage to pick up the kids from school and get home in time for dinner, doing whatever it takes to keep their established partner unaware. Then there are certain dating apps primarily intended for folks only looking for brief hook-ups, and others specifically for people into BDSM (bondage/discipline/ dominance/submission).

I should also point out that there are some more concerning truths regarding online dating, and there's a pretty good chance you may have stumbled across a few of these. According to a survey of over 1,000 internet daters in the US and UK,[23] 53 per cent admitted to lying – most often regarding their appearance (many used younger photos of themselves), but also their employment, usually by falsely representing how successful they are (that they have a better job, for instance). In an earlier study, sociologist Ervin Goffman showed that we actively try to manage how others see us,[24] a phenomenon referred to as *impression management*. All of this deception tends to diminish with age, however. Is this because we become more comfortable revealing our true selves, and less prone towards ideal-izing? Yet another problem with dating apps is that the men looking for temporary hook-ups far outnumber the women. This often messes up the gears of the apps (more on that in a bit).

Appearances often determine who we approach in bars and nightclubs, and we generally strive to sparkle a bit brighter ourselves when meeting others. Especially for a party, or when we're in the mood for a flirt – we know full well that this ups our chances of getting someone's tail to twitch.

So how do dating apps work when it comes to attraction? Your appearance carries a lot of weight here too. Yet we're not just being superficial as we sit there flipping through each others' photos, trying to figure out if we're physically compatible. We're also trying to get a sense of whether we'll be *socially* compatible. We ask ourselves, 'Do I have anything in common with this person?' We notice their clothing style, posture, facial expressions, and so on. We evaluate – even if only subconsciously – whether this is a Cosy Rosie into folding napkins, or a Jukebox Jimmy out to paint the town. How self-confident or dominant is this person? Certain individuals are clueless that they're coming across as superficial. A picture of a guy holding a drink in a nightclub sends completely different signals to a picture of the same man holding a cat on a sofa, and yet another signal if he's lying on a sunny beach reading a spy thriller. We draw immediate conclusions, and a single photo can broadcast hundreds of signals.

There's more. We've also got dating apps that are supposed to match us up with our most viable candidates. These function through the workings of diverse algorithms: we provide facts about ourselves which are used to pair us up. Eli J. Finkel, a professor of social psychology at Northwestern University, claims that these 'solutions'[25] are nothing but snake oil. According to him, you won't find any relationship researchers who consider them to be scientifically credible when it comes to finding Mr Right. The dating sites that employ these algorithms contest this statement, of course, but Finkel spent a year investigating the algorithms, evaluating them against eighty years of research on dating and attraction. His conclusion? The evidence fails to verify the claims that these matchmaking services work. (Sorry!) Matchmaking is a thorny field in general. In one study,[26] over one hundred variables, traits, and preferences were employed to determine whether two people could be matched up. The result? It doesn't work. We can increase the odds of pairing up folks who are attracted to one another, but nothing more than that. Coupledom only works when we feel mutual attraction *and* we sync in everyday life, and matching on both levels just doesn't happen very often. Researchers speculate that attraction – which occurs the moment two people meet – is essentially unforeseeable; it's like a spontaneous chemical reaction that's mysteriously set off by the right combination of personalities.

Not everything in life fits neatly into little scientific boxes or specimen jars, and love, personal chemistry, and attraction still seem to retain a veil of mystique.

All of this means that online dating can feel like tiptoeing through a minefield at times, a place where no one is trustworthy and you're forced to sleep with one eye open. (OK, maybe I'm being a *tad* dramatic . . .) And let's not forget about *this* mirage: 'There are sooooo many people out there – I swipe and I swipe and it just goes on forever . . .' If there are, then how come we never seem to give anyone a chance? It's like trying to pick a movie to watch when faced with too many choices, and you end up just going to bed instead. Psychologists refer to this phenomenon[27] as *choice overload* (or *overchoice*),[28] a term first coined by Alvin Toffer in his book *Future Shock*.[29] Having too many options and the potential outcomes that ensue quite simply throws a spanner in our cognitive gears, overwhelming our decision-making process, and this increases the odds of us choosing poorly. Whew! This is a tough spot to find yourself in, because whether consciously or not (it's just how our brains think), we suddenly feel the urge to weigh up hordes of (equally qualified) candidates against each other, one by one, so that we can filter out the best of the best. Our satisfaction with the potential number of alternatives follows a bell curve:[30] we dislike only having a few alternatives, but having *several* alternatives increases our satisfaction,[31] peaking at between 5 and 9 choices. As the number of alternatives expands beyond this golden number (in other words, you start getting too many potential dates on the dating site) our satisfaction decreases, slowly becoming replaced by frustration and confusion. In a well-known experiment conducted in a grocery store,[32] participants got to see a shelf of jam samples. One shelf held 24 different varieties of jam, and the other only 6 types of jam. There was a 50 per cent greater chance of participants stopping at the shelf with 24 jars; however, there was a 10 per cent greater chance of customers *purchasing* jam from the narrower selection than from the wider one (30 per cent vs 3 per cent). Smaller 'arrays' are more in line with the mechanics of our human psyche.

Studies also show that the design of most dating apps, comparing various candidates side by side, contributes to us going into *comparison mode*, also referred to as an *assessment mindset*.[33] We become more critical under these circumstances, comparing our potential dates against a backdrop of candidates.[34] The alternative, in which one choice is presented at a time, is referred to as *locomotion mindset*.[35] Here, we're inclined to ponder our various candidates more deeply. The plethora of options we're faced with when dating online also leads to us objectifying potential partners. Dating turns into an online marketplace,[36] very different from meeting at a pub or dinner party, and causes our minds to weigh up the benefits, disadvantages, profits, and expenses of each candidate in a sort of equation,[37] all while we run a calculated prognosis of how we *believe* a relationship with each candidate would work out. In speed-dating experiments,[38] it's also been observed that the greater the number of alternatives available, the lazier we become as decision-makers. With a great many potential candidates, we allow ourselves to be guided by more superficial and easily observable attributes. A person's appearance, height, or weight, for instance, as opposed to their internal attributes (which we can't see, of course, but about which we could form an idea if we tried). We become more judgemental and demanding when faced with a whole slew of potential dates,[39] more so than when meeting face to face. Online dating causes us to manage our time poorly too,[40] spending too much time on profiles that aren't good matches for us and less time on those that are. We wander off-track and grow less satisfied with our options.

The reason? Too many alternatives!

This too-many-alternatives problem[41] leads us to say no more easily than yes: we try to weed out as many lesser options as we can. Yet we still feel less satisfied with our choices afterwards,[42] because we wonder if we're not missing a diamond in all that dust. We humans tend to try to leave our options open, even when this behaviour might sabotage our current situation.[43]

I think you can see what I'm driving at: online dating is a challenge and our psychological processing just isn't in line with it – we ain't cut out for the job. Another thing: the selection offered by dating apps makes us less interested in committing to a parter.[44] 'Why settle? A better version's only a swipe away!' We've discussed this phenomenon a little already, but the picture darkens further – this affects us even *after* we've found love. When we see so many gorgeous heartthrobs waiting in the wings, we experience our partner as less compelling, resulting in less commitment, more dissatisfaction, and a greater number of break-ups.[45] Bad news, right? Yet if we experience the number of alternatives as *few* instead of many, we're more inclined to view our partner in a positive light, to harbour more positive illusions about them. The greater our opportunities for changing our minds, the more finicky we generally become. On the other hand, if we perceive a choice as permanent and irrevocable, we tend to be more at peace with it – 'The dice have been rolled, so let's make the best of it.' If we believe that the consequences of our choices can't be undone, then trying to accept them and be content is a natural defence mechanism. So we tend to prefer our freedom, but it comes at a price. *Maximizers*[46] in particular feel worse when facing a greater number of choices. They strive to sift out the best of the best, comparing as many alternatives as possible and setting the bar high. These folks are also often disappointed even after they've chosen. They're hesitant, focusing on what they haven't got instead of what they have. *Satisficers*, on the other hand, are more satisfied with their choices, whether we're talking about a car, an ice cream, or a life partner. They're pretty much satisfied the moment an alternative that fulfils their basic requirements shows up. Once they've got their selection in their hand, they feel no need to keep looking – they don't need to have the best to feel satisfied. Unfortunately, maximizing goes hand in hand with less happiness or optimism, lower self-esteem, and less satisfaction with life in general. Maximizers are often depressed, perfectionistic, and angst-ridden. This is despite the fact that their decision-making process improves their odds of finding better alternatives! When it comes to dating, we should try to stay balanced between being a satisficer (*Sure, I don't have everything I want but the important bits are there*) and a maximizer (*Is there someone better out there?*). Always thinking that the grass is greener leads to rejecting everyone and everything, and your relationships and partners will suffer if you've always got one eye looking else-where. Neither should you just take anybody who comes along without any kind of screening process.

We're *all* small fish in the dating ocean; the next person is only one swipe away. We send out a hundred hearts, funny GIFs, and 'Wassup?'s and get back . . . *nada*. After a few days of this, it starts getting pretty easy to hear what the world's trying to tell you: you are getting outshone.[47]

Allow me to wrap up with a study that points out one of the positive aspects of online dating. This study has revealed that marriages that originated online showed (despite everything) greater stability than those begun offline.[48] The researcher hypoth-esizes that things probably turn out this way because, through dating online, we're able to be more selective, leading to us making better choices in partners. Also, it's believed that online daters are more certain that they're seeking a relationship, as opposed to just accidentally falling into one. That alone may be a reason why these relationships can be more successful. Given the situation we're dealing with, I only hope that we can be sensible enough to hold tight to those quality relationships, and avoid the classic pitfall of seeking greener pastures over the fence.

We've determined that human beings both seek out and need

one another. We hope to gain the emotional intimacy that a romantic relationship can offer us. It's become increasingly common to find each other over the net, and that's a rough path to follow in a lot of ways. But that being said, if you're signing up to an app, it means you're now ready to dive into the exciting jungle of online dating, where the (potential) trophy of landing that love of your life awaits you! Or maybe it's just time for some physical intimacy or the warm glow of a little affirmation. Whatever you need, once you've finished reading this book, you'll be able to improve your chances of meeting those special someones.

Let's DO this! 😎

Part I
BEFORE YOU MEET

1: Mr Right or Mr Right Now?

Or Ms Right vs Ms Right Now, right?

The first question you'll need to ask yourself is 'What am I looking for?' This is a critical knot, and worth untangling. Knowing what you're looking for underpins your ability to search for it.

The three types of daters

There are three main categories[1] of daters.[2] Some are looking for a new partner, someone to couple up with. Others are looking for casual sex. There's also a group out there merely looking for entertainment or confirmation.[3] (Getting right-swiped feels good – it's nice to know that someone's out there making eyes at you.) We feel less alone when we have a lot of internet contacts;[4] however, 'confirmation' daters are seldom interested in meeting up IRL (in real life). There are even folks merely looking for new acquaintances, such as younger adults who've recently moved to a new area, but since groups like these are statistically insignificant, we'll stay focused on our three main categories.

Ask yourself this important question: which of these three types are you?

Once you've figured that out, things will be much easier for you. This allows you to tailor your profile to fit your ambitions: the right pics, the right profile bio, which interests to mention, and how to reply when asked flat-out, 'What are you looking for here?' How to bait your hook, in other words, so you can send out the right signals to attract the kind of people *you're* interested in.

Sifting the wheat from the chaff

You'll hear the question 'What are you looking for here?' over and over. The next important question to consider is whether you and this new match share the same goals. There's an effective method for finding this out: ask! A vital dating skill that you need to develop is the ability to quickly figure out just *who is who*. Allow me a moment here to describe our three types of daters in a bit more detail, to help you more easily separate the wheat from the chaff:

Confirmation Seekers. These individuals want confirmation, nothing more. They're often busy bees on the web, and seduce you with fool's gold when you stumble across them. They'll switch you over to a different app or two, chat away all friendly-like, maybe swap a pic or two. Regular pics, sure, but don't be surprised to get some naughty stuff here as well. The thing is, after a while, things just don't add up . . . They never want to meet up IRL. You try to set up a simple phone call and they say, 'I'm more of a texter, not really into the phone thing . . .' For this group, dating is mostly a fun way to pass the time. Fact is, some of these folks are *already* in relationships . . .

Research supports the beneficial effects of *confirmation*. Receiving signals of approval from others holds an important role in our sense of well-being. In one experiment,[5] participants were given 'greetings' written by close friends or family to read. When they read positively charged emotional messages, such as 'You are the only person who cares more about me than yourself', the reward centres in their brains were activated, as opposed to their reaction to objective statements, such as 'You have brown hair.' That specific study researched messages written by loved ones. But what about strangers? Do their opinions induce the same effect? Surprisingly enough, they do. A related study[6] exposed participants to images of unfamiliar faces on a screen. They were first shown a portrait and then informed that the subject of the photo wanted to chat with them. When participants found out that this stranger wanted to chat, it activated the reward centres in their brains – *whether or not* they desired to chat with the stranger in question. So even strangers we *don't* want to hang out with give us a warm, fuzzy feeling when they tell us they like us.

If you're *not* just out for a little online confirmation, a pen pal, or a way to liven up lonely evenings at home, then forget these little fish – despite the pleasant rush you feel when they nibble your line. How can we identify these small fry in the first place? The solution here is to book a date ASAP (after you've texted enough to know if it's worth it). That tends to be the solution to most issues, by the way. If too much water passes under the bridge before you get that date sorted, you'll watch a 'relationship' run out of steam.

1NS (One-Night Stands). The second group consists of folks primarily focused on casual sex – flings, quick hook-ups. These daters use a lot of code words. *Netflix and chill* definitely advertises a date where underwear is optional. The premise: we hook up at your place or mine, and then wham, bam, thank you, Sam.

A study researching gender differences regarding online dating behaviour[7] on Tinder asked men and women to state what they were seeking through the app. Participants were given five options: 1) I use Tinder to look at profiles; 2) I use Tinder to chat with people online; 3) I use Tinder to find a partner; 4) I use Tinder for casual dating; and 5) I use Tinder for one-night stands. They were then asked to rank these in order of importance, with 5 representing the most important and 1 the least important. According to the results, 49 per cent of male respondents rated 'I use Tinder for one-night stands' as 4 or 5, compared to just 15 per cent of women. (If you're a woman who's been dating men on Tinder for a while, I doubt this comes as a surprise.)

The challenge is that, in the dating apps, all these conflicting attitudes are thrown together in one big, sloppy mix. The apps' inability to differentiate between the intentions of their users leads to many mismatches between people looking for quite different things. The stats reveal how many of our matches turn out to be awkward dead ends: 73 per cent of dating singles have estimated that 10 per cent or fewer of their matches result in real-world meet-ups. (And these figures are virtually identical among men and women.) When one sees figures like those, it's hardly surprising that one of the most common questions asked on the apps is: 'What are you looking for here?'

In the beginning, I always replied: 'I've just got out of a long relationship and I'm probably not really ready for a new one, but dating sounds like fun.' I was thinking, 'Wouldn't it be nice to meet up for a walk, or a cup of coffee, you know . . . Get to know a few new people, see if there's some chemistry there?' But nine times out of ten, my answer was interpreted as: 'So you're lookin' to brush out the ol' cobwebs, eh, firecracker?'

Sometimes this question pops up: 'Where do you want to meet?' Between the lines, what they're really asking is if you want to meet up in public or in private. Your date also wants to get an idea about what you're expecting. This is a way for them to figure out if they've got a 1NS cooking or whether you're looking for something different. If someone asks 'Wanna meet up?', I sometimes reply 'What did you have in mind?' This way I can check what their intentions are. If they answer me with something like, 'A nightcap,' then I know that they just want sex, which makes it easier for me to decide.

It's important to be in control of your dating and avoid undesirable situations. If the 1NS daters aren't for you, then make sure you are very clear about this in your bio text *and* in your pre-date communication. (It can be as easy as writing 'Not open for 1NS,' 'Looking for a serious relationship,' or 'Searching for true love.') 1NS daters make up a very large group online, so *you* need to take charge: be the director of this play, not just an actor. If you're only interested in meeting up for sex right now, be clear about that too. Keeping things honest and safe is important for everyone.

Relationship Seekers. Our third group is looking for long-term partnerships. If this is you, then you need to target your audience the same way that confirmation seekers and 1NSers do, and filter out who you're looking for.

Perhaps you're looking for more than one of these types, or even open to all of them – it may depend on your current prospects, for instance. Maybe Ms Right is your ultimate goal, but Ms Right Now will do for the moment. It's good to know that you can always answer 'What are you looking for here?' like this: 'I'd like to meet up with you, and we'll see how it goes from there.' Or even: 'Meeting new people is always fun, and who knows? You never know where things might lead.'

Date like The Bachelor

Swipe right or left? Who's in, who's out? It's easy to get nitpicky when faced with so many choices. You brood over every profile, wondering things like: 'Will we sync?' 'What if this one's an asshole?' 'Do I *really* think she's hot?'

Here's the rub: it's going to be a real drag if you keep your filter cranked up to 11, jamming every candidate through your mental wringer before you swipe or text. It'll take you forever to pick out the right candidates, and the love express will be gone by the time you've packed a suitcase. Plus, you'll be missing out on unexpected pleasures such as the interesting companions you can meet along the dating trail. Get out there and meet some people! This is a *numbers game* – wanna sell some cars? Most folks are looking, not buying, so more visitors = more sales. This is no different. A lot of pieces need to fall into place before you meet up with someone IRL. You have to like them, sure, but it's important that they like you too. Right?

Perhaps you're newly single and you just don't know what kind of person you'd like. We're all different, with different tastes. (What a relief, right?) One of the most important lessons that my dating journey has taught me is to know myself, what's important to me. What attributes do I appreciate about a date? I've gone from feeling uncertain to becoming someone who knows what kind of people I enjoy spending time with. Dating several people at the same time gives you an advantage because it keeps you from seeming desperate. When you don't have all your eggs in one basket you can relax a little, and it shows: your shoulders appear more relaxed, your posture improves, and your renewed self-confidence gives you a little extra glow on your dates. Now let's make one thing clear: I am *not* suggesting that you walk in bragging about your sex appeal or that you play jealousy games with your dates. Be discreet.

Let's say that you've begun meeting up with someone. The first date went well. So did the second! And one date starts leading to the next – does this mean you're together now? Are you exclusive? *NO*. No, this does *not* mean that you're together. *That* must be stated openly and agreed upon by *both* of you. If this hasn't been determined, then either of you may date – or perhaps *are* dating – other people. We need to know each other a bit before we establish an exclusive relationship – that's just how it is. If thoughts of your dates meeting other people make you jealous, be patient and ignore those feelings. Don't let this negative attitude cloud your judgement, and certainly don't sabotage anything. This is still an early stage of dating, and you haven't established exclusivity yet.

So, figure out what you want, what you need, and what you're looking for. This way you'll always be able to vet your dates. Maybe one person looks good for a little intimacy. Perhaps you had an incredible date with *another* person who looks like relationship material. If you're on the prowl for a potential partner but they're only spreading their wild oats, though, it won't matter how much you clicked – you're not a match. Both sides of the coin are needed: that your *goals* are aligned, and that your *personalities* are compatible.

If a situation isn't working out – even at the start – please don't go around thinking you can fix it with your magical fairy wand. The greater your demands, the fewer candidates that make the cut. But they're out there; it just might take a little longer to find them. Keep swiping, keep texting, and book those dates. Pretend you're on *The Bachelor*. Some dates end there. Some lead to friendships. With a few, you'll click. But a lot of prospects won't make it through the playoffs, so you're going to have to run the numbers game a bit. Think of it as a multi-tiered process, not a single admission fee. You're looking for that person you click with on a deeper, more intimate level, and a series of dates will help you find them.

And for all you hopeful romantics out there, keep your chin up. Lightning can strike from a clear blue sky!

2: First impressions

There are two secrets to dating smart. First, you need to make a good first impression, to stand out from the crowd. Second, you need to learn how to read your dates.

In this chapter, I'm going to explain what first impressions are built on and why we build them. You'll also learn why the ability to read other people plays such a definitive role in human relationships. This is how we operate, after all, and it affects everyone.

Being good ain't good enough

In my role as an inspirational speaker, I often discuss those unconscious questions we ask about each other. How *do* we read each other's personalities?

The ability to express ourselves effectively provides fertile ground for growth in relationships. If we fail at this task, our fruit withers on the vine. I like to explain it this way: *being good ain't good enough*. Don't get me wrong, being good is a great foundation to build on, but the pertinent question is: how do you manage to *express* that to the world? It's crucial to give off the right impression when you meet your dates – otherwise it's like hitting the dance floor with one arm tied behind your back. Instead of letting a *bad* first impression hamper your chances for success, let a *good* first impression be your key to success. Unfortunately, we're not judged for who we are, but for who others believe us to be.

This decisive moment follows a predictable pattern. For starters, first impressions happen virtually instantaneously. After a first impression has been formed, changing it is like, well . . . Ever watch someone try to work a dent out of a car door? Another factor is our generally sceptical attitude towards one another, referred to as the *smoke detector principle*. When meeting new people, we're calibrated to set alarm bells ringing at the slightest suspicion that something is amiss. We're faster at spotting the negative than the positive – a contributing factor to our survival over the course of human evolution. One implication of this is that we need to overcome an inherent barrier of suspicion before we can get someone else's approval, from the second they see your profile, to your first text, to your first date . . . Time to shine for the jury, my friends.

After a first impression has been established, we spend the rest of our time gathering evidence to corroborate whatever that impression happened to be. This is referred to as *confirmation bias* – a tendency in human behaviour to unconsciously and selectively pay attention to information that reaffirms our suppositions. We see what we expect to see, and hear what we expect to hear. Or to be more specific: what I see and hear *confirms* the first impression I got of you. I'm ignorant to the rest.

When you make a good first impression on another person, they are inclined to continue to see you that way. In fact, if you've nailed that first impression, this usually even gives you a little wiggle room when you screw up: 'Katie didn't mean to call me *that* – she's usually such a sweetheart!' Sure, perhaps Katie didn't . . . Katie also made a good first impression.

Besides confirmation bias and the smoke detector principle, there are other psychological biases that it's good to be aware of. The *halo effect* is an important one, about how external factors affect how others perceive us. A good illustration would be to imagine the difference between attending a meeting dressed formally vs informally. They say that 'clothes maketh the man', and if we're talking about how your attire affects how others evaluate you as a person, then there's a ring of truth to this. If you come in wearing a business suit, you're probably going to give off a greater air of competence than if you walk in wearing jeans and trainers. Booking a table at an exclusive restaurant as opposed to the local pub has this same effect: your date will associate you with the surrounding atmosphere, whether it's exclusivity and luxury, or comfort and camaraderie. Posting a selfie online of you and Lady Gaga on a yacht has a different effect on people than posting selfies of you and Kevin at the office party. You can easily use the halo effect to your advantage when choosing your profile pics or locations for your dates. Imagine different types of photos: professional portraits, urban snapshots, nature shots from a hike in the woods. What about dim, blurry, nude selfies shot in your grimy bathroom? Do I still need to convince you that different images give very different impressions of you? You're painting a portrait of your *personality* for people. More than that, your choice of images will affect which types of people you attract. They will predetermine the nature of your conversations and people's expectations about who you are. And since we also have a tendency to live up to the expectations of others, take the opportunity to create a positive feedback loop for yourself!

Warmth and competence

During initial encounters we evaluate two main areas of a person's character:

The first of these is: 'Can I trust you? Are you a good, kind, empathetic person whose heart is in the right place?'

The second is: 'What's your status and level of competence – how capable and self-confident are you?'

In psychology, the first is referred to as the *cluster of warm traits*.

These are related to your *intentions*: are you cruel or kind? Friend or foe? Our evaluation of these aspects triggers our *approach-or-avoid* behaviour. One of the reasons humans exist at all these days is because we function this way. Without this instinct, our ancestors wouldn't have been wary enough to flee from danger and we would have died out. (I'm all for hugs and congeniality, but they don't work on bears.) Trustworthiness still manipulates us in powerful ways: for example, we remember 'untrustworthy' facial expressions more easily than 'trustworthy' facial expressions.[1] Untrustworthy people could endanger us, so we had to be extra wary of them.

The second is your *ability cluster*. What is your capacity for actualizing your (either good or bad) intentions? Can you put your money where your mouth is? This deals with self-confidence and dominance, and capacity or ability – status. So why is status such a big deal for us? Historically, status brought privilege. High rank meant benefits, in a variety of contexts. You got dibs on the mammoth steaks, the best pile of furs to sleep in, and access to greater resources. These social-psychological mechanisms have applied throughout human history – as they do now. We've always been drawn to power and to those who hold power.

But it's rare for us to openly express a desire for power, even though generally we *do* want more of it. The opposite, to feel powerless, is terrible, while having influence benefits us – and can even protect us. Your voice remains unheard without influence. That dream job stays out of reach, your kids ignore you, and you feel like a phantom, bound to the shadows. That hardly makes dating any easier – powerlessness and helplessness are a hard sell on the dating market.

Even if our evaluations of warmth and competence occur virtually simultaneously, warmth still carries a slight lead. Trustworthiness played a more decisive role in human survival than the strength of your ability. Psychological experiments provide further evidence of this: we identify words related to warmth[2] ('nice', 'kind', and 'good') more quickly than we do words related to competence ('ability' and 'capacity'). An untrustworthy date with cruel intentions is more dangerous than an incompetent, bungling date.

You can exhibit these two attributes through various signals: body language, what you wear, mirroring, and the tone of your voice. And these considerations begin with your dating profile too – more on that in the next chapter.

How do you see yourself?

There is another factor that significantly impacts the impression you give. It affects what kind of employment you find, which books you read (although your taste in books is clearly improving), how you take care of your health, and your attitude towards other people.

I'm talking about your *self-image* – your opinions and feelings about yourself. Appeal is about more than just picking the right photos; the background work you do to improve your self-image and self-confidence also pumps up your dating muscles. Look, we've all had our bad days (or a bad year or three, once we get long enough in the tooth) and it's pretty easy to get discouraged and feel shitty about yourself. Everyone feels like a sack of old potatoes at some time in their life, and who'd wanna date a sack of potatoes, right?

Here's the great thing about feeling like a petrol station sandwich: this is an area where *anyone* can improve! I'm not saying it's always easy, but remember that only *you* can set your worth. The value you're projecting outwards is determined in your own mind. Emotions often have a spiralling or cyclical nature, so it can be a bumpy process. But if you keep your attitude steered in the right direction, you'll get that ship to port, no matter if there's a little choppiness in the harbour. How *you* see yourself affects how *others* see you: if you behave as if you have value, others will see you as valuable. When others treat you as valuable, it suddenly becomes easier to recognize that you *are* valuable. Reap the benefits of positive feedback loops!

3: Picking a good 'un

Giving a good impression and appealing to others is one thing, but it's only one side of the coin. There's a flip side to this dating equation too, which is learning to not just grab any old thing that comes along – you're gonna need better odds than the national lottery. If you want to avoid falling in love with someone who's not right for you, learn how to recognize and avoid the most common pitfalls.

In this chapter, we'll examine how you can improve your ability to read the people you meet. You'll learn how to spot the signs if your date has one of the three dangerous personalities, or whether your personalities are bound to clash.

Entering a relationship with the wrong person can cost you a great deal, so reading others is one of your key abilities. Breaking up *after* you have moved in together is going to be a lot tougher than it would have been after two dates.

So who's a good match for you?

While some personalities are always out of sync, others fit hand in glove. Before we examine which personalities might be best for you, though, let's examine the psychology behind them.

First, does personality stay constant throughout your life? Or is it formed entirely in response to your surroundings, such as your upbringing, the stage of life you're at, or the people you happen to be around? Well, the answer is . . . complicated.

A group of researchers carried out a meta-analysis[1] of 2,748 studies, conducted over fifty years, which involved 4,558,903 sets of twins. This is an avalanche of information, and the mystery they were trying to untangle was whether or not we inherit our personalities. Their conclusion? We inherit approximately 49 per cent of our personality traits from our parents. We're born with certain idiosyncrasies.

Our personalities steer much of our lives, affecting many aspects, such as our life decisions, our well-being, our level of optimism, and our health.[2] Your personality consists of your behaviour, emotions, motives, and thought patterns. Some of us are gregarious extroverts, while others prefer the shadows. Some feel enlivened by new experiences and environments, while others find new situations stressful, irritating, or intimidating. In psychology, we talk about *The Big Five*. This is the most frequently employed model used in discussions regarding personality. As thousands of studies have accumulated, five broad categorizations have emerged. We all possess various levels of each of the five; other attributes are generally considered to be variations or nuances of these. The Big Five are also referred to as OCEAN.

1. **Openness** (to experience): curious, clever, adventurous, inventive, creative, and imaginative.
2. **Conscientiousness**: detail-oriented, meticulous, effective, reliable, organized, goal-oriented, planners, productive, disciplined, loyal, traditional, and tend to control their impulses.
3. **Extroversion**: extroverted, gregarious, self-confident, optimistic, chatty, energetic, enthusiastic, social, and are often natural leaders.

4. **Agreeableness:** warm, considerate, empathetic, sympathetic, helpful, kind, reliable, generous, forgiving, and cooperative.

5. **Neuroticism:** people who rank high in this category express many negative attributes, and tend to be anxious, guilt-ridden, nervous, emotionally unstable, moody, easily agitated, and sensitive to stress.

The Big Five model addresses five fundamental human traits. However, I believe that we're missing one, and in the dating world and in conversations with others, I have observed behaviours that exemplify this dynamic within romantic relationships. For example, on dating apps you usually fill in a bio profile – you write a little about yourself and who you're looking for. It's not uncommon to see people write 'dom' or 'sub' here, referring to whether they're dominant or submissive. This automatically implies that they're looking for the opposite – 'doms' want 'subs', and 'subs' want 'doms'. (Exceptions are rare.) For some people this is merely an erotic preference, confined to the bedroom (or perhaps the dungeon). For others, though, it's also a telling sign of their personality in general – certainly regarding where they land on a dominance/ submission scale. And it *is* a scale, obviously, where things aren't always black and white. We all hover over it somewhere. You don't want to be in a relationship with an overly dominant person who exploits, abuses or humiliates you, or disrespects your boundaries. And dominance in combination with cruelty becomes destructive. So I'd like to include *SDO* (*social dominance orientation*) in the Big Five to make it a six-pack: *The Big Six*. (I'm not alone in this, either.)[3]

6. **Social Dominance Orientation (SDO):** a scale of how submissive or dominant a person is in their relationships, including but not restricted to sexual preferences.

All six traits, even dominance, have an ideal level, according to the situation at hand. If you're too dominant, you'll drive your friends away - nobody likes a bully. If you're too submissive, however, others' respect for you will suffer, leaving you vulnerable. Equally, if you're too agreeable, you might be seen as a push-over or if you're too conscientious you may seem like you can't relax.

Often you can already see clear signs of someone's personality in their bios and photos. It drifts out through their tone, the content they choose, and the vocabulary they use. And if you meet up in person, signals will flash all over the place like lights on a Christmas tree - in their body language and posture, their use of mirroring, or in the speed and intentionality of their hand gestures. Vindictive individuals, for instance, can get an itchy trigger finger at the tiniest slights, while forgiving individuals might miss that slight in the first place, and rarely get upset. Extroverts are the life of the party. Meticulous organizers can see in a heartbeat whether or not you've cleaned your bathroom, while some easygoing slackers don't even notice the dishes in their *own* sink.

Here's the thing: I believe that understanding some of the psychology behind our personalities and their traits is important - it helps you determine what kind of person might be right for you. Certain qualities clash. Certain qualities complement each other (doms/subs is an easy example of that). Some qualities may be charming at first, and then the charm slowly fades away. Begin by asking yourself which kind of person you'd fit well with in a healthy, well-functioning relationship. Would you be into the super-open guy who spills his guts? What about a self-improver, or maybe a daredevil? Do you want the girl who inspires parties all around her, or that one who seems so conscientious, who pays attention to the little details? It can take patience to discover these things about your needs. Who do you usually feel best spending time with? The thing is, you'll figure all of this out after you've been out there dating a while. You'll learn to tell which kinds of folks seem right for you.

It's one thing to enjoy the company of a particular type of person.

Another factor will be how your personalities will affect certain aspects of your lives further down the line. Our character traits affect the quality and extent of our lives. For instance, conscientious people generally outlive others, are less likely to get divorced, and (on average) tend to be more successful in the workplace. They've got some good things going for them. On the other hand, neurotic individuals tend to have shorter life spans and divorce more frequently.[4] Negative personality traits tend to lead to negative consequences, positive traits tend to lead to positive consequences, and relationships are no exception to this.[5] Common sense rings true here – temperament matters! Generally speaking, the more positive and the more dominant (it's true, according to research) you are, the better the odds are that you'll experience successful relationships.[6]

A golden quality vs an unfortunate characteristic

We're looking for relationship material and want to avoid dead-ends.[7] Each of these two groups centres on a Big Five Six personality trait.

The trait to keep your eyes open for is *agreeableness*. It's expressed through warmth, empathy, consideration for others, willingness to cooperate, and honesty.

Neuroticism, on the other hand, is the trait to avoid. It's expressed through irritability, capriciousness, being overly critical, stubbornness, bossiness, and emotional instability.

Signs of whether we're dealing with one or the other often appear in texts – agreeable folks spread positivity and neurotic folks spread negativity.

Using texts to interpret personalities

Personality shows, and once you meet them you'll get the chance to read your next date through their eye contact, body language, and how they mingle or react to unexpected situations. Before you get to that stage, you can already read signs of someone's personality in their texts – connections that have been confirmed by research.[8] When it comes to texting, some of us are expressive and tell you how we're feeling whether you asked or not, while others keep our cards close to our chests. Our emojis reflect this: some compose elaborate emoji pictograms, while others won't even tap out a smiley face. Generally speaking, emoji-users tend to be friendlier, more empathetic, and more socially receptive compared to emoji-avoiders,[9] in the same way that some people are more inclined to smile or employ hand gestures.

Texting's got its eager beavers, of course, all geared up to mind-meld with you, but plenty of other folks are more reticent. If you've taken a shine to a quiet type who's slow to reply, you might need 'a reason' to contact them again. And guess what? You've got my permission to make one up. After we finally met up, one date commented, 'I could tell from your texts that you're really upbeat.' What a nice thing to hear! The implication was that he felt this way from how I used my emojis and my !!!s, the tone of my replies, and the questions I asked. And don't miss the universal truth in this: others will draw conclusions about us from our messages – both what we write and what we don't.

Texts often reflect gender as well. While both consider it to be impolite, according to one research study, men are more likely than women to break up by texting. When conflicts arise, though, suddenly men show a greater preference for talking over the phone, whereas women prefer texting. Although gender differences play a role, individual differences in personality outweigh generalizations.

Here are some ways you can spot Big Five personality types based on their texts:

- **Extroverts** are chatty, and their texts reflect this. They're wordier, use lots of positive expressions like 'fun' and 'great', and often refer to social processes and activities. They tend to text more often (particularly extroverted women), use more sexual innuendo[10] and positive emojis[11] 😎🙂☺, tend to make texts more personal by frequently using pronouns (like I, you, they),[12] use fewer negative words,[13] and are more likely to stretch out words: 'Woooop!!! Nooooo waaaay!' They seek social occasions and exciting activities, and often enjoy being the centre of attention.
- **Open** people are curious, creative, and enthusiastic about new things.[14] Consequently, they're less enthusiastic about routines and predictability. So if your date proposes new, unusual activities for your first date – or other factors turn out to be unconventional or unexpected – there's a good chance you're dealing with an open personality.
- People with **agreeable** tendencies use positively charged emotional words,[15] positive emojis[16] 😳☺😊, and fewer negative expressions or swear words.[17] They're reliable, supportive, generally well-liked, and have their hearts in the right place – all reflected in the warmth of their texts.
- Folks who rank high in **conscientiousness** are meticulous, organized, and disciplined.[18] If a prospect's texts always appear carefully composed and grammatically correct, it can be an indication of a conscientious individual. These people are generally *not* in the habit of spontaneously texting random comments, or even misspelling. They enjoy planning ahead and prefer to follow up on their plans.
- People with **neurotic** personalities often use negative words[19] and emojis[20] more often (annoying, tough, shitty, 😫😑😧),[21] and tend to share personal information

unnecessarily.[22] They can be irritable, hostile, easily stressed, and are subject to mood swings. Such characteristics are frequently reflected in their texts too, of course.

Our personality types affect which words we use and how many too. They affect how quickly we get personal and how we use social media: what we choose to share, how many contacts, friends, or followers we have (extroverts have more, of course),[23] and how much we choose to reveal about ourselves.

Naturally, being able to quickly interpret someone's personality is an invaluable tool when evaluating potential dates or prospects, and this is definitely possible. Like DNA at a crime scene, our personalities splash all over the place, offering potential insights into our psychological profiles. But stay focused on the right things. After you've had a taste of their conversational style, make use of that information. You can, for instance, mirror their behaviour – not because you want to manipulate or mock them, but because mirroring (adapting to one another) is a perfectly natural and productive aspect of human relationships. In my lectures, I frequently emphasize how human beings have evolved to be highly socially flexible. This is where our social competence comes into play.

Three types to avoid

There are dream dates out there, and they're the ones you're looking for. Unfortunately, there are also some dangerous people who should only be approached with caution. These three personality types are referred to as *The Dark Triad*:

Narcissistic: grandiose self-image, egotism, pride, lack of empathy. These people think they're better than others – more attractive, more intelligent, and funnier. They love competition (winning in particular) and love being the centre of attention. According to the Austrian–American psychoanalyst Heinz Kohut,[24] narcissism is fundamentally a way of shielding a fragile and damaged self-image.

Psychopathic (*antisocial personality disorder*): Impulsive, selfish, indifferent, cold-hearted, superficially charming. They usually seek dangerous thrills as well.

Machiavellian: Cynical, manipulative, self-serving, exploitative, amoral, indifferent. Con artists are a classic example of this type, telling you anything you want to hear if it maximizes their own gain.

These three personalities overlap and their borders are blurred. You'll find borderline personalities and pathological liars edging into this pack as well.

So how do you figure out if you've got a villain on your hands? I hate to say it, but it isn't always easy. I should probably start by explaining to you how they relate to the Big ~~Five~~ Six. In a factor analysis carried out by Glasgow Caledonian University,[25] the strongest connection the Dark Triad had to the Big ~~Five~~ Six was found to be a low level of *sympathy*. They're neither kind nor sympathetic – no shocker there. There's also a connection between the Dark Triad and a *lack of conscientiousness*: being careless or disingenuous, and failing to show loyalty or impulse control. Another big shocker: *neuroticism* also shows links to the triad. Unfortunately, these folks tend to blind us with their dazzle. They can look pretty good at first glance – who can resist that natural charm, easy swagger, and carefree demeanour, especially when they keep flashing those pretty eyes at you? Don't be surprised if they're socially radiant, mingle with ease, or seem ambitious – this stuff appeals to us.

But don't let these charlatans hoodwink you. Keep an eye out for the red flags – you might not see the signs on the first date, but it's only a matter of time before you'll sense that something fishy's going on. You can't put your finger on it, but something ain't quite right. Listen to your gut.

Someone can seem genuinely kind and wonderful when you first meet them, and then Dr Jekyll turns into Mr Hyde. It's easy to blame yourself in that situation, thinking, 'I should've seen the signs,' or 'What's wrong with me because I didn't pick that up earlier?' But honestly, you just can't always know. There might not have been any signs at all and everything truly seemed perfect. But when the situation turns – when you learn about the other side of this person – it's important that you actively make decisions regarding this relationship. It's like playing Seven-Card Stud Poker – you don't know what card's coming next, but it can change your whole hand. If your date starts misbehaving out of the blue, you'll find yourself facing all-new odds. If that handsome prince suddenly reveals his inner frog, then your decision to date him is no longer relevant – this isn't what you signed up for.

Impulsivity is a warning sign – watch out for dramatic mood swings. Do criticisms or contradictory statements pop up out of thin air? Can't tell where you are with this person? One moment you're God's gift, and the next she's dissing you like yesterday's breakfast? Untrustworthiness is a red flag too. Does it seem like this guy is hiding the truth? Does he break his promises? If you spot one of these signs more than once – yup, that's a red flag for sure.

Having a Dark Triad personality in your life often involves uncertainty, anxiety, and confusion. Before you know it, you'll be feeling like shit, distracted by trying to figure out what's wrong with *you*. You can lose your compass, your sense of who you are. One of my friends dated a guy who turned out to be an expert in avoiding responsibility. At the same time, he was a pro at making her feel demanding and cumbersome. If she mentioned that it might be his turn to do the dishes, he would answer with 'You're so obsessive about who does what – are you going to put a rota on the wall next?' He made her feel indebted, as if *she* was the 'difficult' one – although quite the opposite was true. These people often use manipulative methods such as *gaslighting*, in which a Dark Triad individual causes their partner to doubt their own perception of reality – their own memories, observations, and opinions.

Some dangerous personalities can be hard to detect at first, which is one reason why it's recommended you arrange those early dates in public places. And also why you may want to be cautious about how much personal information you divulge early on in the dating process. Safety precautions are intended to remove uncertainty, so smart planning should help you relax more, allowing you to focus on reading who this new person is. The phrase 'it takes two to tango' doesn't apply to every situation. It certainly doesn't apply when you're dealing with a Dark Triad personality; it's not your fault they are the way they are, and neither is it your place to 'fix' them. It's flight, not fight, that this situation calls for – thinking that you'll be able to sit down and work it all out is only playing with fire.

4: Catching their eye

The other day I was sitting around discussing dating profiles with a friend. We got onto the subject of photos. Getting out his phone, he opened up his dating app to show me his profile. He looked pleasant enough in the first two pics. In his third photo, he was sitting there picking at a guitar, at what appeared to be a traditional Swedish Midsummer celebration.

'This is the photo I get the most comments on. They like this one,' he said, sounding not too displeased.

'Why's that, d'you think?'

'It's like that photo says more about my personality. There's a depth there you don't see in the other ones.'

What's *your* guitar pic?

So why was his guitar pic giving off such positive vibes? Why do some pictures capture folks' imaginations but not others?

For starters, we're dealing with the halo effect we discussed earlier. According to this phenomenon, the qualities of our photos reflect back on us and our personalities. The details of your surroundings and any activity taking place in your photos influence how others decide who you are. I only posted three pictures of myself at first, but upped it to six or seven after a while. It took me some time to find the right photos; I was intent on attracting people who had 'serious' intentions, and initially posted photos taken in work environments where I was formally dressed. Then a few outdoor shots were added to give off the right vibes. My strategy proved successful.

In the dating apps, you'll generally find every kind of picture under the sun. Nature shots, gym shots, the workplace, Halloween parties, holidays, bathrooms. Some people are wearing spectacular outfits – others seem to have forgotten their outfits. I've seen a lot more pics of snowmobiles, reindeer, and snowy landscapes when dating in northern Sweden. Our photos reflect our lives, naturally. We want people to know who we are, to see our everyday realities.

That's the question this chapter addresses: what story do you want to tell with your photos? Which pictures will sell your pitch? For attracting others and standing out from the crowd, your photos are the most important tools you have.

So use them correctly. In fact, get your phone out right now, let's check 'em out . . .

What are your pictures saying about you?

That first impression comes in hard and fast. As I mentioned earlier, we quickly form first impressions based on trustworthiness, warmth, and competence, no matter where we are in the world. These photos are the 'dimensions' we're working in, and you should be conscious of these when choosing your photos. If you want to radiate confidence, for instance, then focus on that. Better to focus on warmth? Choose photos that express warmth instead. I'll give you some tips on how to do this in a moment.

Here's a funny little example of how our photos affect how others interpret us: have you ever heard of the *imbibing idiot bias*? This refers to the fact that we – whether you drink or not – tend to view people (consciously or otherwise) who drink alcohol as less intelligent. In other words, if you post a selfie holding a beer or a glass of wine, you come across as less intelligent. Even just hinting at alcohol has this effect! Comedy or tragedy? The point is that details matter.

The three photos we most want to see

Portrait. Our brains are particularly evolved to be highly attuned to faces. Your face reveals a great deal about your attributes: emotional state, gender, age, etc.

Body shot. People need a look at the goods. Preferably your whole figure, but at least waist-up if nothing else. If they're left wondering they'll skip past you.

Activity. Badminton, breakdancing, wrestling together IKEA bookshelves, rockin' out at the karaoke bar, building a model railway, giving a speech to 5,000 people – we want to see you *DO* something. What do you do? Where do you go all day long? Show us, please! 😎😃😗

Looking good brings results

The glitterati know exactly how to pose on the red carpet: which camera angles make them sparkle, how the light will enhance their cheekbones. They know which backdrops matter, which clothes will say what, and just how to make their hair look effortlessly fabulous. They know how to shine – how to optimize their potential. When taking my portrait for a magazine article, a press journalist once informed me that women rarely want to be photographed from below. Yet this preference to be shot from above isn't shared by men. Apparently, women's chins tend to protrude less than men's (just look at any Disney film), and we're often inclined to employ strategies that enhance our gender identities without even reflecting on it. Selfies taken from above reduce the lower half of your face.

'Beauty is in the eye of the beholder.' 'Don't judge a book by its cover.' I bet you've heard those lines before. The ancient Greeks had a different take on it: 'What is beautiful is good.'[1] According to their mindset, outer beauty and inner beauty were interconnected. Unfortunately, this stereotype seems to run deep in the world.

We tart ourselves up with make-up and fancy threads, trim our beards, dye our hair, and take forever to get that camera angle just right. And this effort is *not* in vain – looking attractive gives you quite a few advantages. We're not all supermodels, but we can all look our best. Stay healthy, look clean and presentable, and choose which signals you want to radiate. Remember that attractive people aren't always happy, but that happy, kind-hearted people have a unique magnetism. So don't let anyone spoil your positive attitude!

Looking and feeling like the best version of yourself gives results. Remember that as you choose your photos, and when you're heading out to meet your date. The research is telling: when you look good, people are more appreciative of your work. Attractive people are more successful, earn more, and find it easier to get hired.[2] They have more success dating and are considered more fun to go out with. We tend to see them as warmer, stronger, more socially competent, more popular, more dominant, more psychologically healthy, and more intelligent.[3] And it gets worse – attractive people are also perceived as showing stronger leadership and better conviction.[4] Attractive criminals are reported less often than their less attractive peers, and receive lighter sentencing as well. We let good-looking people persuade us and win arguments, and we try to appease them by trading favours for their approval.

The list goes on. They have it better. So maybe it's not so strange that we make an effort to look good – it pays off. There's a psychological phenomenon referred to as the *beautiful is familiar* effect. Even if we've never met them previously, beautiful people still seem a little more familiar to us.[5] And we prefer the familiar.[6] The way the researchers describe it, it's almost as if attractive people have an aura.[7] And the magnetism of attractive people doesn't wear off after you've been dating for a while, either, but affects your relationship in the long run.[8] If you think that your partner looks good, it enhances your commitment, passion, intimacy, and sense of satisfaction.[9] And in case you were snoozing back there, I said, 'If you *think* your partner looks good'. In this case, it's in the eye of *you*, Beholder.

Here's my point: the better you can look in your photos, the more you'll end up midnight-texting. And once you start texting, you'll be able to charm them with your personality, and get your foot in that dating door.

Ready for your close up?

Your portrait alone first determines whether others will want to zoom in on you. Everything in your pics – body language, mirroring, clothes, background – sends signals about you and your personality.[10] Here's how to make sure they're the right ones.

> **Body**. Take up a little more space for yourself, using expansive positions such as having your arms akimbo or sticking straight out, or keeping a wide stance. Expansive body gestures signify power, influence, and dominance, but they can also show warmth and expressiveness – it depends on your positioning in combination with your facial expression. Crossed arms can appear dominant. Poor posture signals submissiveness. Open hand gestures convey warmth and approachability.
>
> **Face**. Smiling makes us seem kinder and more intelligent. A measured smile comes across as authoritarian. It's important to look into the camera lens; according to research, eye contact helps people remember us better.

Head. A tilted head suggests subordination. Keeping your head straight expresses competence. Tilting your head back implies arrogance, while simultaneously leaning forward and avoiding eye contact will make you look shy or evasive.

Leaning. Leaning into things that you like (and away from things you don't) affects how others see you in both photos and real life. Leaning back implies a relaxed attitude, but apathy as well. Leaning forward shows that you're interested.

Hair. Short hair seems more authoritarian. Letting your hair down appears less formal or businesslike, and is often considered more attractive.

Glasses. Glasses make us look more intelligent and reliable, and we come across as harder workers. Other stereotypes that come with spectacles: we're less extroverted, less athletic or funny, and less attractive even. However, there is **also** evidence that contradicts this – some research has shown that glasses can make you look sexier and *more* attractive.[11] Like with anything else, the sum of the parts is greater than the whole, and how you combine your specs with your hair and outfit will influence the impression you create.

Sunglasses. Sunglasses hide our eyes, and we can come across as both less authoritative and less honest. It's better to show us the windows to your soul.

Beards. Facial hair tends to make you look more self-confident, masculine, aggressive, and mature. Once again, it's also a question of the total package – is it combined with a sleek blazer, a kaftan, slicked-back hair, perhaps a bald dome? Stubble tends to increase attractiveness.

Clothes. Formal clothing makes us appear more intelligent, authoritative, and trustworthy than informal dress. It also makes us appear less interesting as individuals. A tailored suit suggests self-confidence, success, and a high income. Personally, I've experimented with a lot of different clothing styles for my dating profile photos. Some of my outfits were casual, some more businesslike. In my experience, it's good to show variety in your pics, illustrating the different dimensions of your personality, interests, and preferred activities.

Colours. Dark colours appear more authoritarian. Red is a signal colour, and comes across as both sensual and powerful. We generally tend to wear a lot of black, grey, and beige, so choosing more visible colours is an easy way to stand out, especially with an unusual garment.

Nudity. The scantier your clothes are, the more you'll be objectified. Objectified individuals come across as less competent, and tend to be seen as lacking personality. The message is that you want to share bodies, not minds.

Surroundings. Due to the halo effect, even our backdrops affect how others view us. If you post a picture from your shower, people will get a certain image of you. And whether you're skydiving, skateboarding, or playing darts down the pub, they all paint different kinds of pictures, right?

Shots to avoid

Blurry, hazy, or out-of-focus images.

Faceless body shots.

Dark pics. (Sunny photos make a huge difference to the impression you give off.)

Busy backgrounds.

Old portraits. (This will backfire. Be the new you.)

Bathroom shots.

Not making eye contact. (Make eye contact in at least a few pictures, if not all.)

Revealing photos. (Now let's be clear: this depends on your goals. If you just want one-night stands, then racy pics make sense.)

Grumpy face. (Don't look like a bad time.)

Looking arrogant.

Looking expressionless.

Pictures of you with people of the gender you want to date.

Pictures of you with other people – at all. (I'm seeing you for like 2 seconds before swiping – who are you again? The exception is if it's obvious which person you are, in which case a group photo can signal that you're popular and have a strong social network.)

Hiding your face.

Duck lips.

Close-ups of your tattoos. (If you're otherwise missing from the photo.)

Pictures of your vehicle.

Cigarette pics.

Alcohol pics.

Standing out from the crowd

In summary, having attractive photos brings you a lot of advantages. Professional portraits paint one picture, nature shots paint another, and different bait hooks different fish. Beautiful, exciting, or even exotic environments in combination with a snazzy outfit and a positive glow on your face will improve your odds of scoring that date.

As to how best you can stand out from the crowd, there's one last thing I'd like to tell you about. Many leaders in their fields share common characteristics, whether they're artists, motivational speakers, salespeople, or authors. Ambition, willpower, a strong work ethic, and being goal-oriented are certainly components of success. But another thing often unites them too: something they do, whether consciously or unconsciously, is *look* different, standing out visually in some way or other. They may have a unique style, or a splash of colour such as a tie or a piece of jewellery, just enough to catch your attention. You don't necessarily have to dress like Prince the first time you experiment with new outfits, but it's usually advantageous to include some unique details in your photos. This effect is a result of our fundamental psychology, and a trait we share with the animal kingdom. Alpha lions, for instance, have much larger manes and longer tail hair.[12] The alphas are the trendsetters and tend to be fashion-forward. They dare to be different, and it shows.

Your photos carry serious weight in the dating game.[13] More than your texts.

How will *they* stand out?

5: Your profile bio

Seeking: Wonderful person ☺
Positive qualities: Sunny disposition, cuddly, adventurous, free-spirited 😄
Unique qualities: Rarely drink but can dance for hours, performed in death metal band, goal-oriented, knowledge-thirsty, creative powerhouse. Love saunas and swimming – preferably outdoors
General Info: Stockholm
Into: Empathetic, kind people with a sense of humour ♡

or

I'm into guys who are humble, empathetic, and funny ☺
Superstar chefs get to jump the queue! 😄
NO1NS (no one-night stands)

Instagram @angelaahola

or

Searching for fellow free spirit: kind, fun, passionate, ambitious, charming. Cooking skills a huge plus ☺ I love dancing, knowledge, freedom. Open to something long-term 😊

Those are three profile bios that I've alternated between – that's how I've been presenting myself. These three different bios plus my seven photos are the only glimpse you get on my dating app, and comprise *me*. The same mindset should apply to you too. You need to condense yourself into a brief text and set of pictures in a way that piques people's curiosity. It's tragic to leave the field blank if you want to stand a chance out there.

In this chapter, we'll go over the best way to present yourself in your profile bio.

The ultimate bio text

Let's begin with a stat on bios. An extensive study showed that 36 per cent of profiles lack bio texts altogether.[1] And the majority of those who *did* write bios employed fewer than 100 characters. If you happen to be leaving the box empty, bear in mind that profiles with bios *always* fare better. Particularly if you're a man looking for a woman – men's profiles without a bio received an average of 16 matches from women; this more than quadrupled to 69 per cent when they included a bio. In other words, a bio makes you more attractive.

So what should we write?

I know how tough this can be. But it's time to pick up your digital pen and write something about yourself, a pitch that will interest other people. It's not the time to brag, but you do need to sell yourself here. What should it say?

In order to solve this riddle, imagine you're attending a course for the first time. Everyone is given one minute to introduce themselves. How would you introduce yourself? You have a few deft strokes to paint your own portrait. Which qualities would you like to shed light on? We often present ourselves digitally these days, whether on Instagram, Facebook, or dating apps, and these are more than just brief, superficial presentations. They portray how we view ourselves, and how we differentiate ourselves from the billions of other human beings wandering the planet. Amidst this swarm of strangers, we're torn between contradictory impulses. On the one hand, we're herd animals: we like conforming, dressing like our friends and colleagues do, or sharing their opinions and interests. Blending in gives us a comfortable sense of camaraderie, and our social nature has aided our survival for millennia. The psychological phenomenon of *mirroring* is a result of this. When you and I speak to one another, we imitate each other's gestures, postures, speech patterns, and even dialects. This instinctual behaviour is driven by highly automated cells in our brains called *mirror neurons* – more about this later on. But the other social impulse contradicting our desire for strength in numbers is the need we all share to feel like unique individuals. These contradictory forces – the need to *conform* and the need to *deviate* – push us simultaneously in opposite directions. Imitation vs distinction.

Social media and dating sites allow us a golden opportunity to personally tailor the image that others will have of us. We can choose *in detail* which aspects of our lives we'd like to share, and so steer others' perceptions of us. That's probably why it's so hard to come up with what to write in our bios. What ingredients make a bio text pop?

For starters, bios that give results come in all different forms. Your priority, again, is to know what you're looking for. Generally speaking, the more clearly you can define what you're looking for, the more time you'll save (by not sitting around waiting for answers to questions that your bio could have already taken care of).

The most important function of a profile bio is to make people pick *you*. These texts are teasers – movie trailers, bait. If they wanna watch the whole movie, they'll have to buy a ticket, so let's check out a few strategies for your next box-office hit. In my experience, humour is almost always effective – get me laughing and you got me loving! Another approach I appreciate is when someone is both genuine and mature. A third type of profile bio lessens your chances, so it ought to be avoided – we'll cover a few examples of those as well.

Ready? Here come examples of all three types of bio texts. When you read these, think about which type best reflects your own personality. When your dream date is swiping somewhere out there in the digiverse, don't get caught without a bio. Nor without a well-thought-out presentation text. Your text often tips the scales in your favour! Your bio text isn't supposed to be a complete description of who you are. Its only purpose is to stir up a little interest, to pique a little curiosity. And it should be primarily directed towards your audience – who do you want to meet?

Warm, genuine bios – this works mostly on people over the age of 25

Martin, 38

Looking for a serious man who's driven and honest, yet still has a twinkle in his eye? Perhaps you'd like to meet a mature person who's lived a full life – and isn't afraid to speak his mind or express his feelings?

I'm often told that I'm considerate, charming, respectful, and a good listener. If qualities like these appeal to you, swipe right on me.

What am I looking for in a woman? I have no demands. I do know, however, that I'm attracted to women who are goal-oriented and love to dance. (I'm a former elite dancer, and work as a judge for dance competitions these days.)

Daniel, 54

Calm, creative northerner. I'm a carpenter, and work with dogs as well.

I like nature, cooking, working out, and making things.

I enjoy spontaneity and intimacy.

Fred, 22
Sports Academy
Your prize: Decent, happy, and high-energy future secondary school teacher with a lot of different skills.

I like humour, honesty, and pleasant company.

I always see the glass as half-full, and I like others who share my positive outlook on life! 😎

As you will see in the following pictures, I'm brilliant at reading (and sleeping), making food, picking mushrooms, putting 2-part tables together, and playing football. And all of this in my favourite pair of jogging bottoms. I keep my feet on the ground and my head in the clouds – literally. I'm 6' 5".

Funny crowd-pleaser bios

Rich, 22
I have the potential to be really attractive, according to my mum.

Steve, 47
Consultant
Advantages: Being my only match, you'll get 100% of my attention.
Disadvantages: Can't reach the top shelf.

Anna, 39
Police
Have you ever said 'F*** the police'? Well, now's your chance.

Katja, 29
Respiratory Therapist in training
Cute enough to take your breath away, smart enough to bring it back.

Cool bios that rely on photos to do the heavy lifting

Wilma, 21
DJ
Seriously, chill a bit, how come everyone has to be so ****ing uptight?

Sid, 36
Business exec
I'll give you one more chance.
A skilled man who's seen it all,
difficult to impress. 😐

Toby, 23
Yowie bowie mcfowie, what up, yo?

Anton, 20
Student
6'6" so I got plenty of hoodies you can steal x

Adrian, 21
Haha date me and have the adventure of your life 🤠

Francesca, 18
One, two, or three glasses of wine?

Your language determines where you'll land

Before we start discussing how to compose your bio text, allow me to emphasize the significance of good pics, because your bio text won't matter if you don't catch someone's eye in the flood of faces first – don't expect your Pulitzer Prize-winning bio text to compensate for crappy photos. Photos are the first thing they see, and since human beings are such visual animals, your pictures will always pack a harder punch. If you're in a pinch, prioritize snazzy photos over flowing text.

Our language influences how others see us, and the words you use in your bio will affect how others view you. According to research, impactful words like 'wonderful', 'amazing', and 'fantastic' give others more favourable impressions of us than neutral vocabulary does.[2] In one study, participants chose potential dates with more positive vocabulary three out of four times over their less optimistic or outgoing counterparts. Playing it cool and low-key doesn't always pay off.

Talking in a positive way about other people also has an effect, causing *us* to appear more positive as well. The halo effect of your words quite simply colours your person – using swear words generally leaves stains on your character (despite there being situations in which it *is* more forgivable to use them, damn it).

So no effing and blinding on dates.

There are certain triggers we can sneak into a good bio, words that pluck at the heartstrings of your readers. Imagine what people might be searching for or need. Depending on which type of date you're looking for, different words will be useful. For instance, consider words that give good signals for the mature bio: warmth, respect, listener, nurturing, energetic, follow-through, humour, having a twinkle in your eye, emotionally open, and charming. Funny bios also have triggers, such as employing self-deprecation, or more punctuation and emojis. Cool bios can signal that you have money, fame, or status, or may employ minimal messages: 'I got plenty of hoodies you can steal.'

Choose your words wisely, according to your goal.

Bio benefits

- *Humour*
- *Positive words and positive composition*
- *Authenticity*
- *Well-aimed trigger words*
- *Short and sweet – and comprehensible*

Bio hazards

- *Negative words*
- *Negative vibes* – 'You don't do it for me.' 'Left-swipe if you . . .' 'I hate all the . . .'
- *Long reads* – a lengthy bio signals that you're trying to skip the dating process or that you overshare. Flash an ankle on the dance floor, don't stride naked into a shopping mall.
- *Boring filler* – about you, your life, or what you're seeking. This is supposed to be flirting, not a loan application.
- *Saying you're 'too good' for dating apps* – or that your friends forced you.
- *Tumbleweed* – an empty bio. One funny thing, seriously, you can come up with one funny thing. Anything's better than nothing, so don't waste this opportunity.

Using music to reel 'em in

Were you aware of just how much your taste in music affects how others perceive you? This too has been studied, and if you allow other people to listen to your top ten favourite songs, it turns out that they're able to form a rather accurate assessment of your personality.[3]

Dating profiles often allow you to add an 'anthem'. Choose wisely – you're reflecting your personality here.

Does sharing similar taste in music affect you and your date's relationship? It sure does! When we discover that we enjoy the same songs, we get along better and form stronger bonds than when our musical tastes clash. If we end up together, our bond over musical preferences will make our relationship more satisfying and deepen our feelings of intimacy.[4] Sharing musical taste not only improves the satisfaction felt by romantic partners, but even university roommates who like the same music are more likely to continue living together. Don't move in together if you can't groove out together.

In life, your verbal and non-verbal communication need to sync if you don't want to confuse people, and your dating profile is no different. Your bio text and photos need to speak the same language, and you should let your goals steer this process. Looking for 'serious', for example? Then avoid that photo from the beach in Rio, or any flirty pics. If superficial objectification is the flavour of the evening, though, then those photos might come in handy.

Choose the right signals – get the right responses.

6: Making a match

You've done everything right – your photos were dazzling and exciting, and your bio gave you an air of mystery and showed your potential as a partner. Moment M has arrived . . . M for match! Congratulations! 🎉 Maybe it's your first, maybe not – it's probably not your last. (Do people remember their first match, like they remember their first kiss?) Let's make the most of this opportunity!

What to write, what to write . . . This chapter is all about the chat. Play your cards right, and you'll get a few tail feathers shaking. Mess it up, and IRL will have to wait for another match.

When it comes to the texting process between you and your prospective date, a simple 'Hi there!' ain't gonna cut the mustard. You've piqued their curiosity, now you need to get them intrigued.

Who breaks the ice?

First your photos made an impact and then your bio text brought results, and now you've got a match. It's time to let your personality shine at the next level, to personally and directly communicate that you're charming, fun, interesting, informed, exciting, and unique.

Before we even get to that: who makes the first move? Don't expect a straight answer here – it depends a little on how interested you are and how you want to spin that first date. Many folks claim that the *second* matcher should always write first, but either way *someone* has to make that first move, and today it's you.

You've got different approaches to consider here. OK, I'm going to cross over into personal territory – I think GIFs are the bomb! (GIFs – short for *Graphics Interchange Format*, developed in 1987 by Steve Wilhite – are extremely short, often silent video clips, like living postcards.) Not all dating apps allow them, but if they do, I'm all in. It's such a great way to use that first interaction to create a mood, flirt a little, heat things up a bit, or get a laugh (never a bad way to start). Sometimes I get a GIF back – a good GIF exchange is always fun. GIFs tend to reveal our use of mirroring rather clearly, so they're very effective as a form of non-verbal communication. I think that's why so many of us are fond of them.

Another simple but sweet way to break the ice is to say: 'We matched – that's great! How's your day going?'

What to suggest

Are you looking for sex or a relationship? Do you want a deep-thinker to hash out your life philosophy with, or just a good laugh? Your goal is your lodestar, your guiding light. The first text sets the stage for those that follow. You'll make things a lot easier for yourself if you can write something unique or interesting, and also something that opens up a conversation. 'Yo!' or 'Wanna shag?' is not recommended here. Actually, avoid ALL yes-or-no questions, because they kill any dialogue. Use what information you have from your potential date's bio and pics to write something personal and specific – tailor your question. This shows that you're attentive and interested, that you *see* them. A person who feels seen is more likely to show interest, or if nothing else at least feel inclined to respond.

For those only looking for casual hook-ups, the whole point of dating apps is efficiency, so chatting tends to be brief, shallow, and focused on meeting up quickly. Simple messages like 'You're so hot!' 'What you up to?' and 'We should hook up' are the norm. Even with casual dating, you still need to speak the same language. Geography comes into play here – a beer at the local pub, a walk on a nearby beach, is common. If everyone's on board, then the evening ends by heading up the front steps for Netflix or a nightcap . . . ☺ If you're looking for some hanky-panky tonight, let them know. Not tonight? Tell them. If you'd like to meet up somewhere in public first to check this person out *before* you invite them up for a coffee, then tell them *that* too – ahead of time.

A common query is 'What do you want to *do*?' Here's your chance – be straightforward and don't be shy. Being clear about your intentions will only help you to get what you're looking for, and beyond that it earns you respect. You'll lose a few prospects, but that's a good thing, frankly. The vibe ought to be mutual anyway, so it's better to find out now than later.

Meeting up to do something together in a relaxed environment is always good. It makes it easy to go your separate ways if you don't share the right chemistry. And if you *do* click, it's easy to meet there again next time. My friend has a little trick: 'I have a pre-determined route for walks. If I sense a connection, I can extend the route so that we get more conversation time. And guess what? It just happens to go past my apartment, at which point I ask, "D'you want to come in for a bit?"'

Approaches vary, of course, depending on whether you live in a big city or the middle of the countryside. Age plays a big role too. A rural acquaintance has found this approach to work well: 'It's taco night, may I take you out for dinner?' He also usually offers to pick up his dates and take them home again. This is quite specific to the rural location where there aren't many taxis.

Regardless of the nature of your ambitions, research[1] around dating app behaviour has confirmed that if we do a better job writing texts (both our profiles and chatting), we'll attract more candidates. It's always worth taking the time to improve this valuable skill.

First contact – points to consider

Time to write, but what? Here are a few tips for breaking the ice.

A funny GIF. Make 'em laugh.

Tailor your text. Open with a question or comment related to their bio text or pics. Look first! This shows that you're interested, that you see them.

Be polite. Imagine you just got this text: 'You're hot. We should date' – it's brusque, and cold. Using compliments, positivity, and manners in general will make you seem nicer, friendlier, and more sympathetic. If you forget your manners you'll give a negative impression, so be polite, please. Thank you!

Positive terms. Happy thoughts help set the stage for romance. Put a positive spin on things. Avoid words like 'boring', 'shit', or 'annoying', and instead use words like 'awesome', 'wonderful', or 'lovely'.[2]

Warmth and competence. We immediately and automatically evaluate the reliability, empathy, and ability of others – even in the digital realm. Be warm in general, use positive terms, ask questions, mirror, and show an interest in what people say. (Try to *remember* what they say too!)

Emojis. Emojis soften up your texts and add humour. They give you access to certain subtleties of non-verbal communication, so take advantage of this.

Mirroring. Observe how your match expresses herself, and proactively mirror things like how she formulates sentences, her word choices, sentence length, tone, emojis, or GIFs. Is your date formal or informal? Everything she types out signals something you can reflect. We mirror IRL, but we mirror online too.

Make a splash! Stand out. Avoid boring, one-word texts. Short texts are still good, but at least say something unexpected.

Short and sweet. If it takes over 10 seconds to read your text, it's a chore, not a pleasure. Extended essays scare off prospects, making you appear overly complicated (the halo effect).

Straightforwardness. 'Hey there, I'm Sofia, what a kick that we matched! How cool that you're also into stamp collecting.' (Or golfing, kickboxing, taxidermy – you get the picture. Common interests.) That's all it takes: simple, straightforward texts, served with a pinch of charm.

A consistent thread. If you've put up a 'mature' bio and 'mature' photos, your prospects might not appreciate suddenly getting texted, 'Up for a shag?' Show consistency between your bio, your pics, and your language.

Use the right tools for the job. If you're looking for *sexual* encounters, chatting tends to stay superficial and the focus is on meeting IRL. If you're looking for a *relationship*, you're probably going to be engaging in more heartfelt, genuine, and personal communication. Regardless of your goals, don't chat too long before meeting up IRL to see if the chemistry's there.

Answer promptly. If you're up for it and it's worth it, that is. People who appear available seem more attractive.[3] (This applies geographically too.) Prompt replies improve how attractive you appear.[4] But keep things balanced and in perspective; you run the risk of looking desperate if you seem glued to your phone, scrabbling after crumbs of human contact.

Things to avoid . . .

There are some great ways to break the ice. There are some not so great ways too. Watch out for these potential pitfalls:

Penpals. If you put off meeting IRL too long, you might find out that this IS the relationship . . . Did you only join a dating app to find new friends?

Bitterness. Don't be a moaner. Avoid grumbling, getting upset, and never be demanding. Maintain a positive, humorous tone. If you've been waiting forever and they still haven't written, a funny GIF, or mentioning something that you're doing right now or your plans for the weekend can all work well as a nudge.

Demands. You're not together yet, so making demands is nothing other than rude and unappreciative. Be generous, glad, positive, compassionate, and thankful – *that's* the secret to getting things your way (pleasant relationships included).

Yes or no questions. These are conversation killers – dead ends. If you've already texted previously, you can bring up a topic from earlier, ask them about their weekend plans, a film tip, or book recommendation. Not, 'Know any good books?' but rather, 'Which book can you recommend?'

Egotism. Don't just talk about yourself all the time. Your mum told you that – listen to her.

Copy/paste. Different strokes for different folks – don't be lazy. If you send the same opening line over and over again to every prospect you match, we'll catch on. Make us feel special.

Vulgarity. It's OK if you want to skip romance and go straight to the sex, but people will often be afraid to meet up with you if you seem crude and insensitive. The humour in sexual innuendo is in what you *don't* say. If you want to play adult games, act like an adult.

Expectations. You can take nothing for granted. Matching with a person doesn't automatically mean they want to meet you.

Brevity. Giving really short, uncommunicative answers, like 'OK' or 'That sucks', makes you look nonchalant. Sometimes you need to take the extra time to type out a few more words: 'That must have really sucked – I'm sorry!' or 'That's terrible, what happened? Are you OK now?'

Nagging. It never helps. Be patient. If you're tired of sitting on your hands and feel that this person needs a little prompting, use your little GIF trick or ask them about their day, or maybe their plans. And if they ignore that? Then just move on – they're not interested.

This is where you are supposed to be reading a really short title that, in a funny and perhaps ironic way, tells you to avoid writing messages that are way too long. Long messages make people feel weighed down with expectations, and your prospects will lose patience with you.

Texting tips: Five rules of thumb

1. Use their profile text (if they have one) to personalize your response.
2. Mention something from their photos. Compliment their pics.
3. Ask questions that give results: 'What do you like doing on first dates?', 'Beach or mountains?', 'What aspect of your life are you most proud of?', 'What do you think I should know about you?' Remember to be open, appreciative, warm, and genuinely curious.
4. Give them an honest compliment. Compliments are free, but they buy you success.
5. Keep the dialogue flowing.

Let's finish this chapter by looking at a study that compiled statistics from the profiles of 250,000 female and 230,000 male Tinder users.[5] One of the first behavioural observations regarding these online daters was that women tend to be more selective, which leads to fewer matches. Men, on the other hand, swipe 'Like' on a far larger proportion of women: some men like *all* the women's profiles, and only decide who to respond to afterwards.

This pattern creates a feedback loop, whereby men are driven to be less selective in their hopes of attaining a match while women are increasingly driven to be *more* selective, knowing that the vast proportion of their 'Likes' will lead to a match. When the men keep swiping women and it leads nowhere, it incentivizes them to swipe even more, and the women get flooded with even more empty matches. The men grow less discriminate, the women more selective, and this unfortunate, vicious cycle carries on.

The fact is that a whole 33 per cent of men reported applying this swipe-right-on-every-profile strategy regularly, whereas *none* of the quarter of a million women said they employed this technique. Quite the opposite: 93 per cent of women report that they *exclusively* like profiles that they are explicitly attracted to (which is how the apps were intended to be used in the first place). Interestingly enough, 13 per cent of the men report that whichever strategy they choose to gamble on is affected by how many matches they're receiving.

Due to the game-like nature of this process, a man can up his chances quite a bit with simple improvements to his profile (better pics, for instance). An improved profile improves his chances, and thereby his number of matches.

How about after matching? What do statistics tell us about who's more likely to write – and what?

Once again, differences become apparent. The researchers found that, overall, 21 per cent of female matches send an opening message, whereas only 7 per cent of male matches open up a dialogue. In other words, women are three times more engaged in the process than men. I think this is most likely affected by the men's quantity-over-quality approach on Tinder. In the study, they recorded 8,248 matches where men did *not* pursue interaction. This stands in contrast with only 532 female matches behaving likewise, indicating that they're more particular about who they like, and therefore consider it more worthwhile to send a text.[6] On many other dating apps, you're allowed to write to each other without the need for an actual match first.

Here comes our next little exciting moment: the difference between matching and messaging. The men who send a message do so promptly: 63 per cent of their messages get sent within five minutes after they've received a match. For women, however, only 18 per cent responded as quickly, which suggests that female users often wait to receive a message first. However, the men's messages are incredibly brief. The average message sent by men is only 12 characters long, compared to 122 from the women! And quite a few messages are even shorter: for men, 25 per cent of messages contain fewer than 6 characters (think along the lines of 'Yo!' and 'Hey!').

So, I've got a golden tip for you gents: write something! And if you want to stand out, write something that you've carefully considered (and that's not too long or too short).

The results of this study paint a clear picture: when dating online, men and women employ different strategies, which makes dating that much more difficult. Yet at the same time, these results also reveal plenty of strategic weak points where we can improve our chances for success! 😁

7: Text, call, or 'Let's meet up'?

Did you know that a quick 'Hello!' over the phone is enough for someone to start forming opinions about you? That's not a bad thing; it's just something we all do. Unfortunately, when it comes to dating, people tend to avoid phone calls. This is a shame, because you're missing a real opportunity here. *Phone calls* give far better results than just cranking out emojis day in and day out.

Let a phone call do the heavy lifting

Meeting IRL is the goal for most of us daters. We ought to strive to hit that mark as early as possible. So why bother calling? Texting's good enough until we meet up, right? Absolutely, you can do that. But sooner or later, occasions will pop up when it's more productive to talk. It could be that your match is hesitant and wants to talk ahead of time. Perhaps you can't meet up yet because one of you is travelling, or you live too far apart, or your families are feuding . . . If you can keep those coals glowing, you won't risk letting the fire die out, and phone calls help fan the flames. In psychology, this phenomenon is referred to as *Media Richness Theory* (or *Social Information Processing Theory – SIP*). It describes how interpersonal communication gets impacted in different ways, contingent on various methods of communication: text exchanges, phone calls, or IRL.

Keep in mind that we humans have evolved for meeting IRL, which explains why it's so important. Real life is where you hope to feel that little 'click'. Video or phone calls are the next best thing: hearing someone's voice is nicer than just texting, and you can reach depth in a relationship more quickly this way. What texting lacks is that tonal non-verbal communication, making it less effective. This is the same reason why misunderstandings happen so easily online. A phone call can be just the trick to get that straggler out the door (and into your arms). Studies[1] also show that spoken language affects our neurochemistry by increasing the levels of oxytocin in our body. It makes us feel good, strengthening the bond between you and your date. Talking to someone you trust also lowers the levels of stress hormones (cortisol) in your body. Texting alone doesn't have this effect.

It's not what you say, it's the way that you say it

Advancing to the next level can hinge on how you compose your texts and handle your phone conversations. Get this right and you'll keep that door open for one more day. 'You may be the warmest, gentlest person in your heart and soul, but be short in tone and you'll be judged by that,' writes author Jean Phillips-Martinsson. Being good just ain't good enough, so the question is – how can you reveal your warm, positive personality to your prospective dates?

Keep your eyes on the prize – get that date booked! Phone or video calls help speed up the process. Remember that your goal is to meet IRL, so you shouldn't be only texting as the days and weeks roll by. (Having said that, if you're only looking for a little attention, then I suppose a few texts will do the job.)

There are two things I think you ought to focus on if you want to spin the conversation in the right direction.

Energy levels. We all have different levels of energy. Some people speak in a slow drawl, while others are bouncing with enthusiasm. If you're a ball of energy but your date's a patient thinker, you might not click well. At this stage, it's wise to try to mirror one another's energy levels, frequency of pausing, and talking speed. Although remember too that a calm demeanour projects intimacy and invites a deeper level of emotional contact.

The art of exaltation. Make them feel important. Listen attentively, ask pertinent questions, and wait for the answers. This makes your phone date feel valued. A large part of your personality is expressed in how you sound, so be conscious of which signals your voice and language might be projecting. According to American philosopher and psychologist John Dewey, 'The deepest urge in human nature is the desire to be important.' It's good to make others feel noticed and appreciated. If you make your date feel seen, heard, and appreciated, and they have a nice time, you'll be much easier to like. More than if you're just squawking about your new wheels or fancy job.

Part II
ON THE DATE

8: Got chemistry?

It's Go Time, the big date! Your mind is aflutter with anticipation . . .
Will this *be* something? When it comes to sensing attraction, there's
just no faking IRL. One guy I was on a date with wryly commented,
'Now we're sitting here de-objectifying each other.' It's an apt
description. Judging whether you've got chemistry with someone
new based on a mere phone screen is like judging whether you'll
like New Jersey based on a postcard – dicey odds. Perhaps you've
noticed how people can shout things to the world over the web
that they wouldn't whisper in a crowd? We *do* need to meet up.

What factors lie behind the mysterious process of attraction?

In this initial chapter about handling first dates, I'm going to
explain the innate psychological mechanisms that kick into gear
when you encounter someone for the first time. I've got a handful
of solid tips for you too, to help steer that encounter – how to read
body language, send the right signals, and even how to flirt. It's
important to understand how you feel about your date, and life gets
easier when you can tell how they feel about you.

Mind the gap!

The researchers Liesel Sharabi and John Caughlin have investigated
that tricky leap from the net to IRL, referred to in science as *modality
switching*.[1] According to tradition, this crucial, make-or-break

moment is often regarded as the defining point of when a relationship begins.[2] If you both strike gold, it can be the starting point for a more intense relationship – or else it can be the fizzle-out point.

Among other things, Sharabi and Caughlin examined how *attraction* changes between online dating and IRL, the *similarities* that dates felt with each other (an important component of attraction), their *uncertainties* about the other (does she like you?), and the likelihood of a second date. A striking number of daters felt disillusionment when meeting for the first time.[3] It didn't happen always, obviously, but feeling *less* attraction for a person after the date was par for the course. How many of us haven't experienced that whooshing sound of deflating expectations in our lives when our idealized preconception of someone fails to deliver? It's not completely unexpected, and I can tell you why: our natural inclination is to fill in the missing details, and our capacity for wishful thinking is more than happy to oblige. We even have a bad habit of tidying up how we visualize prospective dates, chalking 5s up to 9s from blurry photos.

I've felt disillusionment many times. I was texting and talking on the phone with one guy. The conversation flowed beautifully. He seemed wonderful, honest to the bone, fun, kind, empathetic, and his personal life and career seemed to be in good order. If a phone call were enough to feel that click, I would have felt it then and there. We met up two days later. No click. None. He was still the same wonderful person – no change in that department. But I just didn't feel it, to my dismay. There is a something you can do to remedy this: the more we've communicated, asking and answering questions to learn more about each other, the lower our risk of disillusionment. The research claims that this enhances your odds of having a good date – talking reduces the uncertainty.

We overestimate our commonalities. Before a date, it can be easy to believe that you're into the same music, films, comedians, and literature, but these illusions fall away as you get to know someone more deeply, and suddenly start to see things as they really are.

Experiencing those similarities isn't just a trick of the mind or wishful thinking, it's also one of the most important predictors for satisfaction on a first date. The reason our minds tend to amplify commonalities while brushing dissimilarities under the carpet is because we want to feel that the people we like have a familiar background.

It's not always easy to make that leap from the net to IRL. If you've got a good feeling about someone, set up a date ASAP, denying your imagination the time to wreak havoc on your expectations and before you're already too emotionally 'in-texted'.

How well can you read people?

A good partner makes you happier in life. A bad partner can make your life miserable. The art of reading other people can literally save your life. So how can we read one another correctly, to avoid setting ourselves up for future heartbreak?

For starters, we're actually pretty good at reading people from that very first impression. Researchers studied how long people needed to spend together before they'd formed an idea about each other: 5, 20, 45, 60, or 300 seconds. In other words, when given more time, do we make more accurate assessments of others? They also studied which kinds of information (signalling) held significance. For instance, is it that first presentation, that first anecdote, or perhaps how you solve that first problem that reveals the most about your personality?

The ability to read each others' feelings played a critical role in human evolution – I might find myself in a dangerous situation if you're especially ticked off today, so it's good to know whether I should avoid you. That's why we're much quicker at reading negative emotions. But we're also pretty fast at reading intelligence, amiability, and conscientiousness. We can read these traits after five seconds as accurately as we can after five minutes (300 seconds).[4] How come? Well, our top priority for survival is to know whether we're facing a 'friend or foe' – someone who's trustworthy or untrustworthy. We're quick at reading intelligence because it's a good gauge for judging someone's capacity for fulfilling their intentions. What those intentions are is another question.

At what point during an encounter should we start judging the success of the date? After we've relaxed into the date a bit? Is it only then that our 'true selves' start to reveal themselves?

I'll admit it sounds a little vague, but the answer is 'after a while'. The researchers found that we were best at evaluating personalities (seeing people's true selves) at around three minutes into a first encounter – once we've got past our initial nervousness, but before an awkward silence rears its ugly head. Another study determined that at least one minute was needed for our judgement to be reasonably accurate. The four minutes spent with each person when speed dating is usually enough time to make pretty accurate character and intelligence assessments.

First date prep list

Birds of a feather flock together. Setting up dates with people you share similarities with or at least have common areas of interest with enhances your odds for good dates – and second dates.

Talk on the phone before you book a date. I recommend a serious, worthwhile conversation, although some people prefer to save that for the date.

Listen to your gut instincts. We tend to make fairly accurate assessments of people in the first few minutes of meeting them. Be careful not to let someone's charm distract you from your instincts about his or her character.

Ask questions! Start getting to know each other, although don't put that first date off for too long.

Date people who are open about who they are. Being open and honest dramatically improves your likelihood of enjoying a quality relationship.

Be ready for disillusionment. Sometimes your hopes get dashed – them's the breaks, kiddo. Be aware that the shift to IRL involves a fair amount of disenchantment, but also that it doesn't guarantee your dance has ended. If you're reacting to negative behaviour, though, it's a warning sign that you should jump ship at the next island.

Chemistry and *LAFS*

You're going on a date! Getting that booked was a victory in and of itself – if you check out the stats, quite a few swipers never go on any dates at all. Lots of folks get left twiddling their thumbs every evening.

So what should you think about before this decisive moment? One rule of thumb – and this is *any time*, not just when dating – is that you can't let your social skills slide. Work on these skills today, because the better shape your social skills are in, the greater the number of people you'll find available to you. Make an effort to learn how to *create* attraction. As your skills improve, you'll master how to steer relationships in the right direction.

It all begins with a powerful entrance. The first impression you give people should snap them awake and send a buzz through the room. Your head should be held high the first time your date lays eyes on you, your posture should reflect pride, and a little smile should grace your lips. You've made an intentional effort to feel confident and fully present, and this should give you a natural rapport with anyone around you. Instead of being alert for 'stranger danger', you should welcome any unknown person with warmth and congeniality. Keep your hands out of your pockets, and don't flash any suspicious glances. When greeting your date, let your positive attitude shine through as you make eye contact, like you've merely forgotten about a pre-existing friendship. If someone looks at you, look back with a friendly smile. Own the situation, but do so with humility.

The behaviours I've just described signal both warmth and self-confidence. In our physical encounters, we communicate in dual ways: verbally and non-verbally. Parallel conversations take place over these two channels, and several hundred non-verbal signals can accumulate over a mere half-hour meeting.

We'll discuss body language later on in the book, but for now let's take a minute to look at the psychological properties of *chemistry*. After all, a decisive factor is whether or not you and your date feel that magic. But what is it? 'Chemistry' refers to the feeling of having a special connection with another person. This doesn't always have to be sexual; the important aspect of it is the feeling you get that you need to meet this person again. It's the sense that you've clicked, and you usually feel it right away.

On rare occasions, you might even experience *love at first sight* (*LAFS*). LAFS has been a repeated theme in art and literature for over 3,000 years, and in the Western world at least one out of three people say they have experienced it. Fascinatingly, that same feeling continues to affect a subsequent relationship over its lifetime, even in its later stages. Why's that? Experiencing that click of chemistry increases a couple's level of passion, which in turn is linked to a greater sense of satisfaction and more stability in the relationship. LAFS is real and is grounded in attraction – and attraction is necessary if there's ever going to be a second date.[5]

Beyond physical attraction, we also need to connect on emotional and intellectual levels. Think: heart, mind, and body. It's important that we find the other person hot, smart, and kind. With friends, 'kind' or 'smart and kind' is often enough. At work, the emphasis is often on 'smart' and 'competent' (depending on your line of work). If you're after a late-night fling, then 'hot' might be enough, but for something that will pan out in the long run, you'll need to hit all three bases: intellectual, emotional, and romantic/sexual. Here, the word 'sexual' implies sexual tension, lust, flirting, and sexual attraction.

To start with, we need to find people who are emotionally available. And we need to be emotionally available ourselves as well, at least if we hope to feel a deep, true connection. The first date plays an important role. Show that you're interested in more than just pleasant small talk or a new friendship. You can help bring the date to life by creating a light, playful atmosphere, making more eye contact, initiating a little physical contact, sitting close, making jokes, offering compliments, and avoiding work discussions by steering the conversation towards something more charged. There's a difference in how you radiate an erotic connection as opposed to an intellectual one, through non-verbal communication.

What's next? You shift between playful, light-hearted moments and moments of deep silence, moments of tension. For your date, flirting is nothing to do with being skilful, smart, hot, or impressive. It's more about your ability to be present in the moment, to have a fun time with them. If you've tried in the past to play it cool, look happy, sound smart, and play your cards just right, aim instead for a mode in which you feel calm, warm, content, and fully present. Cheerfulness and wit are great qualities to have, but not always inroads to sexual contact. If you've mainly talked about work in the past, try other conversational topics such as your dreams, your ambitions, your joys, your fears, or the worst or best things that have happened to you. Reveal your inner world, and take charge of setting the atmosphere. Before a date, prioritize taking a moment of pleasure for yourself: dance to a little music that puts you in the right mood, spray on your favourite perfume, luxuriate in a hot bath, or have a nice cup of tea. Find a way to focus on the present and get yourself offstage for a bit, back to your real self. You certainly don't want to do the opposite: rushing straight from work directly to your date, your head still swimming from something your boss said. Which version would you rather present? In other words, be happy, conscientious, kind, and flirty, and balance it by showing that you're vulnerable and human.

So what leads to LAFS? Well, like it or not, appearance is unquestionably a factor. Appearance consistently affects our feelings of attraction and how we choose partners, regardless of gender, culture, or even the length of our relationship. Add to that how we can almost instantly read appearances (the speed-dating studies have helped confirm this),[6] and you can see why physical attraction is a critical component for LAFS to occur. Physical attraction has been defined as 'subjectively experiencing positive feeling towards another specific individual based on their physical appearance'. And you recall the halo effect from earlier, right? Attractive people are (fairly or not) appreciated as more interesting in a variety of different ways.

I'm aware that all these facts regarding the impact of appearance could cause anyone to lose heart. But don't worry, I'm telling you this because there's some good news: you *can* affect your potential for experiencing chemistry . . . By looking your best. And the power to look your best is already in your hands. As I've said already, all the things we can do with our appearance (hair, clothes, beard, make-up, etc) add up to more than just what we're born with appearance-wise. With a spritz of hairspray, a new pair of shoes, and a little luck, you just might get a kickstart to your next relationship.

Three levels of contact

No matter what you do, you're flashing signals all around you. Choose which aspects of your personality to radiate on your date. Your vibes and energy can make or break this date, although the other person also has to add components if you want to wire up a love bomb.

Sometimes it goes off, sometimes you get a dud. Contact on these three levels will help you enhance attraction and stir up chemistry. The contact you manage to establish often makes the difference between friendly interest and romantic attraction – a nice date vs a hot date, or a superficial date vs a meaningful date.

Find balance in all three:

♡ **Emotional contact** – Slow down the pace, increase eye contact, be present, attentive, open, and authentic. Share your feelings, including your vulnerable side. Offer personal details about yourself, perhaps telling a story from your life that reveals your humanity. If you don't feel comfortable sharing your deeper feelings with this date, perhaps that's a sign you ought to pay attention to.

🧠 **Intellectual contact** – What's their take on the world? Careers? Relationships? Values or priorities? Do you enjoy conversing, and seem generally in agreement? Whether or not you see eye to eye on these subjects will hint at whether or not you're an intellectual match. If you are, you can continue to learn from one another, your conversations will be more satisfying and rewarding, and your relationship will be more than just a physical pairing. Your date should be finding out what a thoughtful, wise, intellectual, and diplomatic person they've stumbled across. Be open about where you stand on issues, and focus on the ones where you agree the most.

😏 **Sexual contact** – The third level of contact regards flirting, physical intimacy, and erotic undertones. It's the playfulness, magnetism, spark, lust, and physical attraction that you hopefully will feel for each other. Lower your voice, communicate with your eyes, dare to pause and be quiet – create that classic film scene where the kiss is waiting to happen. Meet eyes. Switch gears from intellectual to sensual. Sometimes the hottest thing you can do is say nothing at all, and just stay quiet for a moment.

The art of alchemy

Let's imagine that you and your date have set a time and place. As you're arriving, you can see from a distance that she's already there, waiting for you. Perhaps you've got butterflies in your stomach, and really, really hope you won't be disappointed. Obviously you're hoping that you'll click, since it will certainly make a big difference to how you feel during the next hour you'll be sitting there. (Even though you can still have a nice time without chemistry.)

So the question is: can you *make* chemistry between the two of you?

Before we get ahead of ourselves, let's remember that we can only steer the set-up and try to influence our date – we can't control their feelings. There are no guarantees. You're facing four potential scenarios. You like them but it's not reciprocated. They like you but it's not reciprocated. You don't like each other. Or – and this is our goal – you both like each other. But don't worry; you've got some tools at your disposal to help tie up any loose holes in your net.

Since physical attraction is so vital here, start off by looking good! Wear flattering clothes (pay attention to your shoes, fellas), get your hair done, and your make-up all glowy. Don't overdo it (which can make you seem desperate) but *do* maximize your potential. It should seem like this is just *you*, how you look – it's not your fault you look good, and it's no big deal. In the words of the iconic fashion designer Coco Chanel, 'Dress poorly and everyone will notice your clothes; dress well and everyone will notice *you*.'

Your next tool is upgrading your personality. Which traits are worth emphasizing? Let your outfit reflect this. And if your appearance happens to catch their eye, that's all well and good, but it's your personality that'll keep it there, so be sure to flash that smile![7] Smiling has a powerful effect on our brains at a primitive, reptilian level. Smiling causes your date to relax and see you as less of a threat, so consequently shows you in a better light. And even if you don't think that smiles look good on you, crank out a few anyway – it still works.

Making eye contact is important, although staring is taking things too far. Your greeting and use of eye contact are your sharpest tools for inspiring others to evaluate you positively. Among other things, eye contact makes you seem more self-confident;[8] public speakers who inspire confidence make eye contact three times as often as their less confident seeming peers.[9] Another interesting aspect of eye contact is its connection to warmth. A study was performed in which subjects were shown film clips of couples talking.[10] In the first clip, a couple maintained eye contact 80 per cent of the time. The subjects of the study evaluated the pair as friendly and natural, and felt that they had a positive self-image. The couple in the second clip only made eye contact about 15 per cent of the time. The study participants qualified this second pair as cold, defensive, immature, and submissive. We tend to feel most comfortable at around three seconds of eye contact; holding eye contact longer than that makes us uncomfortable. If we like the person very much or agree with them, we instinctively increase how long we maintain eye contact.

Greet your date in the manner that seems the most appropriate. If a hug seems possible (which may depend on whether we're in a pandemic or not), remember that hugs release *oxytocin*. This is a natural neurochemical substance that promotes a warm, pleasant feeling in your body – and in the body of the person you're hugging too. We're talking about the same effect mentioned earlier regarding phone calls,[11] although the effect is more powerful when we touch each other.

Getting the conversation off to an immediate start helps you skirt any post-greeting awkwardness. Comment on something right there on the spot, or ask your date how they travelled there. You can comment on the beer selection or the view, and honest compliments are highly recommended. Show your playful side, 'cause if there's one thing that turns a tea party into a fiesta fast, it's humour! Laughter loosens the heart. Acting standoffish or playing it cool is a terrible strategy, so even introverts need to come out of their shells on this occasion.

The first seconds and minutes of contact can set the tone for the whole evening. There's a scientific term, *sensitive dependence on initial conditions*, which means that tiny changes in the initial stages of an event snowball into enormous changes later on, which implies that those first few minutes are crucial. But don't let the pressure intimidate you; the more relaxed you come across, the better. You want to create a warm and happy feeling for your date. If your date is a bit tongue-tied today, then doing a little extra legwork to lighten the mood is your responsibility. Do you also get nervous? Distraction tends to be a good strategy here: try watching funny film clips right before your date, or listening to some favourite songs. And keep a good posture too – stand up straight. You can even give yourself a little shoulder and neck massage. By affecting your neurochemistry, all these little tricks will improve how you feel right before you slam-dunk that first impression!

Emotions are infectious. Turn that frown upside-down, turn that attitude right-side-up, and infect your date with joy and enthusiasm.

Radiate for your big date

Your goal is to feel a wonderful connection with your date, which will inspire positive feelings in both of you. So let's end this chapter with a summary of the solid tips that give you a leg up on the stiff dating competition out there.

Humour. Get 'em laughin' and you got 'em lovin'. Better early than late. Not taking yourself too seriously and irony are usually considered attractive.

Smile! Smiling makes you appear more intelligent and trustworthy, and increases your popularity. We respond innately to smiling – flash those pearly whites!

Be hot. Look your best today – this is the moment when it counts. If you're unsure about your outfit, ask a friend for feedback. You could consider going to a stylist or having a make-up lesson if that would make you feel more confident.

Smell nice. According to research, if perfume is sprayed at people when they view faces, the faces appear more attractive to them (vs odourless attempts).[12]

Good posture. Straighten up – it sells you. Body language speaks louder than words.

Eye contact. Making good eye contact makes you appear more self-confident and accepting.

Greetings. However you greet someone, look happy and mean it. And the more (appropriate) touching involved, the more oxytocin gets sloshed about – smiles all round.

Flirting. If you sense a friend-zone situation looming, it's time to bring out the big guns. Try flirting, looking deep into your date's eyes, or switching to a better subject. If you're out of tantalizing topics to discuss, you could try out something like this instead: 'Excuse me, sorry for interrupting you, but I just have to tell you that your eyes are beautiful.' Self-confidence is alluring, and flirting makes us feel great. Be charming, playful, humorous, warm, and sexy!

Talk. Find something clever or funny to say.

Listen. Listening is more important than speaking.

Show enthusiasm. Enthusiastic people are way more fun to hang out with than cynics and moaners. Enthusiasm is magnetic, but it doesn't necessarily mean high-energy; you can be enthusiastic and mellow at the same time.

Be expressive. Poker faces do well in casinos, but faces with a range of human emotions will outcompete them almost everywhere else.

Mirroring. Similarities inspire connection and attraction. You can mimic the way your date is sitting, or gesture as frequently, or find crossovers in your taste in music, holiday destinations, or sports teams. Find common ground.

Leaning. Leaning forward makes you appear more interested; leaning backward less so. Cocking your head while listening makes you look more empathetic, and holding your head high appears more authoritarian.

Go with the flow. Try to let your feelings guide the conversation, not your ideas. Go with the flow so that you're more relaxed, and also so that the date doesn't turn into an interrogation.

Touching. If there's a natural point in the conversation where touching your date would be appropriate, do so. But sensitivity is key here, so be cautious.

Hot drinks. Having a cup of tea or coffee with your date can kickstart feelings between the two of you – warm drinks and warm feelings about people activate the same regions of the brain.

Consideration. If you're going to pour another glass of water or wine, offer some to your date first. Use your best manners.

Generosity. Offer to buy your date a drink or a bite to eat; never wait for *them* to ask *you*. You're the beneficiary of this deal – first impressions are priceless.

Focus. Pay 100 per cent attention to your date here and now, and nothing else. Anything less, and you're sabotaging your date and wasting everybody's time. Lose the phone. Don't think about work, chores, your parents, or global warming. Be here now, with all your heart and mind.

Employ the contrast effect. (Conditions permitting.) This may sound a bit harsh but we judge one another in comparison to others. After test subjects were required to stare at very attractive faces for a long time, they showed a reduced desire to meet people who were only 'average' in appearance. Need to get a few years back? Make sure your qualities and appearance get compared to people you consider 'aesthetically inferior' to you, and enjoy the beneficially positive light that the comparison provides.

Priming. You can prime the pump by mentioning or hinting at something romantic or erotic – depending on which direction you want to move in – before you meet up. Subtle innuendo and charm are your tools here.

Have an end time. Always have somewhere else you need to be afterwards, and inform your date ahead of time when you'll be leaving. If it turns out to be a terrible date (and many do), you've got an easy way out. And if this person turns out to be your dream date? Excuse yourself to make a phone call and . . . Well, gosh, who'da thunk it? Turns out that meeting got postponed . . .

Walking or sitting – which makes for the best date? Different strokes for different folks. Ask them what they like to do on a first date. And have some answers ready for when *you* get asked. A good date doesn't have to be exceptional or original – a good date is just a good date! But you should unquestionably meet somewhere you both feel safe and secure, and you should do something of *mutual* interest too. Also, it's important that you get the chance to talk – afterwards is fine if you attend an event or watch something. That being said, exceptional or original occasions tend to make you seem more interesting.

9: It's about finding things in common

Or was it that opposites attract? When it comes to relationships, compatibility means overlapping in some areas, and complementing each other in others. In general, the more similarities you share with a partner, the greater the odds that you'll be satisfied with your relationship.[1] We've already discussed the psychological phenomenon of mirroring. Now let's look at the bigger picture regarding similarities.

I like you – you remind me of someone I am!

Mirroring refers to how we imitate each other's gestures, postures, and speech patterns. I've caught myself imitating other people's dialects many times without having any reason to do so. This deeply instinctual behaviour (not unique to the human species) is driven by highly automated cells in our brains called *mirror neurons*. When our tastes in food, clothing, or activities sync, or even just the way we conduct ourselves shares a rhythm, we sense a feeling of togetherness. And a feeling of togetherness is important – as I mentioned previously, groups survived where individuals didn't.

Mirroring has been shown to affect the results of negotiations.[2] In one experiment, researchers studied pairs of individual negotiators; certain negotiators were instructed to mimic their counterpart discreetly so that it would be undetected (for instance, leaning back in their chair after their counterpart had done likewise). Subtlety was key. So did mirroring affect the outcomes in negotiations? Did it ever! The negotiators who imitated their counterparts were *five times* more successful in brokering deals. And almost *none* of the negotiators who avoided mimicry managed to hash out a deal. Mirroring creates a sense of rapport, and works as a social adhesive. It breaks down our sense of 'us and them', leaving both parties feeling closer and more connected. The subjects who were mirrored felt more comfortable and satisfied.

Studies have shown that speed daters who mimic the linguistic style of their dates enjoyed a threefold increase in their odds of getting second dates.[3] Couples who enjoy matching linguistic styles are 50 per cent more likely to still be together three months later. It makes us more persuasive as sales reps and earns us better tips, in fact up to 70 per cent better tips![4] Mirroring also affects how we text. Research has confirmed that mirroring greetings over texts (responding to 'Good evening!' with 'Good evening to you!' instead of 'Yo!', for instance) improves our odds of being positively received.

Mirroring unites us. It causes people to take a shine to us, makes us seem more helpful, and when we get mirrored ourselves, it spins our opinions of others in a positive direction. We're nicer to *every-body* who mirrors us, whether we like them or not.[5] Getting mirrored amplifies our sense of sharing common ground.

And we can find so many similarities! Similarities in appearance would be the low-hanging fruit, but beyond your clothes and physiology, you've got lifestyle choices like diet and exercise, education or employment, reading habits and tastes, preferences in entertainment, personality, values . . . The list goes on. According to the *similarity-attraction effect*, the greater our similarities, the greater our attraction.[6] We feel more accepted by those we feel similar to, creating a sense of belonging which both enhances our self-identity[7] and implicitly corroborates our perspective on the world. (She thinks so, I think so . . . Sounds like we're onto something.) Naturally, we get along more harmoniously – and fewer conflicts arise[8] – when we feel a sense of togetherness. If we all agree, what's there to fight about, right?

Gesturing, leaning, and adjusting your posture are just the bare bones of it; you've got other ways to mirror too:

Activity preference similarity:[9] If you and the person you're talking to enjoy the same activities, chances are you'll like each other more than if you don't.

Attitude preference similarity:[10] When we share similar opinions about things we feel greater respect for the other person than when we disagree. Try to focus on conversational subjects, opinions, and ideas where your feelings overlap.

Another applicable theory here is *social exchange*,[11] which purports that we make a cost–benefit analysis of the 'resources' each person brings to a relationship, regarding professional success, academic background, even attractiveness. This implies a sense of symbiosis, such as: I bring the good looks while my partner has the keys to the castle. The crux is whether we bring *balanced* resources to a relationship, irrespective of whether they're the *same* resources. Income vs appearance, age vs status – anything's on the table here. Perhaps I sport my Olympic gold medal while my husband has a star on Hollywood's Walk of Fame. Somewhere in our minds, we're attracted to the notion that we ought to at least get what we deserve from a relationship.[12]

According to the research, we *do* tend to choose partners who are similar to us, such as being equally good-looking, sharing similar attachment patterns (to be discussed later on),[13] political or religious convictions, or a similar social or economic class, or level of education.[14] Our similarities can also involve our values, interests, lifestyles, and intelligence.[15] Similarities provide payoffs, because the science shows that they lead to healthier, happier relationships.[16]

The most common reasons people give for breaking up with a partner are 'We're just too different' or 'We grew apart'. One of several studies corroborating this is from the Netherlands, which found that 40 per cent of divorces were motivated by claims that their ex-spouse's personality was just *too* different.[17]

In fact, the only time we truly deviate from this instinct is when we are actively avoiding any connections with the individual in question. An interesting example: we're *less likely* to mirror attractive individuals – of the gender we're into – if we're already in a satisfying relationship.

These facts about mirroring mean that when other people meet you (or even before that, when they're texting you), they're thinking: how similar are we? What do we have in common? This is why focusing on similarities in your tastes and interests is a rewarding strategy. For instance, let's say that you noticed a dog in his photos. Tell him about your lovely little chihuahua Bling-bling, or the dog you grew up with, something like that.

Ask questions – be loved!

Around 30–40 per cent of the words spilling out of our mouths are intended to inform others about our feelings, thoughts, and opinions. Since we happen to find this form of chit-chat very pleasurable, when you give your date a chance to talk about themselves, their brains receive a little shot of dopamine. That makes them feel good, which reflects well on *you*.[18] Make a great impression – just by listening!

Worthy equals or two sides of the same coin?

What initially floats your boat is one thing. Whether being similar in all things makes for better relationships is a different can of worms.[19] If we compare sharing similar values to having similar personalities, are both equally beneficial? (They're like apples and oranges, you know.)

Let me answer this way: having different values, opinions, and moral positions on the important things in life can often trip us up in our romantic relationships. Anybody who has been in a long-term relationship has probably realized this already. There are enough things to split hairs over as it is (like child-rearing, holidays, balancing careers) without adding further points of contention.

Personalities, however, don't work the same way. Having *different* personalities can actually be *better*.[20] If two partners are equally dominant, for instance, every little decision can turn into a boxing match – something's got to give. And if two people are equally withdrawn, relationships can easily stagnate. According to the research, for example, if both partners have low levels of the ~~Big Five~~ Six trait of *agreeableness*,[21] effective communication becomes dicey. Complementary attributes provide a more diverse and effective toolkit for a relationship. (No soccer team ever won a match with eleven goalkeepers.) Instead of focusing on similarities when it comes to personality, focus instead on *compatibility*. It may sound complicated, but it's just a matter of seeing whether two jigsaw pieces go together. You should *fit* well. It's true, on the other hand, that extroverted, sympathetic, and open people are generally popular,[22] which logically implies that dating them is a lot more fun than dating meanies or duds.

There's something important to point out here: what we *think* we're attracted to often doesn't match up with what we're *actually* attracted to. Vibes are vibes, and the gap between the desires of the mind and the desires of the heart is considerable.[23] Romantic attraction is just terribly unpredictable (no matter how the matchmaking TV shows try to sell it). And just because you've had a super date doesn't mean you'll have a super relationship. I've had a slew of fantastic dates along the way, but only a few of those had the potential to develop into an equally impressive relationship. Follow-up dates are the only way to figure these things out.

I have to admit that I reflexively keep the Big ~~Five~~ Six in mind, and it's made me self-aware enough to more easily recognize who I like, who I'm drawn to, and who I absolutely wouldn't want to date. Texts, profile pics, bios – they all informed me about the personalities of my dates. The ability to predict with reasonable accuracy *who* one should be able to form a healthy relationship with has been the Holy Grail for psychologists studying romantic relationships since the area of research first emerged in the 1930s and 40s.[24]

Hardly surprising. Imagine the headaches you'd avoid if you could spot a perfect match at a moment's notice!

Similarities play the biggest role early on as we're romantically drawn towards them, often believing we're more similar than we actually are.[25] A sense of commonality is important while we're getting to know each other – similarities create attraction.[26] Once you're knee-deep in a relationship, however, they play a less significant role. Despite this, we still tend to emphasize the areas where we're similar,[27] and even the sense that we share similarities goes hand in hand with a successful marriage.[28]

In relationships, we're generally more similar in certain areas, and less so in others.[29]

More frequent similarities:

Age, ethnicity, religion/level of spirituality, attitudes.

Frequent similarities: Education, values, interests.

Less frequent similarities: Personalities – we're often each other's opposite in this regard. This is good, because certain personalities clash.

Tricks for teasing out similarities

Finding similarities will create a sense of closeness between you and your date. So what are you supposed to do if it doesn't seem like you have anything in common? If you're interested in this person anyway and want to keep the ball rolling, my first trick is just to ask questions. Eventually, you'll always find *something*: similar interests, similar experiences, or just similar preferences. Something you have in common will eventually rise to the surface, such as having been on similar holidays or shared similar pastimes.

Another trick is just to employ basic mirroring. Be subtle here – don't show your hand. Once you've found those similarities, get talking about them, whether it's opinions on the environment, your favourite brand of trainers, or childhood camping trips – anything where your feelings and thoughts might overlap.

10: Body language that attracts

Despite the tapestry of fascinating images you're weaving with your words on your big date, subconsciously Mr Maybe has already read you by this point. He's already made up his mind regarding your trustworthiness and self-confidence, and whether or not you've got good intentions.

Just be yourself

What do other people see while you're talking?

Among the first things someone focuses on is your facial expression. Another important aspect is what you do with your hands. Keeping your hands visible and away from your pockets makes the other person more relaxed. It signals that you've got nothing to hide – not just symbolically, but literally. As far as your facial expression is concerned, try to keep things loose and easy, and obviously on the sunny side. Avoid ambiguous or contradictory facial expressions – you should be focused on creating a sense of security. Bear in mind that those little micro-expressions that occasionally whisk across your face can do damage if they're negative or crop up at the wrong time.

Don't crank up the hand gestures; try to keep things nice and slow instead. You don't want to talk in slow motion, but taking your time is an excellent defence against looking desperate or nervous and signals self-confidence. Self-confident people aren't in a hurry, and there's no problem you can't solve, right?

To find a good match, you'll need to do a little fieldwork before you're sure just who you might be looking for. My first priority when I became single was to figure out what sort of person I enjoy spending time with. I didn't feel pressure for every date to be perfect because I needed to know as much about myself as I did about my dates. If you see dating as an ongoing *process*, then you avoid the risk of feeling desperate. Keeping this perspective, you avoid the anxiety of wanting to be liked, and don't need to put on airs, agree with everything they say, or cross your boundaries in order to feel affirmation.

You don't want to fall into those traps. It's not good for your own self-worth and does nothing to make you more interesting. If anything, the reverse is true – you come across as insecure and lacking willpower. Do the opposite – show up as your best version of yourself: confident, dignified, optimistic, and reliable! ☺

Use body language to express warmth and competence

If a picture paints a thousand words, then your body paints a thousand pictures. So make sure that it's giving off the right signals. Warmth is the most important quality to project on a date. It's also excellent if you can project self-confidence, status or influence, and competence. How you project warmth differs from how you project these other qualities.

Warmth and reliability: Use open gestures, show your palms, make positive eye contact, use mirroring, nod sometimes, tilt your head, and (of course) smile.

Competence and intelligence: Have a firm posture, straighten your head, take up more space, use targeted gestures and strong handshakes, and gesture showing the back of your hand. Avoid fidgeting, or unnecessary movements that might distract. Use what you need to communicate what you want, but otherwise keep it simple. This applies to what you do or say, and even your outfit.

Choosing to play the authoritarian card (which is intended to emphasize strength and power) runs you the not insignificant risk of appearing arrogant or overly dominant. For instance, holding your head straight projects self-confidence, but tip that head back just a tiny bit more and now it's arrogance that comes across. Warmth should also be kept within a certain threshold. While a genuine smile hits the bullseye, if you throw a little too much enthusiasm into that grin or get the timing wrong, you can seem pathetic, or even a pushover. Pushovers might make great room-mates, but they tend to have a tough time attracting partners. We tend to be drawn to people who have a clear vision of what they want, or who seem to have a natural dignity about them.

Communicate harmoniously – and smile!

Verbal and non-verbal communication need to harmonize. Words matter, but if your body language doesn't back them up it will confuse your date as to what signals you're trying to send, and you'll come across as insecure or potentially even dishonest.

Spencer D. Kelly,[1] a neurology researcher, employed an EEG scanner to measure how gesticulation affects the electrical activity in our brains – our brainwaves. The lowest value on the measurement scale, N400, registered when test participants witnessed gesticulation that contradicted what the speaker was saying. The same effect also registered if the film clips showed someone gesticulating while speaking gibberish. Saying one thing but doing another is confusing to us – there are no two ways about it.

At Duke University, a research team revealed that we have an easier time remembering the names of people who smile at us, and regard them as more sincere, gregarious, and competent.[2] According to their results, the reward centres in our brains light up when we try to learn and recall the names of smiling individuals. This tells us that it's rewarding to look at smiles. Even thinking about smiling people improves our mood.

Smiling is your ace card! If you take advantage of that lovely grin, your dates will be fonder of you and you'll better your chances of ramping up the dating process.

So close, yet so far away . . .

OK, I probably won't write an entire book called *The Art of Leaning* (no promises!), but it really is a useful tool in your kit. I've mentioned it previously, but let's look at it in more depth.

Cocking your head a bit to the side shows that you're listening sympathetically. You can lean *towards* someone to tell them something in confidence, or lean back with nonchalance. We instinctually lean towards people or things we find interesting, and lean back from things we're wary of, or people from whom we prefer to keep our distance. What happens if we lean towards or away from something that we feel indifferent about? Does leaning affect us emotionally too? It does. Seriously, merely leaning forward tickles warm fuzzies in your brain as *if* you're interested. This means that by leaning forward, we can become more engaged in what's happening.

So on a date, you can covertly check which way the wind is blowing: how interested is this date in you?

Take a little step back – *while maintaining eye contact* – to increase the distance between the two of you, and see how she responds. (Losing eye contact means you might be perceived as standoffish.) If she takes a step to regain lost territory, then you're all good; she's interested. If she leaves the void between you, then you've only got a nibble – not a fish. Keep baiting your hook and try again a little later, to see if there's anything worth reeling in.

Here's an example of how *proximity* can affect us. If your date suddenly takes a step backward, it's a good indication that you're making them uncomfortable. You may be coming across as over eager, or taking things too fast. If you're unsure of what's happening, take a little step back to increase the gap. If your date doesn't step up after a while, wait until they seem comfortable again before you reduce the separation between you. If they sense that you're not trying to pressure them, it's usually easier for your date to relax. And it's natural for you to take a step back yourself if it feels like *they're* encroaching on *you*. This ebb-and-flow process is a dance, and you have to keep in step with your partner's rhythm. This applies to texting as well, both prior to and after the date. Two-steps-forward-one-step-back is just part and parcel of finding a mutually comfortable level of intimacy.

I know it's counterintuitive, but . . . if you want to turn up the heat? Chill out a little.

Passion vs dispassion

Sometimes you think, 'Man, I must've seemed totally superficial jabbering away at that strong, silent type', while other times you're on the flip side, thinking, 'Jeez, If I'd been any less interesting last night, that poor guy would've fallen asleep in his beer!'

It's legit to feel either way, and it reveals just how differently we can act under different circumstances. And we all have different personalities to start with: some of us are highly strung, others are mellow yellow. But don't worry, you should just be who you are, of course. That being said, do people share a general preference regarding *passion* vs *dispassion*? (Psychologists normally use the terms *aggression* and *passivity* in this context, but I'm going with less clinical terms here.)

In one study, recruiters were asked to take part in a filmed presentation, tasked with choosing a candidate for a CEO position.[3] In the films, men and women presented themselves as if applying for a job, but the presentations given by these 'candidates' varied in their levels of intensity, from fairly neutral up to measurably intense. Both male and female 'candidates' received the most glowing evaluations when they displayed the highest levels of passion. We like people who burst with life and energy, the way passionate people tend to come across. The men and women who delivered dispassionate presentations received the worst reviews, of course.

But Angela, this is a date, not a %#'#&%€ job interview!

OK, that's true! But if you look at how your success will be secured by how engaged you seem, it sort of *is* an interview. Other studies confirm that people are attracted to expressive behaviour. After all, doesn't that explain the celebrity afforded to actors in the film and TV universe? A study titled 'Impression formation: The role of expressive behavior' describes how we enjoy being with people who are extroverted, competent non-verbally, casual, confident, expressive, and appear visibly focused.[4] So on your next date, you can see what you might want to focus on revealing, right?

Self-awareness opens doors

Being conscious of the signals that you send is enormously beneficial. What kind of behaviours and body language have you been using? What kind of habits (or bad habits) do you have? Do you belittle yourself? Do you come across as arrogant or unsympathetic? Your level of self-awareness affects whether you open doors in your life or not, and strong self-awareness increases your odds of entering relationships. It also causes people around you to take you more seriously.

Study the behaviour of other people in detail. How do they appear, how do they greet people, how do they speak? Learn how to read social situations and how to react accordingly – master your social competence. So on your date, just be you. That is, the *new* you – the keenest, slickest, sexiest you the world has ever seen . . .

The image you project

In his book *The Political Brain*, Drew Westen[5] discusses the role of emotions in politics. He describes an attribute which he's dubbed *curb appeal*: 'One of the main determinants of electoral success is simply a candidate's curb appeal. Curb appeal is the feeling voters get when they "drive by" a candidate a few times on television and form an emotional impression.'

It's all about gut reactions; long before you've shown people that you're the right person in the right place, they've already made an emotional decision as to whether or not you're a leader, whether or not you're trustworthy, and whether or not you've got a chance for a second date. Besides political affiliation, Westen found that our emotional reaction – our gut feeling – is the dominant factor for determining whether we vote for a candidate or not. So, considering how powerful gut reactions are, pose this question to yourself: *Do I have curb appeal?* What gut reactions am I inspiring?

Bolster your curb appeal

It's time for a tip on how to beef up your curb appeal when you're playing the dating game. You can encourage the development of a relationship by linking eye contact with a positive feeling. Try this: give your date a compliment while you smile and make eye contact with them. If you can, make them laugh. It sounds simple, but this little combination will 1) create a warm atmosphere through your message and facial expression, and 2) allow that warm feeling to become associated with your (lovely) eyes, which 3) reflects back on your entire person. Conditioning at its finest.

Having a positive attitude about yourself gives your feathers extra lustre. And it's *important* that you like yourself. Your self-image has an enormous effect on how others see you. When you're an open and happy person, it makes the people around you feel comfortable being open and happy themselves. If you're insecure and withdrawn, it makes the people around you nervous and withdrawn too. You're forming your own social environment whether you like it or not, so if you're interested in attracting someone, then you need to give off the same vibes that you'd like to get back. If you decide to stampede gung-ho with guns ablazin' on a hunt for eternal love, you're setting yourself up for a lot of disappointment and heartbreak. Desperation has earned its crappy reputation. If you're relaxed, satisfied with your life, and can find peace in your heart, it gives entirely different signals than if you seem like you're looking for your missing half. If you can maintain a casual attitude, on the other hand – if life and death don't hinge on this one magical date – then you'll be all right if it goes bad. Even getting dissed isn't the end of the world. In fact, try to never take it personally; when other people reject you, it's often just a knee-jerk reaction on their part. Perhaps they got dumped recently, maybe they've been overwhelmed by too many responses and took it out on you, or maybe their mum just sat on their guitar – you have no idea how this person's day has been. Give them the benefit of the doubt, for everyone's sake.

Stay focused on moments where you really connect with people, and keep things playful. Be present for your date, be yourself, show interest in them, and show them that you're interesting too. Give yourself good advice ahead of time, and use it as your guiding star. Tell your date about exciting personal incidents from your life. Ask questions. Listen to the answers to those questions. Don't try to over-sell yourself and impress your date, rather just share with them the things that you're passionate about. In the dating jungle, light-hearted, happy, engaging, passionate people are the cream of the crop.

How present are you?

As I mentioned, being *present* can be crucial. If you want to make a memorable impression on people, you need to give them your full attention. The more engaged and focused we are towards others, the safer they feel around us and the more magnetic we become.

One thing that usually helps me to feel more present before a date is to put my phone on *Do Not Disturb*, tuck it away, and ignore any impulses to touch it. I stop thinking about whatever I've got going on later and forget about everything that went wrong earlier, and just let my thoughts and ideas pass by like wandering clouds. After that, I make sure I turn up a little early so that I'm not flustered. (Or at least I try! Sorry Håkan, Erik, and Magnus . . .)

When you stay fully in the now, completely present, it improves your success in your relationships and personal interactions. Research done in America has shown that doctors who are intentionally present and listen carefully to their patients get sued less often than others.[6] Sounding dominant or unconcerned, on the other hand, increases their risk of getting sued.[7] This same ability to be present makes us more attractive as partners, and healthier both physically and psychologically.[8] People who are able to stay in the present moment come across as calmer and more reliable, feel better in general, and suffer less from stress.[9]

So, as you can see, presence (or the lack thereof) has conse-quences. We've got everything to win by discovering tools that help us manage to stay fully present. People might not *understand* why they find you so compelling and irresistible, but they'll feel it.

11: Pumping up your charisma

Is charisma attainable, or is it a magical talent only gifted to the lucky few at birth?

Along with his colleagues, the psychologist Howard Friedman[1] conducted research into how charismatic people differ from uncharismatic people, and as a result discovered that highly charismatic people affect how less charismatic people feel. A particularly interesting detail is that when charismatic people are happy and spend time with less charismatic people, the less charismatic people feel happier afterwards. This effect only goes one way, in a positive direction.

Friedman's studies reveal that charisma (and you can call it passion or a glowing aura if you like) rubs off on other people. Highly charismatic people tend to express themselves in more optimistic terms, regardless of the form of communication, because they *are* optimistic – that's the whole appeal. Their enthusiastic, charismatic vibes warm the others around them like heaters in a pub garden. Surprisingly, it doesn't matter whether they've been recorded or are speaking live – charisma has influence.

A charismatic person's communication is more effective since they can persuade others more easily, and this affects getting to second dates as much as it does your performance in the workplace. Charisma lets you stand out from the crowd – people remember you. You have more influence, are more convincing, and people like you more. Your opinion carries more weight.

Luckily for you, charisma can be developed, and here you'll find tips on how to do just that![2]

Create a vision and communicate it. Tell a story. Make sure it is directed towards your listener so that they feel included in the excitement.

Use expressive, coherent gestures. Speak with your whole self – face, body, eyes. Be energetic and engaged. Avoid overdoing it, though, as this can make you seem nervous or scatterbrained and reduce your authority. If you focus on quality, not quantity, you'll calmly and compellingly exude authority. Keep a light touch, making sure your gestures are appropriate for the circumstances, and avoid seeming forced. If you'd like some training, watch video clips of successful, convincing speakers, and study their movements. Research tells us that we judge emotionally expressive, extroverted (and even physically attractive) people as more charismatic. These are areas you can improve in.

Use eye contact. Look at the person you're speaking to. Don't stare (remember, three seconds is considered optimal), but using eye contact appropriately shows that you're paying attention. If there are other people there, be sure to make eye contact with everyone in the group.

Express your feelings. Emotions drive our decision-making process, not logic. Humans generally use logic to *justify* their conclusions, not to make them. So you'll have an enormous advantage if you can manage to stir up some positive emotions in your date. For example, consider ahead of time what kind of emotions you'd like to inspire, and see if you can't think of an anecdote or two that might tug at the heartstrings.

Smile! Because we love it when you smile! No BS here, though – you have to mean it. Also, there's a balance here too: running around with your gums exposed in a permanent grin will cost you some authority. Just smile – it's easy! ☺

Keep the conversation flowing. Gaps in the conversation are awkward with people you don't know well, and today's the day to impress. If you can keep that dialogue flowing, you'll be dating like a pro. If you find it difficult to come up with topics of conversation spontaneously, keeping a few ideas or stories up your sleeve can be useful for kickstarting the chit-chat. Or try a joke!

12: In touch

How physically entangled you'd like to get on a date (and I hope this is obvious) is up to you. Forget what your date may or may not be anticipating – it's not a determining factor. You are under no obligations, and your body is subject to no one's will but your own. If you feel that you're getting coerced or pressured into sex, then there's never been a better time to stand up for yourself.

I've covered a lot of ground on my 100 dates. I've had some great adventures, wonderful dates, meaningful close connections, and plenty of occasions that were missing any or all of these things. I've met all different kinds of people, and the physical contact varied as well. The vast majority of dates ended without any physical contact beyond a handshake and a goodbye hug. That's how I felt, so I acted accordingly. That should always be your guiding light: that it feels right and you're comfortable. Regardless of whether we're talking about a lifelong relationship or a one-night stand.

The magic touch – oxytocin

Humankind's most primitive language is *touch*. In an experiment at Purdue University, a female librarian was assigned to examine what the students in the library were reading. However, she was also assigned to brush against them as discreetly as possible half of the time. For example, she would lightly brush visitors' hands when receiving or returning their library cards. After the visitors had left the library, they were asked to evaluate the experience they'd had there. Among other things, they were asked whether the librarian had either smiled or touched them. Strangely enough, those who had been touched remembered the librarian *smiling* at them, but not the touching itself; it didn't register. More than that, the visitors who had been touched described having had a more positive experience at the library, and even that they felt better about life in general. It's also the case that touching their customers is another way that waiting staff can earn greater tips.[1] Touching has a nearly mystical effect on us.

So what goes on inside us when we are touched by someone?

Being touched causes our brains to release the neurochemical *oxytocin*. The librarian, like the server, stimulated the release of oxytocin in her customers. Oxytocin creates trust and emotional ties between people. When people touch you, you feel better. And if you like someone, you usually like touching them too. These things are connected, and often form a positive feedback loop.

When two people become a couple, the amount of oxytocin circulating in their bodies increases. The higher the levels of oxytocin the couple experiences, the more they exchange physical affection and experience behavioural synchronization. Research teams have observed that higher levels of oxytocin also contribute to longer and happier romantic relationships.[2] And when other people trust us, our oxytocin levels go up.

All of us are born with individual, predisposed levels of both oxytocin and *vasopressin*, a related hormone that shares a common evolutionary origin. Certain individuals are quite simply predisposed towards stable, monogamous relationships, are more actively engaged as parents, are better than average at seeing things in perspective, or are naturally more empathetic than others. I don't know about you, but personally, I think that sounds like a pretty good catch! Wouldn't it be awesome if you could just pop up at that first date and spot signs of these fantastic qualities right there and then?

How can you apply this knowledge about oxytocin on your next date?

Although touching is a wonderful elixir for our relationships, touching someone you've barely met can be like stroking a cat the wrong way. You need to be sensitive towards your date and read the situation. There's good touching and there's bad touching, of course. Showing the way or leading someone down a corridor, for instance, is usually a situation where touching them is OK. Leaning into someone occasionally, or even patting them lightly on the back for just a moment are also usually nice ways to show affection. Still, anything beyond a handshake is entirely contextual and needs to be entirely consensual. A wrong touch can easily create misunderstandings, make you seem too touchy-feely, or suggest that you don't respect your date's boundaries.

And there are other ways to become physically closer without going too far and seeming invasive. You can lean in as you tell them something, which shows that you're comfortable getting closer. Placing your hand gently on their forearm as you say something tends to inspire trust. Or pat them a little on the arm when they say something funny. Another good occasion where it's often OK to touch your date is if they've just said something surprising, something you wholeheartedly agree with, or something particularly personal.

If the pheromones are flying and the air is charged with romance, touching each other in these situations often comes quite naturally.

Getting Physical

Oxytocin has a way of changing our attitudes, making us kinder and more generous. We become more cooperative and more considerate, and we also tend to smooth things out more quickly after we've argued. It's good stuff.

If it turns out that you both like each other, getting physical is a common, natural next step. Sometimes just a little kiss is the perfect boost, and sometimes a little more where that came from hits the spot. It's hardly a secret that there are some eager daters out there who are more than ready to jump between the sheets. Others prefer to take their time. Take things one step at a time and see how they build up. A stroke on the shoulder, walking arm in arm, holding hands, or even a little stroke on the cheek can string Cupid's bow. And if you've taken it easy in the beginning, then going in for a kiss won't come as a shock, but instead feel welcome and exciting.

Taking your time is good, but relationships also build in an arc, and without sexual tension you risk getting friend-zoned. If you find that you're slipping back down the relationship rainbow, lean over, look your date in the eyes, and ask about – or comment on – something that she's told you. I'm not saying that the ground should be quaking from the erotic suspense you're radiating every second you're together, but you *do* need to keep those love butterflies flitting about in your stomachs. Touch your date occasionally, look meaningfully into his eyes, and don't be afraid to garnish your humour with a little sexual innuendo. Listen attentively, and don't be pushy. Be discreet, polite, but also straightforward about your intentions. If your date rejects your advances, *never show it* if you feel irritated or upset.

In fact, since we've broached the subject, never get irritated or upset on dates *at all*. Just don't. Shit happens, I know, but flipping out makes any situation worse because people turn defensive, and defensive people are usually 100 per cent uninterested in your opinions. Also, it can make you look like a jerk, which certainly clashes with your new role as queen of the dating scene.

In summary: tips for a successful date:

- Don't talk all the time without pausing or listening to your date.
- Don't talk exclusively about yourself.
- Never talk about an ex. Or anyone else you've been romantically involved with.
- Never talk about previous sexual escapades or your sexual prowess.
- Don't sit tongue-tied so that your date is forced into a monologue.
- Ask questions back. You're not being interviewed; it's a conversation. Avoid speeches, interrogations, or any other unbalanced communication.
- Don't interrupt. Let your date finish their thoughts, and leave a little pause in the air. After a moment, you'll know it's your turn.
- Don't talk about work; it tends to stale the conversation.
- Never show up drunk, or out of it in any other way.
- Don't be late. It's disrespectful.
- Don't smell bad. Come showered and clean – good hygiene is a *must*. Check that breath too.
- No dirty clothes.
- Don't scan the room all the time. Focus on your date – everyone else is just noise.
- No fidgeting. Keep those nervous habits in check.
- Don't finish each sentence with a laugh. This is a telltale sign of insecurity, and insecurity is a turn-off for most people.
- Don't mention the war. No politics, hot-button issues, religious opinions. This is neither the time nor the place where disagreement is a good idea. The only politics involved should be your remarkable diplomacy in

avoiding conflict. That said, if you disagree with something and feel the urge to respond, then do so. Being a people-pleaser only pushes disagreements into a pile-up down the road.

- Don't talk about money. Like how much you earn, for instance, or how much the bill is. Just pay and move on, or split the bill 50/50 and shut up about it. Or if it's your treat, enjoy the honour of hosting a meal and don't make a thing out of it – no one owes anyone anything.
- Don't be evasive, but don't brag either.
- Don't try to impress your date. People with status don't need to show it every chance they get. It's the ones who ain't got it who try so hard to prove the opposite.
- Don't stress the time. Avoid planning dates for when you've got a million other things to do.
- Never ask anyone's age, and never mention their weight. If your guess falls shy of the mark you'll look like a creep, and if it flies high you'll embarrass or humiliate your date. Should they ask you to guess, say you haven't a clue and change the subject. Don't ask anatomical questions at all – age and weight are just a part of this rule.
- Don't be a cheapskate. Offer to buy the first round or to pay for something to eat. Do *not* wait for the other person to treat you.

Part III
DATING

13: Booking the next date

It turned out to be a great date! You made a good impression, kept your cool, and scored a few laughs. So when is it time to get in touch again? While you don't want to seem overkeen, you certainly want to keep the momentum up.

One smart way to handle this is to book a second date right there on the spot. That way both of you avoid the awkwardness of what to say and when. But if the cards fell differently and a second date hasn't been pencilled in, unfortunately there is no officially accepted waiting period, such as two or three days. Personalities and circumstances bring in too many variables. If you didn't feel a deep enough connection on your date, or didn't find time to get the next one booked, then texting and seeing each other sooner rather than later is important to keep that steam building up. But if you nailed your first impression and spotted that glint in their eye, then you've probably got a longer grace period before the sparkle wears off.

Personalities play as much of a role in this as situational vibes. Some people run hot and can't wait to get back in the same room as you, while others get easily overwhelmed socially and need more space. The most important thing is to contact them politely, and without any expectations. Sending a text afterwards on the same day to thank your date for a good time or to just share something relevant is usually appreciated. If your date seemed a bit apprehensive, though, wait for the dust to settle first.

But once you get the communication flowing, you'll figure out what level of contact your date is comfortable with soon enough, whether it's frequent or more sporadic. Do your best to keep a balance in your response times – I'm aware that waiting four days to answer someone might feel risky, but the introverts out there need more downtime to let the intensity wear off. It's better to leave them a little hungry if the alternative is making them feel suffocated. A good tip to avoid uncertainty is to say *when* you'll contact your date again: 'OK, great, I'll get in touch with you on Wednesday!' Then, on Wednesday, you can set up your next date. If you're way too revved up to sit on your hands for four days, you'll have to work out some kind of compromise. If a mutually satisfying tempo still feels out of reach, it's time to admit that you're dancing to the beat of different drummers and don't really match. I hate to break it to you, but if you're struggling against cross-currents this early in the game, this isn't the relationship for you.

Suggesting a second date

When everything goes well, we usually want to meet up again. It's good if you can get a handle on the situation and steer the conversation to keep things percolating. A lot of us are busy these days and lack the time or patience for a messy or tentative scheduling process. If you keep rescheduling, the situation will get complicated and this reflects on how they imagine a relationship with you will be – demanding, uncertain, or annoying. So take the initiative. Cook up a solid plan and present it in a humble but unambiguous way. If there's a scheduling conflict, offer *one* alternative. Seriously – *one*, that's it. It's human nature to want someone else to fix things for us (as long as the person in question is decent and sensible). It's a relief to sit back for a few minutes. That's why driven, goal-oriented people score way more points on the 'sexy' scale.

Watch out for hesitant or evasive answers. This may mean that your date is looking for a way out, or perhaps they're date-aholics trying to squeeze you into their crowded calendar. A certain type overbooks dates the way (pre-Covid) airlines overbooked flights. Players only looking to cut new notches in their bedposts bump the dates they judge least likely to jump in the sack. Not OK. Don't accept getting knocked to the bottom of their dance card. Unless they got hit by a train or waylaid by a family emergency, you're likely looking at a bad apple. Someone who values you won't leave you on standby, so never accept preliminary bookings, in which they propose a *possible* meet-up but will confirm it on the same day. You're getting juggled. If you get an uncertain answer, demand clarity. You're Plan A, not Plan B, so tell them that if they don't know, you've other things on your agenda for that evening.

Here's a few playful ways to get that next date booked: 'I'm at the game and you wouldn't believe this energy! Wish you were here! 😳,' or 'I'm checking out that new joint. It's packed, how come you're not here? 😎' By hinting for them to join you, you're offering them an indirect invitation. It keeps the pressure off, but also opens the door for them to invite themselves to meet you – maybe not right then and there, but the day after or next weekend. Don't overuse this little trick since there's a risk of looking desperate, but it's totally worth a shot once in a while.

Getting stood up

You're all done up, you've got on a crisp shirt, your teeth are polished, and your hair's on point. You're psyching yourself up for your date, letting your imagination fill in details that you'd blush to admit. Just as you're putting on your coat – *ding*! Ooh! A message!

'Hey there. I'm so sorry, but I won't be able to make it.'

Shit.

There's more, but the only thing that matters is you got *stood up*. Your heart drops into your stomach like raw steak falling off a kitchen counter. Maybe his boiler's broken or he got called on an urgent mission for MI6, but the odds aren't in your favour. As disappointment floods through you, take a few deep breaths before you start hammering out your response. It's crucial here to *not lose your cool*. It sucks, yeah. *They* suck, yeah. It hurts. But we all get stood up or dissed on occasion. Firing off an angry or passive-aggressive answer, or making a desperate plea for him to solve the situation and meet you anyway would be a mistake. Let a little time pass and you'll see things in a new perspective, and realize that the situation isn't as bad as it felt when the hammer fell. I can give you two good reasons why it's in your best interests to politely reply that it's OK that he bailed on you. For starters, although you were looking forward to the date, you've got a busy life and your happiness doesn't hinge on waiting around for him. And the other reason is to show that you're an understanding person. If he's sensible, he'll realize that he's ruined your plans. You'll demonstrate what a noble, kind, and generous person that fool's missing out on. Use patience and etiquette to gain a victory for your reputation.

Include these three elements in your reply:

1. Let them know that it's OK that they had to cancel.
2. Ask if they'd like to rebook the date a few days down the road (although don't start rearranging your schedule on account of this unexpected change of plans).
3. Wish them a pleasant evening or good luck.

Busy people with interesting, complex, and exciting lives are more attractive to date. Sending vibes that you're just a potato on the shelf with nowhere to be doesn't sell you as an appealing catch. If she's capriciously bumping dates on every whim and you're always ready and available, it's only a matter of time before you'll get taken for granted.

If getting stood up is the final straw for you, though, and you realize that it's probably for the best that she cancelled, don't say something hurtful or crass. You're the rising star of the dating circuit, so show them how the pros shake hands after the match. Give her a pleasant and gracious goodbye, and then flush that empty memory out of your mind forever.

Here are some practical suggestions on how to deal with various scenarios when you get stood up:

If they're 'too busy': 'Hi Enrique, that's fine, I understand that something came up. I've already made plans for the next few days, but I'll be free this coming weekend if you'd like to meet then instead. Have a great night!'

If they give you an excuse: 'That's OK, I get it. I hope you get it all worked out! I'm pretty busy this week, but let's see how things look in a few days. Have a good one!'

If they don't give you an excuse: 'No sweat, we've all been there. We can try for next week instead. Keep your chin up!'

If you're done with them: 'OK, have a great evening! And a great life too!'

If they stand you up more than once: 'Hey there, Martin, sorry you got sidetracked tonight. If it's possible to give me a little more notice when you cancel in future it would make things easier for me. Have a wonderful night!'

When you have to stand *them* up

Shit happens. Sometimes *you're* the one who has to cancel a date. Hopefully you can give them plenty of warning, but on occasion you might be forced to cancel at the last minute – you missed the train, or your kid is unwell, who knows? When it happens, there are a few useful things to keep in mind: be apologetic, make it clear that you value their time, and let them know how sorry you are. Tell them *why* you can't make it.

Not all cancellations are equal. For example, 'Hey Nicole, sorry I can't make it' is hardly optimal, leaving question marks dangling all over the place. But messages such as 'Hey there, Lucian, I'm really sorry, but my work deadline got pushed up,' 'My sister is in a mess and needs me to babysit her kids tonight,' or 'I think I'm coming down with flu – raincheck?' are all reassuring and spare your date from speculating *why* you had to cancel. This tells them that it isn't personal, and that you haven't lost interest. It's also important to work in a rebooking of your date right away. Something along these lines:

'Hello, Alex. I'm so sorry, I woke up this morning with a bad migraine and probably should stay at home today. I'm really excited to see you, though – I was looking forward to our date! How's Saturday evening look for you?'

'Gerome, hi. I'm really sorry, but my boss moved our deadline, and I'm going to have to stay at work for a few more hours. I was so looking forward to seeing you tonight, so this really sucks. If you can ever forgive me, would Friday night work for you? A new restaurant opened round the corner from where I live, and everyone says it's fab. Can I bribe you with a meal to make it up to you?'

When they give you zilch to work with

'Hi there!'
'Hi'
'How's things with you today?'
'Cool'
'How's your day been?'
'Fine'

B - O - R - I - N - G. You've had this conversation before. Just because she responds doesn't mean she's interested – she might just be trying to be polite. Starting a conversation with someone new is hard enough as it is, without having to cobble together conversations out of monosyllabic answers. But it's not the end of the road! There are clever ways to pose questions that tease out more complicated answers or get someone's tail to twitch. For instance, instead of asking him how his day was, ask him what *the best thing* about his day was, which forces a specific answer. Ask what she's planning for the weekend – people usually get excited talking about their plans. Her answers to these questions will reveal whether she's interested or not. If trying to get answers is still like trying to squeeze blood out of a stone, try switching topics. For example:

'So what did you do for the rest of your trip?'

'We rented a car and drove to a vineyard an hour away.'

'Cool! So what was the vineyard like?'

'Interesting.'

'So what was your favourite wine, and why that one?'

He likes wine? Let's talk about wine, then. Wines, grapes, regions, pairing wines with food . . . The trick is to find something that your new friend is into and build conversation around the topic. You've found something to work with here, so run with it.

Another approach can be to circle back to a previous topic – music, sports, films, anything you've already brought up. Just make sure to have a relevant new detail, such as: 'I finally checked out that bookshop. You're right, their crime section is incredible!'

Words and phrases to help get you another date

Some words make you look uninterested, weak, or indifferent. Other words make you seem like a go-getter who gets stuff done.

Words to avoid:
- 'maybe'
- 'I guess so'
- 'eventually . . .'
- 'sure . . .'

- 'whatever'
- 'why not?'

Avoid vague words in general, particularly if you're talking about meeting up again. Hesitant, ambiguous, or ambivalent words weaken your ideas and opinions. Instead, choose words that express clarity, positivity, and decisiveness.

Words to employ:
- 'absolutely'
- 'of course'
- 'obviously'
- 'that sounds great'
- 'perfect'
- 'then that's what we're doing'
- 'I'll see you tomorrow in that case!'
- 'I can't believe you're also into ice skating! I love it! They've got an ice rink about two miles from my house. Why don't we meet up there next time? I'll drive – I can pick you up Tuesday evening if you're free.'
- 'You know, this is something we definitely need to talk more about. And I think we should discuss it at the Grand Hotel over the best brunch in town, what do you say? My treat!'

Using the mere-exposure effect to your advantage

Some aspects of love aren't as magical as you might think, and in my book *Your Hidden Motives*[1] I describe the following study[2] executed by Professor Richard L. Moreland, from the University of Pittsburgh. Moreland asked his study participants – both men and women – to look at photos of four women, marked A, B, C, and D. Afterwards, they were asked to answer a few questions about the individual women. How attractive were they? Would the participant be interested in spending time with this woman? Would they like to be friends with her? Aesthetically, all four women looked like average college students of more or less the same age, were considered to be averagely attractive, and wore a casual style of clothing typical of the other students – as if they were classmates. Which they sort of had been – at least three of them. While Woman A had never sat in Moreland's class, the other three women had attended his lectures. They showed up several minutes before class, walked slowly to the front row, and sat quietly taking notes during the lecture. Afterwards, each woman quietly packed up her things and left the lecture hall with the other students, who were unaware that Moreland's hired imposters had been in their midst.

But the experiment hinged on an important detail: the number of lectures that each woman attended varied, ranging from none to fifteen lectures. So what did Professor Moreland's study find? A pattern emerged in the evaluations, based on how many lectures each woman had attended: the more often the women had attended lectures, the more often they were deemed to be attractive. Woman D (who had attended fifteen lectures) was rated the most attractive, followed by Woman C (ten lectures), Woman B (five), and Woman A (none). *Seeing someone often* causes us to like that person. It wasn't as if the woman who attended fifteen times *looked* better than the other three – they had been selected for the study because they were considered to be equally attractive. And the students never met any of the imposters during the lectures. The women were present, sure, but they had never interacted socially, either verbally or non-verbally.

Exposure encourages acceptance, and this has been proved repeatedly in hundreds of experiments covering much more than college lectures. Whether we're talking about clothes, phrases, soft-drink brands, ads, it boils down to the same principle: the more we see something, the more we like it. Researchers have dubbed this phenomenon the *mere-exposure effect*. And fascinatingly enough, we're pretty oblivious to it. When Moreland's students were asked if they'd seen the women in the photos before, almost none had any memory of them at all. When the researchers then asked the participants how they felt about the results of the study, their replies were along the lines of: 'Seriously? Seeing someone a few times makes them more attractive? Yeah . . . I doubt that.'

But they were wrong – that's *exactly* what happened.

You know what I'm trying to tell you, right? If you wanna get that fire lit, make sure your prospects see you. Meet up if you can, talk on the phone, or make sure they see pics. At the same time, be careful, because going on dates just for kicks involves repeated exposure, which increases the risks (or chances) of your dates growing attached to you.

And no spamming, please! A little photo now and again is cool, but putting your life on a slideshow will freak people out. Subtlety is key.

So, how long before you should text?

This guy impressed you on your first date and you don't want him to slip through your fingers. But you don't want to seem clingy either. Are there any guidelines regarding timing here? Certainly you could just wait until he texts you first, but even then: how long should you wait to answer?

It's all about *timing*.

Your phone chimes at lunch after last night's great date and you give it a peek: 'Thanks for last night! What a blast! 😆 I'd love to meet up again, what do you say?' As your heartbeat quickens, your immediate instinct is to hammer out, 'TOTALLY! LAST NIGHT

ROCKED LIKE NEVER BEFORE!!!! LET'S MEET UP TONIGHT ALTHOUGH I DON'T THINK I CAN WAIT!'

Stop!

Here's my message to you: 'DO NOT SEND THAT TEXT.' I don't care whether you used all caps or not, the point is that you need to *chill out* before you reply. We understand – we've all been there. It's easy to feel ecstatic when your enthusiasm gets reciprocated! But you need to stay level-headed and collect yourself before you answer. Whatever you're doing – eating lunch, yoga, trimming the hedges – finish it first. You're not underwater and their attention isn't air. There's no perfect length of time you should wait, just answer when a natural chance to do so comes up. Don't approach this like a game with hidden rules – if your response times reflect each other's rhythm it creates a good atmosphere. Did they reply after three hours? Wait a few hours yourself before getting back to them. Sometimes you've both got some downtime and ping-pong texts for a while, and then one of you gets interrupted by something. Don't blast out multiple texts when this happens; if you do, you'll be crowding them. Keep the friendly ping-pong action in play: you text – she texts, and so on. We live busy lives and not many people are looking for pen pals these days, so save any lengthy stories for when you meet up face to face.

Personally, I consider texting to be a tool for booking dates, and for keeping the spark alive *between* dates according to necessity. If text exchanges start taking up too much of my time, it feels like a relationship with that person will also gobble up my time, and why let things drift in that direction?

Now, if a few days have gone by and you're chewing your nails down to the quick, go ahead and lob them another text. If they don't answer this follow-up message, you can send a third and final message – yes, *final* – and don't stay up all night waiting for an answer. You can't grow bananas in the desert, and not kicking dead horses is a hallmark of self-respect. A partner worth being around will make sure you know the score.

14: Good Text/Bad Text

BORING	FUN
'What's up?'	'Life just got interesting. Got the car all ready for a summer road trip and there's room for one more . . . ☺'
'Wanna hang out sometime?'	
'Watching TV'	
'Sure'	'My friend just bailed so I've got an extra ticket to the match on Saturday. Any takers? ☺'
	'I saw your Instastory! Sounds like a wild day! ☻ If only I could have been a fly on the wall . . .'
	'I like how you think. But I'm at least going to wear clothes on the way over . . .'

You can ask 'How was your day?' or 'What's up?' and you can answer with 'Fine' or 'Dinner and TV' but minimalistic texts don't give people much to build on. There are myriad ways to answer that are more fun; it's completely within your power to inspire curiosity, create interest, and provoke positive responses. You can even be seductive. Use your words to paint a picture, shape a mood, or be clever and funny. If spinning vocabulary isn't your thing, mention interesting experiences you've had, or even just ask questions that inspire your date to tell *you* exciting stories.

Now, before you start cranking out texts like Shakespeare reincarnated, take a second to consider something: what is it that you *want to communicate*?

If you're not careful, it's easy to send texts that would be better suited to friends or family, not your romantic prospects. Excessive enthusiasm, such as throwing around hearts and !!!s like confetti, can make people think you're overzealous and scare them off, particularly this early in the dating process. This is different from texting new friends. If he's the kind of guy who holds his cards close to his chest but feels obliged to answer you in a similar fashion, he'll find it awkward. You want to avoid the extremes of either babbling away or sounding like a robot. Of course you want your personality to shine through, but you also need a light touch. Perhaps you're a high-energy, expressive person who *loves* emojis – you want to be *you*, sure, but you also need to consider that we're all different, and that being overly forward might not always be appreciated.

Instead of sending texts that just sound like grunts – 'Yo', 'Wassup?', 'All good?' – try to tickle their funny bone. Keep your texts short and sweet (just like your bio), and remember that giving off warm vibes enhances your appeal. Keep it easy for your date to answer – people are busy, and it's far more likely that people will put off answering you until tomorrow if they have to untangle complicated thought patterns. They might need their morning coffee first . . .

Be aware that certain types of texts will help your cause, and certain types won't. That said, try not to pick apart your texts with a fine-toothed comb or overanalyse everything – if your phone's in your hand already, trust your gut. Just bear in mind what your goals are, and try to see the situation from your prospect's perspective. Otherwise? Be authentic. Be *you*.

Pro-level texting

When it comes to texting like a pro, I recommend five steps:

1. **Double-check and edit.** Is it obvious what you're trying to say? Did autocorrect screw up any of your words? Does your tone seem genuinely positive, or is there a risk that you sound passive-aggressive? Take an extra second to read your text one more time before you send it. You can even read it out loud if you want; the point is to avoid having to send correction texts because – even if those extra texts are legit – quick-fire texting can feel in-your-face. And unnecessary spelling errors unnecessarily downplay your intellect.[1] Give those texts a little polish first, so that your date can focus on your mind, not your eager thumbs.

2. **Sweat the small stuff.** Little details in your texts can make or break how interested others will be in you. For example, using exclamation marks makes your recipient more likely to write back. At the same time, if you use them in every other sentence, they lose their effect – you'll have more icing than cake after a while. What about full stops? In texting, don't bother with full stops unless they're necessary – the punctuation police aren't tapping your phone. A full stop can even give a text a cold tone, like you want to end the conversation. A perfect example of this is the difference between

   'OK'
   and
   'OK.'

   Do you really need a full stop here? If you're unsure, delete the dot. Conversely, make sure to always add a question mark if you're asking something, because otherwise it causes confusion. Right

3. **Be funny.** We love funny people! As you're rolling out those one-liners, though, take care not to be rude or disrespectful. Referring back to something both of you have laughed about previously is usually a safe bet. Letting him work a little to impress you and win you over can also heighten the expectation, and your humour is a useful tool here. If you don't know this person well, avoid anything sensitive or taboo. (The folk wisdom of avoiding discussions about religion and politics applies here.) But as long as you're careful not to step on any toes, go ahead and try to make 'em laugh.

4. **Paint pictures with your words.** Using visual language makes your texts more fun and vibrant. Instead of just asking 'How was your day?' you can write something like 'Tell me about your day! I've still got a smile on my face from your comment about [chipmunks and eggs] last night.' Every text can be a little bit inspired or amusing for the recipient. Simple texts like 'Hey!' don't express what makes you unique, but taking the time to write something funny, creative, or more personal stands a better chance of piquing their curiosity. Being descriptive makes it easier for them to visualize what you're telling them, and makes you more interesting. And use those cliffhangers! Leaving a little info out will help keep them engaged. Don't act like you're hiding something or trying to make them jealous, but use hints to keep things alive. If you dish out your whole story all at once, they've got nothing to come back for. Select what you'd like to share, consider what your words are saying, and realize when it's time to end a discussion without seeming rude.

5. **Focus on the positive.** Negativity has killed plenty of promising romantic opportunities, so put it back in its place and create a warm atmosphere instead. Be a source of optimism,

kindness, and good feelings. Be the person she can't wait to hear from. Show that you can listen to your date, and that you care about how she feels. Keep things light-hearted, and let your texts show that you're smart, driven, fun, and the kind of person who gets things done. Be empathetic, curious, and warm. You want her face to light up when she hears that ping. I was texting with a guy the other day, and we discussed what we were doing right then and there. He mentioned how he was making food, filling his lunch boxes for the week. I could tell that he'd been looking at my bio, and was mentioning things relevant to what I'd written. This made me smile, and that attentive kitchen handyman earned himself a date!

The impression you want to give is that your life is already fulfilling and inspiring the way it is, that you haven't been waiting on tenterhooks for *them* to bring you happiness. There's no need to mention that you're fighting with your ex over your kid's screen time, or that you've got an old debt hanging over you which is keeping that bank loan out of reach. That energy thief at your office is a conversation to have with your coworkers, not your romantic prospect. Eventually we need to open up and share some of our heavier struggles, but that's not material for texting after a first date; conversations shouldn't be clouding over this early in a relationship. It's always better to tackle heavy stuff when you're meeting IRL. If you're not in a good mood, you can always text something along the lines of: 'I'm sorry, today's been a rough one. Can I text you tomorrow and pick up where we left off?' Perhaps you'd like to talk about it over a cup of coffee the next day, opening up an opportunity for your relationship to deepen beyond standard chatter. Doesn't sound so bad, eh?

CD FLIP – your formula for texting

Before you push that little button, make sure your message passes the CD FLIP test, consisting of the five following criteria:[2]

- **C** – **C**heck and edit every text before you send it, please
- **D** – **D**etails matter – use them to bait your hook . . .
- **FL** – **F**unny **L**aughter is always a crowd pleaser
- **I** – **I**llustrate with your words – imagery gets their gears spinning
- **P** – **P**ositivity makes you appealing

Using texts to keep the fire smouldering

'Want to meet up for a drink this weekend?'

Two minutes go by and still no answer. Should I have added an emoji there at the end? Or written 'a glass of wine' instead of 'a drink'? Shoulda, woulda, coulda – your head won't shut up! A few more torturous minutes go by before you suddenly get that golden text: 'Absolutely ☺'

Phew . . . You feel relief for about two seconds before the next battery of questions explodes in your mind. Should I propose a when and where? Or should I play it cool, and wait for her to take the initiative? How long are you supposed to wait to answer? Did she really mean it, or is she just being polite?

Texting has definitely changed how we date. Let's pretend that you've got into the habit of texting with someone all day long.

'Good morning!'

'What kind of trouble are you getting into today?'

'I just watched a powerful documentary about the mating rituals of those walking stick insects. Seen it?'

And then that same afternoon they're suddenly AWOL for a few hours and you're tortured by uncertainty. Did something happen? Did I scare them off? Am I annoying, or too available? Too *un*available? Are they pissed off at me? Are they cheating on me?

Do you really need to maintain constant contact like that? When you start to develop feelings for someone, texting can be stressful because you don't know where you are with them. Every little word or emoji can feel like an indicator of your prospect's interest level. This is why it's important to understand how to handle your texting – even when you're caught up in the thick of it. Keep in mind that it wasn't so long ago that folks often had to wait *months* to hear from one another, yet they still got together and had kids and we're all here now. So maybe it's OK to set your phone down for a while, instead of jumping at every little sign of life?

What I'm hoping to help you understand is that texting with a romantic prospect isn't particularly neutral – you're generally either fanning or dousing the flames. The risks for miscommunication are greater with texting than with talking on the phone. Firstly, you're dependent on the art of composition, and secondly, there's a void of non-verbal communication – you don't even have pauses or your tone of voice like you have in phone calls. You've got words, that's it. How do you express the richness of your emotional life or depth of your mind in mere texts? How can you be sure that they can interpret what your heart is trying to say? It's easy for texts to be misinterpreted, considering that they have to penetrate an unknown filter of biases, expectations, experiences, and uncertainties on the recipient's part. Texts often fall flat because your emotion or warmth doesn't come across; they're confined by language, and lack the emphasis and subtle cues that smiling and gesturing add to the process of communication.

Ask yourself: if you received this text, would you understand what message is supposed to come across? If you've written something long and complex, perhaps it's better to trim it down and follow it up with 'Do you have time to talk for a few minutes?' Generally speaking, the less you write, the less risk there is for misunderstandings. Avoid foul language or trigger words, and as a rule of thumb, keep things simple and comprehensible. Avoid vague messages, and wait until you've cooled off a bit if you get caught up in a conflict that threatens your relationship. Give it an hour or two, so that you have time to consider the consequences of what you write.

When used properly, texting will help you to strengthen your bonds with the folks you're dating. Flirting and keeping things fun in between dates is the way to fan those flames when you won't get to see each other for a while. A good point of departure is expressing, through your texts, what a great day you're having as it is. You're not looking to find happiness, you're just looking to spread it. And hearing from her just made your day even better! This attitude will be appreciated and make you more compelling. Two good examples:

'I'm having a great time here, and your text just made it better.'

'It's great to hear from you! I hope your day has been as fun as mine! ☺'

15: When words are not enough

As we've already discussed, human communication is both verbal and non-verbal.

A significant portion of our communication is done through texting these days, and with texting many people stick to words alone. When non-verbal communication falls by the wayside, you miss out on giving or getting that little smile, warm look, or well-timed nod of acknowledgement. As forms of social interaction go, texting is flat and lacks nuance, leaving plenty of room for misunderstandings.

Because this lack of non-verbal communication was a shortcoming in texts, visual enhancements rose in popularity. One of these was the emoji.[1]

Can emojis improve communication?

Playing with type goes as far back as typewriters, but the first *emoticons*, short combinations of characters such as :) or :-), were officially born in 1982, when Scott Fahlman, an artificial intelligence researcher at Carnegie Mellon University, added :) to a post to articulate that he was joking in an early online forum.[2] Eventually a Japanese company came up with the idea of pimping up emoticons into the colourful *emojis* that we're so familiar with these days.

Emojis help to clarify our intent, reducing the risk of misunderstandings. You can soften up texts, add warmth and humour, set the tone, and express most of the feelings that you'd like to express.

The words you choose still command the stage when it comes to appealing to your date's emotions (not taking into consideration texts containing *only* emojis), but emojis have tipping power and can tweak the volume of those words.[3] Positive emojis amplify positive messages,[4] and negative emojis amplify negative messages.[5] You can take the edge off bad news or give requests (which aren't directly negative) a softer tone by adding a positive emoji. If you want to thank, praise, congratulate, or give positive feedback to someone or wish them luck, emojis beef up your message.

Researchers refer to *facial emojis* and *non-facial emojis*, which most often pop up at the tail end of texts.[6] Facial emojis have been well studied, and proved to awaken our feelings in much the same way that real faces do – we respond to them on a deeply primitive level. (Among others, researchers used the 🙂, 🙁, 😊 and 😁 emojis in their experiments.)[7] Even non-facial emojis do a good job of clarifying what we're trying to say, and help to remove potential confusion. They can still affect the emotional content of a message to some degree too, particularly in expressing joy,[8] softening negative messages,[9] or expressing playfulness.[10] But if it's emotional impact you're looking for, facial emojis are your tools of choice (with more studies to prove their effectiveness).[11]

So, to sum up emojis: they facilitate communication, making it more accurate and effective. Emojis *are* non-verbal communication. When we can't meet up and are stuck with texting, they can be worth their weight in gold. Using !!!s or ALL CAPS are also tools that can get the job done. Simple tricks like these still have an impact on your content and emotional expressivity. Emojis can even affect different areas of the brain as opposed to written words on their own.[12]

A few emoji tips to keep in mind

Just like saying 'I love you!' to everyone you meet, emojis will stop meaning anything if you chuck them willy-nilly all over the place. They're the spice, not the rice. Launching ♡♡♡ or other emotionally charged emojis after a first date will most likely spook your prospects.

1. Instead of composing complicated visual puzzles, think emoji haiku instead. Usually less is more. Don't water down their impact.
2. Remember mirroring. Using emojis in the same way and with the same frequency as your date will make them feel closer to you. You're welcome to do your own thing (for instance, if you feel that they're 'misusing' emojis), of course, in which case whether your prospect mirrors you or not is up to them.

16: Communication in the early dating stage

Relationships go through phases, which my friend John has correlated wonderfully to our seasons here in Scandinavia. The *outset* phase comes before the first date, and correlates to spring in Sweden – blink and you'll miss it. The *initial* phase, when you're getting to know each other after the first date, is like the Nordic summer – a little longer but still too short, and you never know what you're going to get. Perhaps the attraction was only physical, or you get ghosted. The *courting* phase is after you're officially together, and, like autumn in the north, it can be extraordinarily beautiful, but always seems to start a little too early. Expect a few storms and cold snaps – getting to know each other can be a challenge. Yet it can be easy to reminisce about that courting phase once the fourth phase kicks in: a *long-term relationship*, which – like Scandinavian winter – might just never end. And when the realities of life become unavoidable, you simply cosy up together and make the best of what you've got to work with. Stick with it, however, sunny days will soon be here again!

We're concerned here with the time prior to and after your first date. Once you've become a *couple* you've entered the third phase, and a final phase begins after your relationship has been weathering the tides of life. Sometimes these phases go smoothly, and sometimes you face rough seas. But what's nice to know is that by learning how to use your communication skills to your advantage, you can have an enormous impact on how your future relationships turn out. And one reality of the digital age is that we communicate extensively via the written word – and texts in particular. Here's how to improve your texting ability and how to avoid common pitfalls.

The words that form our relationships

When we start dating, we're trying to figure out if we should be a *We*. Our communication should be focused on awakening interest, creating positive tension, and fostering warm feelings. Your messages should make the other person happy to hear from you, and make you seem appealing and attractive to them. If you want to take things to the next level, then you need to keep this mindset and let your skills work for you.

Start off simple and gradually let your texting become more substantial. It takes a little time to learn who your date is anyway, so avoid emotional or heavy topics. Seriously, this is the place to keep things easy-breezy, light-hearted, and fun. However your first date went, remember your main objective: to keep this little love moth circling your flame (without coming across as desperate). Balance the timing of your texts against his to reflect the rhythm of the dance, following each other's movements. Your personality comes out in your texts (yes, your prospect is mentally profiling you) and this affects your future together. If you send anything too upsetting, dark, or off the wall, that door might close forever – so be nice!

Let's imagine that you've been seeing a new girl. You've gone out four times already and everything went well. Lately, however, her texts have begun tapering off. You ask her if something's wrong, but she only tells you that she's been busy. That may be true, but you know she's been managing to post on social media, so it smells a little fishy. You feel hurt, and get the urge to write an accusatory, passive-aggressive text.

Don't.

Your focus ought to be on sending something that makes her miss you and think fondly of you. Something that she can't resist responding to. This can be a bit tricky. You don't want to look like you're begging for a response, despite any wounded feelings or anxiety over watching your situation backslide. Yet you don't want to seem aloof, either, as if you haven't noticed.

Before you write anything, take a moment first to review your last text. *What* was it that she didn't reply to? Was your text time-consuming, overly complicated, or difficult to comprehend? Did you send something that she couldn't think about while at work? Here's a little trick: try sending a text that doesn't need an answer at all. Or send her some exciting news, just for the heck of it. Another strategy is to ask an entertaining question that's easy to answer. Remember that people prefer simple messages and cherish their free time, so keep things light. Give her the benefit of the doubt if she doesn't answer right away – she could be a meticulous composer, or possibly dyslexic, needing extra time to double-check her spelling. Maybe she's just having a bad day and shut her phone off altogether. Folks live busy lives filled with challenges and respon-sibility, so be patient.

Here's an example of light and breezy: 'Hey Jordan! Hope you're chillin' in this lovely spring weather! Quick question: my folks are about to spend a few days in Milan, and since you know that city so well – got any good restaurant tips?' Or something like this: 'Hiya! Doin' alright? You mentioned a really interesting article on popular psychology from some website – any chance you could drop me a link? Have a nice weekend!' While you're in the process of evaluating each other and considering a relationship, don't play games. Instead of messages that are confusing or obtuse (having to crack codes could put anybody off), keep things simple and relevant. Don't text too much (they shouldn't eat up someone's time), and avoid boring or annoying subjects. Whether you're feeling like a bed of roses or a sack of potatoes, when you text you're an interesting and positive person, OK? As I mentioned in earlier chapters, referring back to something they mentioned previously shows that you're interested in them as a person: 'Did you enjoy dinner at your parents'?' or 'Get those tyres changed yet?' They'll see that you're paying attention and thinking about them. There's nothing special about neutral messages like 'What's up?' Bring optimism to the situation. Here's another idea: try a hypothetical scenario. This is a playful way to talk that can put us in a good mood, and it tells us a lot more about our date's dreams for the future. You know, something like, 'If you won the lottery and had five million quid, what's the first thing you'd do?'

Right away is too early, but gradually you can start showing your emotional side: 'I just heard a ballad on the radio, and thought about you' or 'I'm really happy that we met each other.' This usually helps your prospect open up about their own feelings as well. Mention little observations about the other person, things that show you're attentive to who they are and what you like about them. There are lots of little things you can pick up on, such as their work ethic, charming idiosyncrasies, attitude towards life, generosity, fitness routines, kindness, their love for their children or passion for some other aspect of their life, even their relationship with their parents: 'I think it's so sweet of you to take your dad out fishing every month' or 'When I hear how passionate you are about your dance lessons, it really inspires me!'

Everything you ever wanted to know about texts but were afraid to ask

The more often a couple uses text-based communication to express their devotion and love for one another, the *fewer* conflicts they experience in IRL.[1] Notice that I said 'couples' – you're not there yet, but it's good to keep this in mind for when you are.

After receiving a text from a partner expressing devotion, both men and women experience a stronger sense of devotion them-selves.[2] Little love affirmations like this strengthen the bonds and sense of security between the two of you. Knowing that our partner feels love, warmth, and affection for us means a lot for our sense of well-being.[3] In fact, researchers even recommend that couples' therapists instruct partners to send positive messages to each other as a relationship tonic.[4] I can't emphasize enough the importance of paying careful attention to how you choose your words and subject matter when you're writing to someone you have feelings for. It plays an undeniably crucial role in how you set the tone for your relationship as you walk into the future together.

What to consider when texting that certain someone:

- Don't let texting be your *only* form of communication. Squeeze a few phone calls in, and meeting up often is important too.
- Be careful about *how* you say what you say – stay positive, and choose your words carefully.
- If a conflict arises, set up a phone call or meet up as soon as you can to resolve the situation.
- When you're spending time together, be present and focus on your date. Pretend your phone is radioactive, designed to poison romance.[5]

The four best types of texts

Here are four things to consider when texting a love interest:

1. *Questions – get to know this person.* Questions are great, but remember that it's not an interrogation. 'Kite surfing is a splendid pastime! What got you interested in that?' 'I go out dancing every Friday. I can't get enough! What are you into?' 'What's the best film you've seen lately?'

2. *Nab that date!* The whole point of texting early on is about stirring up those dates. But there are some real dead-end approaches here, like: 'Want to hang out sometime?' or 'I'm free all weekend.' Good luck with non-invitations like that. Have a plan, something like this: 'Are you up for dinner on Thursday – remember, that cool little Vietnamese place we talked about?' or 'There's an outdoor concert on Friday in the park near my house. Wanna come with me?' These messages show that you've got a clear plan, and showing your decisive and goal-oriented side is attractive. Coming up with something unexpected, unique, or even a little exclusive creates memories. A coffee is great, but even better if you know a place that does the best pastries in the city. You can make it more memorable than *just* coffee. If you feel like it ought to be *her* turn to propose something, at least be very clear you're looking to meet up. For instance, 'I really enjoy talking to you, and I'm looking forward to seeing you again IRL.'

3. *Humour.* They say each laugh extends your life. One thing that's for certain is that we love being around happy people. If you're going to be relying on your sense of humour, check that it's coming across. Is it obvious that your little 'textual' innuendo is meant to be funny? Referring back to previous dates tends to work. Don't be nasty or creepy, please, and try to 'read the room' first if you're edging towards the provocative. Don't push your humour too far, and remember that not *everything* is a joke. Chucking a 'Ha ha!' into every text is not good. Imagine if you wrote, 'I really enjoy talking to you' and then added a 😔 – that would be a confusing message. And don't forget your GIFs, especially if things have been quiet a little too long. (OK, this is a book, but imagine I just texted a GIF of a cartoon cat breakdancing. 'This is what I look like when I imagine our last date!' or 'Me – after a day at work 💀'

4. *Positivity, self-confidence, and passion for life.* 'Remember that work presentation I talked about? I just knocked it out of the park! Just wanted to spread the good news. Hope you're having a great day too!' A message like that reflects a passion for life. In 2012, Stony Brook University released a paper revealing that individuals who tackle life with energy and enthusiasm are much more likely to enjoy better relationships.[6] So if you want more passion in your relationship, then put your emotional energy into your interests, work, or political activities. Passion for life carries over into passionate relationships, so whatever it is you're passionate about, enjoy and harvest that energy.

These kinds of messages express what kind of person you are: a positive, ambitious, confident individual who gets the job done. Keep the language positive, and use words that express joy, enthusiasm, and determination, regardless of whether you're sharing your accomplishments, planning your date, talking about your great day, or even just expressing how thankful you are for all the good things in your life. The feeling that maybe life isn't quite so bad after all is infectious, and this is one of those *good* viruses. It's highly likely that the recipient will think, 'Wow, it's hard to imagine life being that hard when I'm around someone like this, who spreads so much happiness and joy around!'

And don't think that your little act of seduction here is merely bait on a hook – keep doing this as long as your relationship lasts. Little words of encouragement, affirmations, and warm words will make everything better in more ways than you can imagine: 'I know you've got that big meeting today, but I'll be thinking about you. Go get 'em, tiger!' Watch out that it doesn't become one-sided, though, because if you're bringing the flower power but your partner is a grouch, then you're looking at a problem. If keeping things moving in a positive direction falls entirely on your shoulders, then you're slipping into an unhealthy relationship and your zest for life will eventually suffer. We're establishing patterns whether we like it or not, and the longer they spin, the deeper the grooves we'll need to climb out of.

Texting errors to avoid

We've discussed what to focus on in your written communication. There are certain things I recommend avoiding too.

Long messages. These are turn-offs – people get bored, frustrated, or distracted.

A passive-aggressive tone or angry messages. 'If that's what you want' or 'OK, so you had time to get drunk with Julio and Mike, but you didn't have time to meet me?' Ouch! Dead ends. Texts like this make you look negative or envious. We're human, and we get prickly or piss each other off sometimes, sure. A common concern is feeling under-prioritized too. But try to keep your frustrations to yourself, and by no means respond passive-aggressively. Take a break from contacting this person – just leave it be. Radio silence can be quite a powerful and effective tool. If you leave the other person to stew in their thoughts, a sensible person will take the hint. But this isn't just a ploy to tease out their attention, it's also an opportunity for you to cool down and collect your own thoughts, saving them up for a face to face. Your feelings are your feelings, but you won't gain anything by lashing out. Showing that you're understanding, patient, and optimistic is the best way to turn this ship around.

Predictable or boring texts. When people write in their bios what they're looking for, have you ever seen anyone list 'Boredom'? I've matched with over 10,000 people, and I haven't seen it yet. You'll get to know each other and have a boring time once in a while later on, but that's then, not now. This is early, and boredom has no place here. Maybe creativity isn't your thing and you find this hard, so here's a trick: take notes. You can get tips from your friends, or jot down little ideas you get randomly during the day, and then see to it that your texts aren't predictable or repetitive. Because if you can pull this off, then your date will get excited every time your name pops up on their phone. Sounds nice, right?

Confusion. Or would you rather I had titled it: Unfathomable missives of abstruse entanglement? People need to understand you. For instance, what does this mean: 'Meet up or tomorrow?' Umm . . . Are you making plans, or have I forgotten them? Remember your CD FLIP rule (Check, Details, Funny Laughter, Illustrate, Positivity) and only send the text once you're sure he'll understand it. Otherwise it might look like you don't care.

Jealous or inappropriate texts. There are all kinds of inappropriate texts. Some of the more sensitive themes revolve around former relationships, money, political views, medical issues, or religion. If you're jealous and you show it, you won't get very far. You can discuss certain sensitive topics when meeting IRL (although once again – read the room), but when you're texting, keep things light and positive.

Overtexting. Just because you're walking around all day long with visions of this lovely person floating around in your head doesn't mean you should text him all day long. Making him wait to hear from you helps build up the tension, which makes you more attractive. If you genuinely have something to say or there's a pressing issue you need an answer to, that's one thing, but if you're only desperate to hear your phone chime, then perhaps you ought to invest in a Rubik's Cube to keep those hands busy. Try to stick to a 1:1 ratio – you write to him, then he writes to you, you write to him, he writes to you . . . You see the pattern here, right? Patience isn't just a virtue, in dating it's a golden aura. And the best thing? Everyone has patience – all you have to do is wait!

17: How *could* you!?

I don't care how clever you think you are, eventually misunderstandings are going to arise. At some point one person's going to have a problem with the other. Or you both blow up. In these situations, you can't just gloss things over. So what should you do?

In this chapter, I'm going to cover some of our more common points of friction and what we can do to resolve these situations.

Can't I just tell him how angry I am?

I've said it a million times and I'll say it a million times more: never send an angry or aggressive text. It. Will. Not. Help. Compared to the benefits of meeting up IRL, texting in situations like these is just digging your own grave, one thumb-tap at a time.

'Shit, Emily, what an idiot you are!'

'Nice work, Emily. Thanks for fucking up my day.'

Not a good idea, cowboy. Shoot yourself in the foot while you're at it. Here are some better texts to send:

'Hi Emily. I'm writing to say that I'm really sorry about this morning. I hope you're having a good day at work. Let's talk later, OK?'

'Emily, I'm so sorry about how I overreacted today. I've been a little on edge lately and woke up in a bad mood and took it out on you. I regret the things I said. Can you forgive me?'

'It's me. I regret what I said – it was unacceptable. I hope you realize how much you mean to me, but my behaviour today did not reflect that at all and I feel terrible. Please accept my sincere apologies.'

If you know that you're to blame for the conflict (even partly) – let's say you overreacted or said something mean – then own up to your responsibility and ask for forgiveness.

If your relationship isn't all sunbeams and rainbows at the moment, keep in mind that one angry text might be the straw that breaks the camel's back. We need to explain why we're angry without acting defensively or aggressively, and to stay focused on *resolving* the conflict. You can get through this rough patch together. Remember the good things that you like about this person. Be kind and keep your heart open. She's not perfect, but neither are you. Here are a couple of good ways to respond when you're upset:

'You know I'm pissed off, and you also know why. But I'd love to get through this together with you.'

'I'm really disappointed in you right now. I need to sit down with you so we can understand each other's perspective on this. I believe that we can fix this together.'

The feelings you two share transform over time – that's an unavoidable development in any relationship that has the potential to go long-term. At some point our partner's negative traits need to come out, and that usually means that your love for your partner will get put to the test. Is he worth it? Be prepared that you're going to lock horns on certain issues with no resolution in sight. In these situations, writing an email or text can be beneficial. Take the time to tell your partner what's troubling you, and explain things in detail. This way you can think and talk without getting interrupted, without having your feelings shaken up while you're trying to express yourself.

Show your appreciation for your partner, don't criticize them as a person, and explain that you're trying to cooperate. Being patient and listening is worth it – resolving conflicts helps your relationship come out stronger, deeper, and better integrated.

A simple misunderstanding?

Tone is a subject worth spending a little time on here. Your *tone* (*how* you say what you say) helps guide the person you're talking to. If you start to get the feeling that this relationship is skidding towards the ditch, then you've probably got a misunderstanding on your hands. If this is happening over texts, *stop texting at once*. The two of you need to sit down face to face, or if that's not possible, then you at least need to talk over the phone. If you keep texting, you're just piling on more trouble. In order to stop the carnage and salvage the situation, send something along these lines:

'It seems like we're just not understanding each other. Can I call you so we can work this out?'

'Texts are really easy to misunderstand, and it looks like that's happening right now. I'm done texting for the moment, but I'd like to keep talking about this when I see you tonight. Are you OK with that?'

These texts show your partner or prospect that you'd like to smooth things out, that you care about their feelings, and they also give you both some breathing space. Clarity is more important than urgency.

And no matter whether you haven't been on a date yet or you've been married for forty years, try to keep things simple. Be effective, pleasant, and stay confident. Make sure your tone is optimistic and let your personality show as well. You should also expect this from the other person. Listen attentively to their troubles, understand how they're feeling and why, and be there for them. When someone opens up to you like this, it means that they trust you.

When you need a little comfort

Everyone has tough days, where the clouds follow you, the buses don't stop, and the heel falls off your shoe. And on a day like that, you really need a hug and a little TLC, damn it. But moping around with sad puppy eyes or whining for attention is definitely not the right way to go about it (even if it's exactly how you feel). You need to talk, but you don't need to spill your guts about everything that went wrong. It's good to tell your love interest that they always help you feel better. Isn't that something that everyone likes to hear? Below are a few ways to formulate messages to help your heart-throb understand that you could use a little extra care right now:

'Today's been a killer. All I can think about right now is how nice it feels to hug you.'

'Not my day today. The only thing cheering me up is thinking about you. I could melt in your arms right now.'

And when *they* need to be comforted? If you've been paying attention to your date's tone and recognize that they need a little comfort and encouragement, they'll appreciate you for it – a lot. Many of us have a lot of difficulty admitting and expressing our emotions, but you can get around these obstacles by creating a warm, open atmosphere. Especially early on, when you still don't know each other all that well. Be the warm embrace that's always waiting, the rock they can depend on – on the bad days as well as the good. And just like in IRL, a kind-hearted text can work miracles:

'Thinking of you. Things should get better soon.'

'Sweetheart . . .'

'Is there any way I can help?'

'I'm here if you need to talk.'

'When one door closes, another opens. I believe in you and you're going to be OK.'

And if you're not being attentive but instead dominate the

conversation, only talking about your own troubles? Then this person might not open up to you so readily in the future. Listening to each other is how you build trust. Trust builds confidence, and confidence leads to happiness.

18: Sexting and naked selfies

Did you even read the rest of the book, or did you just skip to the fun part? Sexting and naked selfies are pervasive in the dating world.

If you're starting to date for the first time, or for the first time in ages, be prepared, because someone, at some point, is going to send you an erotic proposition. (Or will it be *you* who sends *them* an erotic proposition?) This is not something you have to take part in: it must be entirely voluntary. Rejecting such approaches doesn't mean you're boring. Period. *The desire must be consensual* – no exceptions. You never owe someone an apology for declining something you don't like or want. You date on your own terms, and if someone isn't respecting your boundaries, *that is not love*, nor is this someone you should be dating.

That being said, I think it's time now to give you some advice regarding *sexting*. There are plenty of ways to handle digital eroticism, and when done right – with respect – sexting can be a good way to arouse emotions, attraction, passion, and titillation. Keep an open mind here, because there are some things you can learn.

Double entendres and other erotically charged texts

So, if you're a complete sexting amateur, where do you begin?

A simple way to ease into it is just to write something suggestive

– there's a lot you can say without actually saying it. This is almost always the best way to get that ball rolling. The idea is to put an image in your date's mind:

'I just had a long walk in the cold snow and need to warm up in a nice, hot shower . . . ☺'

'I'm under two blankets but I'm still freezing . . . I guess I should put on some clothes?'

'Any ideas on what we could do after our date tonight?'

'I'm wearing those black knickers you love . . . and nothing else'

'I had a dream about you last night . . . Could I act it out with you later?'

'I'm in the bath . . . thinking of you . . .'

'I get so turned on thinking about you'

The answer you receive usually gives you an idea about your next step. But whatever you do next, use stimulating language. If you're looking for physical intimacy, you can tell him how you'd like to hold him, how you'd like him to hold you, or where you want to kiss him. You can describe what you're wearing (or not wearing), or what you'd like him to put on or take off. Maybe this sounds a little ridiculous to you, but trust me, it's the way things go down. Let your hair down a little:

'If you were here right now, tell me what you'd do to me . . .'

'Get home quick tonight – the bed's half-empty . . .'

'Guess what's on MY mind right now? ☺☺'

'I just can't stop thinking about you . . .'

How risqué you feel like getting is your own business – maybe erotic undertones will suffice, or maybe it's time for the juicy details. Self-confidence makes a huge difference in how much you'll enjoy sexting, but remember that leaving details to the imagination heightens the sexual tension. (Which is the point, right?) Sometimes just a simple '. .' or a flirty emoji does the trick. And there's no need to always end on a sexy note. Ending with something sweet and innocent or with a compliment works just fine. You should also be aware that sexting with someone will lose its erotic effect if you do it too often.

What feelings are you trying to inspire? Let your sexting reflect that.

Nude pics

Do you want to send that special someone a naked selfie?

It's your call, of course. Whatever you decide, feel confident about it and enjoy it. Do not apologize if you receive one and *don't* want to send one back. Never let yourself be coerced into sending pics (or anything else) you don't want to send. When you refuse, a date might try to coerce you by claiming that 'Everyone's sending them these days, so what's the big deal?' Well, everyone is *not*, and it wouldn't make any difference if they were. I've had guys ask me to send naked pics in their very first text, long before I would even consider the thought. Personally, I tell those *jävla skitstövlar* where to go (or refuse to answer at all).

Friends, listen to me, please! Anything you send can turn up on the internet – you can't control where it might end up. Unfortunately relationships can sour fast, however passionate, and once those pics are out there, there's no getting them back.

Dick pics

Dick pics are getting their own section. Sad, but true.

What's your reaction to dick pics? Same here – I still feel a little shocked each time. Best case scenario, there's some misguided advice out there convincing these guys that sending these pics gets women interested. Sending a phallic photo to someone you already know – who won't be surprised – is one thing, but sending it to a woman you *don't* know? What the hell are you thinking!?

An unwanted picture of a penis gives you an immediate snapshot of the guy's personality: obsessed with getting laid as fast as possible and doesn't give a hoot about who you are as a person. He seems to think that merely exposing himself is a form of seduction, but uninvited dick pics are probably the least effective method of attracting women. And let's not forget that by sending unsolicited dick pics, you're breaking the law in most places, because *unsolicited dick pics are a form of sexual harassment.*

When you get that unwanted picture, listen to your gut reaction and respond accordingly. If you're offended, say so. If you're enraged, say so. If you no longer want any contact with this creep, then just block him – no need to respond. If you're not explicit in your reaction – if you don't say exactly what you think – you'll risk appearing uncertain or weak. Stand firm in your response, because a guy who's into crossing boundaries is a recipe for trouble. If you *do* appreciate the gesture, we're all happy for you – cheers, mate. However, if you should happen to like dick pics in general, it doesn't mean that you need to accept inappropriate behaviour. There are different ways to handle getting unexpectedly exposed; here's a gentle, forgiving and straightforward response:

'Um, I guess that pic was meant for me, but we're not at a place in our relationship yet where I'm cool about it. I'm being as straightforward as I can here – do *not* send me any more pics like that.'

So what happens if you're already dating someone and they send you a dick photo? Well, either you don't appreciate it and respond as I've previously described, or else you decide that it's cool – that's totally up to you. If you like it and want to get the sexting going, you can send him back a nip slip or something else you'd like to advertise. Now, if you give his pic the OK, then it's likely that he'll be looking for you to return the favour. So be ready and don't flip out when he asks. Keep in mind that accepting doesn't mean that you're automatically compelled to reciprocate. Communicate clearly and set your boundaries. If you *do* accept it, though, also know that you've lowered the bar a notch or two.

OK, next test: you've been together for years and suddenly – out of nowhere – you get a photo of your dude's penis. What now? Well, let's see . . . You've been together in a respectful and healthy relationship long enough to know each other pretty well by now, and you've seen this thing like a thousand times. So it looks to me like somebody wants to turn the heat up a little. (C'mon, admit it, *you* sent that pic, not him, right?) How this affects you is something only you can know. Sexting may be just as new to him too – he's trying to figure out an angle, and this is the best he could come up with. If you don't share his enthusiasm for this new approach, keep his motives in mind at least. Here's a good way to handle it, should that be the case: 'Babycakes, I love ALL of you, each and every bit! I can't wait to see you tonight, you handsome devil.'

Drunk texts

You wake up hungover, fumble for your phone, and then it hits you right away – you were drunk-texting last night. Shit.

Rule of thumb: never text a love interest while you're drunk. Certainly not if you've been seeing each other for a while already. Just *receiving* drunk texts is enough to cause cold sweats. How should we react to this? Reply? Ignore it? Should you take what they wrote seriously, or just write it off as whiskey babble? Text exchanges mixed with alcohol can go south fast, and often end up in misunderstandings. Personally, I vote that you ignore it. If you still feel compelled to say *something*, at least keep it short and light-hearted. The inebriated don't have access to all of their brain, in fact, they could even have blacked out, so keep it simple and keep them smiling.

If she's written something that upsets you, hold your horses, bite your tongue, and wait until the next (sober) day before you tell her what you *really* think. Until then, leave her to her own chaos. Tomorrow is a new day.

19: Friend-zoned or ghosted – which sucks worse?

Getting to know someone new might involve awkward, confusing, or frustrating situations. There are plenty of pitfalls along the dating trail: jealousy, misunderstandings, moving too fast, being insensitive . . . Anything that can go right can also go wrong.

And one thing we need to address is getting *friend-zoned*. Your heart's getting all worked up over someone, you've been chatting and hanging out a bit, and then . . . you're just friends. No spark. It sucks, but I think I can help you avoid skidding into this ditch. With a little perspective and determination, hopefully you can dodge this and other hazards along the dating highway.

Friend-zoned?

If you sense that you're sliding into the friend zone, it's time to raise your flirting game to a new level. One technique is to take a step back and leave him hanging for a bit – give him a taste of life without you. It's risky, but it's better than the cruel purgatory of the friend zone. When we don't have access to people, we get more curious about them. (I cover this in more detail in the upcoming chapter 'Wanting what we can't have'.) Forcing your prospect to make a little more effort can make his reward seem greater. Maybe he can't stop wondering what you've been doing, or maybe the little break makes him think you've lost interest – having an air of mystery can kickstart *his* interest.

If you've only met recently, keep your texts short and sweet. No long essays or babbling, and don't get soppy with emotion at this point either. Keep your texts to a minimum but don't disappear altogether. This is effective because it plays on how we function as human beings. Always have 'legitimate' reasons for sending a text and try to inspire warm feelings. For example, 'I'm going to see that robot film if you'd like to tag along. The premiere was last week!'

But maybe you've been dating for a little while when you sense that friend-zone looming? Longer relationships are also friend-ships – ask anyone who's been in one. Passion isn't always front and centre when you're spending time together. The good news for you is that you can try heating things up with your texts. If you feel that she's slipping away then it's time to take charge, ASAP. If you sense that taking a step back might backfire, then you're going to have to flip the equation and become the greatest partner in the world. It's going to take a little magic, but you can make magic with your thumbs: send her texts that make her happy or laugh, or flatter her in a way that you know will boost her ego. That way she'll start looking forward to your texts. Don't go overboard or this too might backfire, but if you play it subtly, she'll feel like the renewed attraction is coming from *her*!

If it seems like you're only treading water – getting weak feedback and the feeling just isn't there – would it be a good idea to let it slip that you've got other candidates out there? It might help you figure out where he stands, but this is a desperate, last-ditch option. You don't want to get sucked into a serious jealousy situation, because jealousy can feed on itself, and there's nothing fun about that. But if you think you can pull it off with some subtle sophisti-cation, then it's your call. If you're going to pull that trigger, here's one way to do it: 'Damn, we had a great night last night! 😄' That ought to set off a few alarm bells. What were you doing? With who? What exactly does a 'great night' entail? When it works, your date will realize that it's time to bring his A game if he doesn't want to get bumped. Make sure to keep a positive tone, keep things light-hearted, and don't push your point. You won't bait him successfully if he knows you're baiting him. It's risky – this could easily kill the whole thing. Being too devious can backfire because he might think that you're hiding something for real. Guarantees are for new washing machines, though, not relationships. It's a tough situation and you're walking a tightrope, but who knows? Your best might actually work for once! So pick a strategy and I'll cross my fingers for you!

Ghosted?

Having to utter the words, 'I don't think we should see each other any more' or 'This is over' to someone you've only known briefly can feel so intimidating that some folks just don't bother. They simply stop responding, like ghosts that have gone up in smoke – poof! Hence the term *ghosting*. They don't answer the phone, they don't text . . . It's probably the cruellest, most cowardly, and most immature way to dump someone. Particularly if you had something going. Having someone say 'I'm dumping you' to your face usually hurts less than getting ghosted. It's a peeling-off-the-plaster situation – fast, and it's over. Slow, and the pain never ends. The uncertainty over what's happening or whether a relationship is ending or not eats you up from the inside.

It's not the greatest silver lining ever, but at least now you've gained insight into this person's level of maturity. You've been given a cost-free analysis of that former prospect's character, and knowing that they weren't all they were cracked up to be should at least make it easier to leave this episode behind you.

So what do you do when you get ghosted?

Sorry, but there's nothing you really *can* do. Getting angry won't help. You dated the wrong person, and now you know. You might long for a resolution, but sometimes it remains out of reach. Just leave that ugly burning question mark alone, ignoring it until it fades away. And guess what? The pain *will* go away. You'll be back on your feet soon enough, and hopefully next time you'll get to date an adult. The sooner you can admit to yourself that you've been ghosted, the sooner you can leave it all in your rear-view mirror and rid yourself of the pain.

OK, I hear you: it's itching at you, you just can't . . . do *nothing*. You're plagued by an irrepressible desire to give 'em the ol' what-for, to fire off that text. Do it – you have my permission. Here's one way to say it: 'It's too bad that things fell apart – I thought we had a good thing going. I've enjoyed getting to know you, but let's make one thing clear: I'm looking for someone who has time for me, and who also has the spine/balls to speak the truth, instead of ghosting people like a coward. Take care.' If this will give you more solace than just walking away, fair enough. You got it off your chest, and lord knows it's a hell of a lot less than they deserve.

Sometimes (if you haven't blocked them) that little dose of straightforward honesty brings your ghost back to life and they come knocking on your door. But this person just hurt you in an immature, cowardly, and irresponsible way – is this really someone worth having? My advice is to keep on walking. And frankly, the same goes for any other kind of hurtful, disrespectful, or mean behaviour. Know where to draw the line.

When they take forever to get back to you

When we've met someone and they give us the warm fuzzies, it's super-easy to want to stay in contact with them all the time. It can be incredibly frustrating if it takes forever for her to get back to you. If all this waiting is really getting under your skin, remember that we all run at different speeds. You might not like to hear this, but you just need to sit on your hands and keep your text-exchange ratio at 1:1. You don't know why she isn't answering. Maybe she's got something difficult she wants to say and needs time to think, maybe she's dealing with a family emergency, or maybe rats have invaded her cellar – you just don't know. Whatever the reason is, you still need to back off a bit. Imagine yourself in a complicated situation where you get a text from your sweetie and you think, 'Well, that's nice! Once I'm done with this brain surgery, I can't wait to read that!' And you pocket your phone – something to look forward to! But then, five minutes later, your pocket buzzes again. And after five more minutes, it buzzes again. And again. Less than half an hour has gone by but you're already thinking, 'What on earth is going on? What's with that idiot? Chill!'

But if you decide that you've been patient, stuck to the 1:1 rule, and yet you still feel like it's time to take a new stab at it, well then, it'd better be good. It's important that you send something that catches his attention and gives him a rock-solid reason to answer. The right text varies a bit depending on how deep into the relationship you are. If it's early days and everything's been grooving along and then suddenly your phone doesn't even squeak for a few days, well yeah, I suppose something doesn't feel right. Try this one: 'Hello! How's your week going? Any plans this weekend? ☺' (Sure, it's not my greatest work, but it's simple, effective, and easy to answer.) If you're actively dating and a few more hours have gone by than you'd expect, pop off a little: 'Got your nose to the grindstone, I see. School? Work? Basketball? Whatever you're caught up in, I hope it's fun. Just wanted to say that I'm thinking about you and looking forward to seeing you tomorrow! ☻'

The important thing is that you have a sense of control over the situation. If you can see that they've read your message but still haven't answered, it's irritating. And each hour that goes by doesn't help, but you have to leave that phone undisturbed. Don't lay on the guilt trips and accusations, or sound upset:

'Where have you been?' – bad.

'You sure do like to take your time' – bad.

'Is it that hard to answer?' – no good.

'Slowcoach' – nope.

Keep a positive tone, and don't mention the war. We live in the real world too, though, and after a few days just about anybody would be at the end of their tether. This works: 'Hi there. Did you get my text about ultra bodybuilding?' or 'Did you get a chance to think about what I wrote the other day? I'm curious to hear your thoughts. ☺ I hope you're doing OK!'

These are positive, happy, gentle reminders. If they get back to you – great! If not – there are other fish in the sea.

Is she dating other people?

This is a shitty situation to be in. Sorry, but in the early phase of dating, a lot of us date several people. Maybe you're sensing that your prospect is falling for someone else – on the one hand you want to be that happy-go-lucky whistler, the positive type that people get attracted to, but on the other you're slowly falling to pieces. Now's the time to decide: is this one worth fighting for? The best way to win this battle is to send them a series of texts dripping with self-loathing, jealousy, and baseless accusations. JUST KIDDING!

For the love of all things sacred, *do not do that*. No, what you *want* to do, of course, is to try to present the best version of yourself you can. Think about what kind of feelings you want to awaken in this person – the kind of feelings that make you more interesting in their eyes – and compose your messages accordingly.

Tips: keep 'em short and to the point. Be charming and alluring, and uncomplicated. Act self-confident and assured, not clingy or attention-craving. Write unique texts that linger in the recipient's head long after their screen has died. You have to pretend that there's no one else – no bad vibes, no jealousy. Today you're the happiest, cheekiest flavour of joy that this city has ever seen. *She's* the one who should feel like she's missing out on the party. You're a positive person willing to give her a chance to be a part of your busy, fascinating life, so let your text reflect that. These positive vibes are highly alluring and tend to spread to those around you. Who doesn't get cheered up by receiving a bubbly, vivacious text? We want those kind of people around us. Don't bullshit anybody, of course – *be* that person: optimistic, enthusiastic, and actively doing things that interest you.

Some terms you should know

So we covered a couple of the worst ones, friend-zoning and ghosting, but there are plenty of other expressions and terms out there in the dating jungle. It's almost like you need a manual . . . Oh yeah, this IS one! Let's learn about some of these situations and how to navigate them:

Breadcrumbing. It seems like she's got you in her sights and wants to date you, yet in reality she harbours no intention of getting together with you. That being said, all her texts and signals imply that she *is* interested. Hopefully, you'll eventually see the light and realize that she's only leaving a trail of breadcrumbs to string you along – a reference to the fairytale *Hansel and Gretel.*

Catch and release. These folks are only in it for the hunt. They love to flirt with you and work their tails off trying to score that date. Eventually you agree, but once you're on the date they lose interest – you're no fun once you're 'caught'. Or they keep on a while longer until they've got you to start falling for them. The second they see those feelings in you, they're out the door.

Catfishing. When you're swiping, you'll sometimes run across ridiculously hot people. Unfortunately, there's a reasonable possibility that the picture has been reappropriated – it ain't who you think it is. Using someone else's photo is a deceitful, dishonest thing to do, but folks do this to get more nibbles on their line. I matched up with a fair number of catfish while researching this book, and I even fell for it once. That was *not* the same dude who showed up on a date, and you can only imagine how shocked I was.

Airing. This is when someone takes foreeeeeeeeever to get back to you. You send a nice text, and then days go by before you suddenly get an answer – as if the conversation never paused. Most singles have experienced some form of this tedious waiting at some point.

Cuffing season. It starts around October and ends in the second half of February. This is the official it's-getting-dark-out-and-I-want-a-cuddle-bunny-to-keep-me-warm season. Having someone around for Christmas, New Year's, and Valentine's Day sounds nice, right? The term *cuffing season* first showed up in the crowdsourced Urban Dictionary, and then in Collins Dictionary in 2017 (where it nearly earned Word of the Year), which describes it thus: 'the period of autumn and winter, when single people are considered likely to seek settled relationships rather than engage in casual affairs.' Empirically and scientifically, the support for this phenomenon is a little mixed,[1] but researchers claim a possible evolutionary explanation. It's a bit like going into hibernation – according to the theory, we're shacking up for warmth and support, especially when SAD (seasonal affective disorder, or 'winter depression') tends to affect us in the autumn. A winter relationship supposedly helps alleviate some of this suffering.[2] Just being cold in general attracts us to warm food and drink. From a psychological perspective, these cuffing relationships warm the heart over those winter months. On a similar note, a study in the *Journal of Consumer Research*[3] showed that when we feel cold, we're more inclined to watch rom-coms than usual. 'Be mine.' (Until March.)

Cushioning. You're dating someone and you see the bad news coming. But instead of just being upfront and breaking up, you start flirting and chatting with other people, to cushion the blow when the curtain falls. I think that a clean break is much better than this kind of sloppy overlap – it's inconsiderate, if nothing else.

Fauxbae'ing. Now this one's a real doozie. These folks pretend that they're in a relationship on social media – even though they're single. Two reasons why they might do this are that they're trying to make an ex jealous, or their family won't stop pestering them about finding a partner.

Flexting. This is when you try to impress someone before you've met up IRL. This is one of the most common reasons why we lie in our bios. Men tend to lie about their height, and women about their weight. A classic gimmick for both genders is using old photos.[4] A friend and I noticed the other day how common it is in profiles for people to mix old and new photos. While we might all include the odd favourite snap from a few years ago, on these profiles the older (and more attractive) portraits show up first, and are placed there to pique interest. But then, as you flip through their photos, it becomes obvious that these people no longer look the same – old pics. However, it's still more honourable than *only* using old photos.

Gatsbying. This expression comes from F. Scott Fitzgerald's classic novel *The Great Gatsby*. It refers to posting a video, photo, or selfie on social media exclusively so that an ex or new flirt will see it: Check out how cool I am, how much fun I'm having, how hot I look . . . Or it's intended to show that you're on a date with someone else (two glasses of champagne or two place settings at a restaurant, for instance).

Ghostbusting. The indefatigable – folks who never give up. They get ghosted but still don't get it, texting onwards nonetheless. According to the dating site *Plenty of Fish*, 78 per cent of millennials (born between 1981 and 1996, also called Generation Y) have been ghosted at least once.[5] 38 per cent have also had to put up with those poor souls who don't realize that they're 'talking to the hand'. Don't waste your time on either: no ghosting, no ghostbusting.

Kittenfishing. A softer form of catfishing. Here people use actual photos of themselves, but from years before or so heavily retouched that they distort reality. They lie about their job, their age, their weight. The second you show up for a date the gig is up, so it's pretty pointless. It's on a par with flexting.

Serendipidating. This is when someone keeps rescheduling the date for later on. And why's that? It's because they're trying to fill up their dance card, and are always ready to bump you down the list. This is inconsiderate and selfish, and you shouldn't put up with it. Don't agree to only booking dates preliminarily – these folks are only interested in the greener grass on the other side, which is why they keep you on the fence.

Side-barring. You're both at a party. From out of nowhere, your date whips out their phone and starts messing around with it, either secretly or in the open. Suddenly you feel shoved aside, uninteresting, and neglected. Not surprisingly, many of us have been affected by – or guilty of – this behaviour at some time or another.[6] Research has proven fairly definitively that we're all terrible at multitasking.[7] Using your phone at the same time as you're talking to someone is a bad way to do either.

Slow fade. This is a weak form of ghosting. These folks have no interest in pursuing anything with you, but instead of either breaking up or ghosting you, they just drift further and further away. They answer a little more slowly each time and say a little less. They ignore texts and break off plans without committing to new ones, letting the relationship slowly dissolve. Mature? I think not.

Stashing. This is ugly behaviour. A stasher won't introduce you to any of their friends or family and never mention you online. You're like a sex toy that they feel ashamed about, 'stashing' you in the corner anytime someone looks in the window. They don't love you but they don't like to be alone, so they hide you while they're waiting for someone else.

Zombie-ing. You got ghosted, and just started moving on with your life. And then, poof! Back from the dead! These creatures just act like nothing ever happened and everything's cool – dropping a text and liking your posts. Where were they, jail? This, my friends, is *zombie-ing.* I'd avoid these folks – you've been duped once already. You've learned where this person's heart lies, so they're obviously just bored and figured they'd play with you again.

20: Wanting what we can't have

Does it seem like you're always falling for people you can't have? And the more they retreat, the more you want them? What's up with that?

Why disinterest interests us

This phenomenon is a result of how our vanity and self-image, combined with a lack of access, distort how we perceive another person's worth. Really, their worth is an invention of your own mind. When we stumble across a resource that's difficult to access or obtain, or is in high demand, it often becomes more desirable to us. The less there is, the more we want it. So when someone declines our invitations, we mentally enhance their value, which can cause us to try even harder – this person is *worth* it, right? The Holy Grail! In other words, they become a limited resource. It explains why we often place a higher value on busy people; we believe they're popular, and if they're popular, then they must be important and highly valued, right? It's a common unconscious bias – a hiccup in our perspective.

When we like someone, our brains get a little hit of dopamine when they text us. Uncertain outcomes inspire especially strong reactions in us – will they text, or won't they?[1] In my book *Your Hidden Motives*, I write about dopamine spikes caused by these uncertain outcomes: 'Did I get a text back? Did someone comment on my post?' – our brains get hooked on the 'maybe' of it all. From an evolutionary perspective, this encouraged our prehistoric ancestors to forage for food. When they ventured out to gather resources, they seldom knew whether their hunt would be successful or not. By delivering convenient little kicks of dopamine, our brains encouraged us to look a little further and try a little harder, and our extra efforts were rewarded with juicy berries, plump fruits, or protein-rich prey.

Our smartphones have become the ultimate 'maybe' device; in fact, you get a bigger kick just from *getting* a message than from reading it. How many times have you checked your phone today – just to check? A lot, at least most of us have. (This also explains why we're such suckers for getting breadcrumbed.)

So when we let ourselves get treated like doormats, blame it on the dopamine. Sure, they never write, but when they *do* . . . Oh yeah, that feels *good*! Except then the cloud of anxiety comes: 'But when will the next time be?' 'Now it's been four days and I haven't heard from her, and I know she's back from her work trip' or 'If we're going to hang out this weekend he'd better let me know. It's nearly Friday!'

It's tempting to fall into this 'foraging' behaviour – the hunt – but ask yourself: is it worth it? He's giving you berries, but you need a moose. Hightail it out of there, realizing that your brain is using you for its own amusement. The very fact that this person is avoiding you is the cause of your attraction, and this phenomenon leads us to bond with the wrong people – people who toy with you or don't genuinely care about you. Let it go now, because the pain will only get worse. Stay focused on the people who are genuinely available.

Should *you* be the disinterested party?

We want what we can't have. We take what we *do* have for granted and don't miss it till it's gone. Do the math.

If you want to seem more appealing, make sure you don't get taken for granted. You need to feel that you're the object of desire – the interesting one that everyone wants. Unfortunately, we often have a poor self-image which causes us to think the exact opposite. This makes us try too hard, answering texts immediately to show that we're easily available, or making up for every little thing that upsets our (so-called) prospect. We become desperate for this person's approval, to be chosen. Stop it, wishful thinker! In terms of attraction, this behaviour is about as fruitful as fishing in a corn-field. Being at their beck and call 24-7 decreases your perceived value; your neediness increases the likelihood of getting rejected. If you want to be attractive, don't be *too* accessible. You have a unique value and are worthy of respect.

Instead, you can use this to your advantage. By striking a balance between being available and unavailable, you can make yourself more interesting. But before you start getting all superior, I recommend reserving this magical power for only those occasions when you feel like your prospect is taking you for granted. If you find yourself in this position, it's time to suddenly not be so predictable. Let's assume that you've been accessible for quite a while. Do you remember the *mere-exposure* effect? The more often someone sees you, the more they like you. But now that he's seen you, make him sweat a little. Suddenly you're not there every time it's convenient for him. 'Tuesday? No good. Maybe Wednesday . . . I'll get back to you.' Your date's going to freak out a little as the alarm bells go off: 'Shit, what's happening? I thought she was into me . . .' You can display a little standoffishness with your body language too: turn away a bit and shift your legs to the side (as if you're preparing to leave). He'll interpret this as if you've only got a limited amount of time, and therefore perceive you as more sought-after. The less of you there is, the more desirable you become. You can fine-tune the situation, leaning in a little again and flirting a little more. Say something funny or charming (with love, of course), or even touch him lightly – an 'accidental' brushing of the hand, say. Whoops!

Stay pleasantly fun, just dial the flirting up and down. Make him just a little unsure of where he is with you. Don't push things too far and only do this to increase the attraction while you're dating, *not* when in a relationship. In a relationship, it only creates uncertainty and confusion, not curiosity or a playful atmosphere.

As I mentioned in a previous chapter, the first two clusters of traits we interpret when encountering someone new are 1) warmth/trustworthiness and 2) competence/status. When it comes to competence, human beings desire to appear meaningful, important, and successful; very few of us wish to feel unimportant or ignored. It's common for people to include pictures of exclusive cars or fancy watches in their profile pics, hoping to impress us, and we also do our best to conceal our weaknesses. Since people are accustomed to us projecting unrealistically flattering images of ourselves, we can surprise folks by admitting our weaknesses. They might get a little thrown off at first, only to become even more attracted to us: 'This person's really genuine – nothing to hide.' If you know that you're valuable, then you don't need to show off every time an opportunity rears its head. For the self-confident, the approval of others carries a lot less weight. You know who you are and what that's worth. It's those who *don't* have a strong sense of self-worth who try so hard to prove the opposite.

Part IV
RELATIONSHIPS

21: Your relationship toolkit

As I'm sure you've already noticed, this isn't just a book on how to pick up chicks or snag dudes. It's about finding happiness in your relationships (and this applies, of course, even to those of you only looking for a little confirmation or for short-term hook-ups). It's about providing you with the tools you need to enjoy loving relationships with people who are worthy of that love.

Dating well is an art that we can all improve in. Just figuring out what you need and who'll be good for you is important for establishing rewarding relationships. A key component of dating well is understanding yourself and recognizing personal behavioural patterns that may be holding you back. Unlocking these psychological mechanisms requires self-reflection, and facing up to personal truths about yourself can often be awkward, uncomfortable, or downright painful. But believe me, it's worth the effort.

Let's say you've begun dating someone and you're falling in love; you've got butterflies in your stomach and you've been seeing a lot more of each other lately. A relationship is blooming. But entering a new relationship isn't just dancing on the moon – it also means sleepless nights and biting your nails sometimes. Experiencing a chaotic mix of emotions is familiar to many of us, and it can be so much easier just to give up than to continue on with all the baggage we carry from previous relationships. Romantic relationships, of course, but often we also carry baggage from our childhood relationships. Sometimes breaking it off *is* the right thing to do – certain relationships ought *not* to continue, and certainly not if they're destructive. Luckily for us, though, there's been a great deal of study about which factors contribute to good relationships – and which don't. We know which challenges are likely to appear in budding relationships, which challenges are likely to crop up a year or two from now, and which ones tend to strike at that 'seven-year itch' point.

In the following section, you'll be provided with knowledge that will make it easier to build your castle in the clouds with a wonderful person, fully prepared for most of the risks that might threaten the peace of your romantic sanctuary.

OK, everybody, grab a partner . . .

Time for the talk?

'So, what do you think about this, then?'
'Think about *what*?'
'Us.'

The talk, the day you dare to broach the subject. Are we both thinking the same thing? Where do we stand? Are we a *we* now, plural? Or do we keep dating other people? (This isn't the same conversation if a long-term relationship isn't your goal.)

The fact that you're both willing and eager to develop a relationship is still no guarantee of success; there are many pieces to this puzzle. For one thing, you both need to be emotionally mature enough to be *in* a serious relationship, and even then you still need to be ready. In order to enjoy a good relationship, it's important that you and your partner prioritize each other: that you spend enough time together, that you hear from one another often enough, that your needs for attention are compatible, and that you agree about moving in together or living apart (when that time comes).

Let's learn about the processes that take place *inside* us as we grow closer to one another. Unfortunately, things aren't as easy as I wish they were. This is why I've included a few tools for you, meant to help you navigate some of the most common obstacles and traps.

Togetherness – delightful and nerve-wracking all at once

When I found myself single again after many years and two kids, I thought, 'Never again!' I had given relationships the best I had. My separation was unavoidable, and my heart felt like roadkill.

In their book *The Answer – How to Start a Relationship and Make It Last*,[1] Dan Josefsson and Egil Linge describe how young children cannot survive without intimacy and supervision. Our interpersonal emotional bonds are quintessential components of our survival, both as individuals and as a species. We've already touched upon how our social nature as human beings is one of the secrets to our success, and this explains why relationships have such a powerful effect on our emotional lives. They give us our highest highs and our lowest lows. Losing a loved one is often the worst moment in your life. And if *losing* a relationship weren't tough enough, even *forming* a relationship is hard. And there aren't any shortcuts. A life of romantic isolation – staying single forever – is your alternative. There's nothing wrong with that – we respect that decision – but let's take a moment to examine *why* people throw in the towel on love. (And just because you're single doesn't mean a life of celibacy, by the way!)

The other day I heard it said that we can only *really* live a full life if we establish intimate relationships. This by no means implies that you need to have a *romantic* relationship – being close to family or friends is enough. It's true that romantic relationships have a different character to them, though. They're unlike our other relationships, sharing the most similarity with the relationship we had with our parents as children. And there's a recipe involved for allowing them to develop. Among other things, a certain level of contact is necessary – spending only two weeks together every five years when your wife comes home from a moonbase isn't going to work for either of you. And a continual series of short flings won't offer you the benefits of a long-term relationship.

So what happens internally as we pair up?

I'm going to explain the mechanisms that get activated when we enter romantic relationships. We'll examine some of the most frequent road bumps encountered as we become more intimate, and naturally I'll give you some tips on handling these. Sometimes you can date quite a few people and yet none of your prospects seem right. Truth be told, though, sometimes you could meet every potential partner on the *planet* and still not be satisfied. Or maybe you're on the flip side of that coin, and seem to fall in love with everyone you meet. What's up with that? All of this, my friend, is a result of your internal mechanisms, the processes our brains unleash when we're forming relationships.

Who are we in a relationship?

Josefsson and Linge describe a number of 'characters' in *The Answer*,[2] all of whom face different challenges when forming relationships. To keep things simple here, I have given these character types a name based on the nature of their relationship challenges. (Keep in mind that these characters are not gender-specific, and have only been given alternating genders for the sake of variation.) Do you recognize yourself or any of your potential dates here?

Glass Half-empty is pleasant, social, likeable, and has a good job where he does well. Although he has a lot of friends, he's romantically lonely. The problem is that Glass Half-empty is never satisfied. His relationships never seem to last for more than a couple of months. The early dates are a lot of fun, but as the novelty wears off, his prospective partner starts to show significant flaws. She might harbour the wrong opinions, be uninformed on subjects he cares about, or maybe she just dresses badly. Glass Half-empty is convinced that it just isn't going to work and backs out. He tells himself that he's a little pickier than the rest.

Over-doer is a sociable person and meets many people through her work. She's currently single but has had a number of relationships, including quite a few long ones. Yet they always peter out into nothing; they often begin with a great deal of love and intimacy, but grow increasingly distant. Over-doer is great at making others feel good and has been called 'the perfect girlfriend'. She does everything to please her boyfriend and cater to his whims, and yet he still tires of her. They grow apart. It turns out that some boyfriends have cheated on her. Over-doer doesn't understand why bad luck keeps following her around.

Grass-is-greener is hesitant. While Glass Half-empty is focused on his partner's flaws, Grass-is-greener is distracted by other opportunities. He's had a few relationships – mostly shorter ones, maybe up to a year sometimes. He has no trouble entering relationships, but the problem is that, throughout the entire relationship, he's uncertain whether he's selling himself short. Grass-is-greener obsesses over whether or not there's another girl out there that would be a better match for him, someone he'd feel *more* in love with. In fact, he gives credence to the slightest doubts: 'If I like this girl so much, why would I be looking at other girls?' His insecurity and hesitation cause him to avoid commitment or making future plans. This is obviously frustrating for his partner, and the relationship implodes. (Remember behaviours like *breadcrumbing*, *serendipidating*, *stashing*, and *catch-and-release*? Who wants to put up with all that?) But Grass-is-greener still doesn't want to be alone.

Clingy wants guarantees. She's had a few relationships, and they're always launched with explosions of passion. Watch out, though – she's jealous. To feel good about herself she needs confirmation all the time. She's heard in the past that she's clingy and demanding so, over time, Clingy has learned to hide this a bit in order to not scare her dates away. But her anxiety over the potential to get dumped plagues her.

1NS lives alone, but he's the hook-up king. Mostly 1NSes (one-night stands), although a couple have lasted a few weeks. He's a wham-bam-thank-you-ma'am kind of guy who gets bored and claustrophobic right away. 1NS feels an emptiness in his daily life, though, and is tired of being single. Will he become *that* dude, whitening his teeth when he's 65, hooking up with lone women in the same sleazy bars? The thought frightens him. He really *does* want a relationship, but hasn't a clue what to do about it – he can barely stick around until the sun comes up. Even 1NS's 1NSes have lost their old charm. Is there any reason why he shouldn't just throw in the towel and become a monk?

The Other [Wo]man, in recent years, has been almost exclusively interested in men who already have wives and children. She values passion in her relationships. These relationships have had plenty of passion, but each time she eventually realizes that this particular guy just can't give her the focus and intimacy she desires. Let's not forget that she doesn't *like* being 'the other woman', always standing in the wings and spending Valentine's Day and Christmas with her sister. It feels humiliating. But the good guys are already taken, right? Single guys just seem dull, like the broken bits at the bottom of the biscuit tin. She gets bored with them in the blink of an eye.

No Self-confidence is a sociable fellow, and his friends are perplexed as to why this popular guy can't seem to meet anyone. Even though he is socially competent, he has terrible self-confidence when talking to women. He's usually relaxed until he sees that someone is interested in him, at which point he grows increasingly anxious and uncomfortable. Interactions with dates usually end with him pushing them away, excusing himself, or just plain leaving. Afterwards he's relieved – 'I prefer my own company anyway' – but he regrets his actions the next day. Sadly, No Self-confidence begins avoiding parties or social occasions where he might encounter women he's never met before. He knows how things will end – no more shipwrecks, thank you.

The relationship stepladder – the stages we climb to reach partnership

Now we're going to discuss a process all romantic relationships go through, referred to as *the relationship stepladder*. There are all kinds of problems we can encounter while trying to develop lasting relationships – I'm sure the previous examples made that pretty clear.

If you scratch below the surface, almost all relationship troubles share common roots. Successfully creating long-lasting relation-ships out of initial dates with virtual strangers entails repeating a process of transforming distance into closeness and isolation into togetherness. It's this process that resembles a stepladder, with a rising series of phases (steps, stages – take your pick), each of which involves greater intimacy:

The *outset phase*: we're on the ground floor, all alone, not really in a phase at all yet. Lonely hearts drifting in the tide, free for the moment.

The *initial phase*: we meet someone who piques our interest. We're more or less strangers, and still don't share any serious emotional bonds. We meet sporadically. The more often we meet, the better we start getting to know one another, and we realize that we'd like to meet more regularly, which brings us up to . . .

The *courting phase*: we're in love as we become an official couple. We regularly spend time together and have an increasingly complete idea of each other's personalities. We explore new sides of one another. We're still questioning whether or not we're ready to go all-in, and these are testing grounds for this relationship (even if some couples may have jumped the gun and made it official already). When we truly know that our hearts are in it and agree to our togetherness, we advance to . . .

The *dedication phase*: we promise one another long-lasting intimacy. Now we can relax a little, in a way that usually doesn't come easily during the earlier phases. We are a *we* now, and in our daily lives we can rely on each other for security and support. We find it difficult to imagine life without the other. We've created an intimate, long-lasting relationship.

This process, from the outset to the dedication phase, manifests itself differently in different parts of the world and varies depending on where we are in our own lives. Every relationship has its own unique trajectory, of course. But underneath it all they still develop according to a stepladder pattern. The timing of our phase-climbing varies considerably, and it depends on the individuals involved. Some couples advance quickly, having made their minds up early on. But for a relationship to develop so fast, it's crucial that both partners are emotionally synced from the very start – which is quite unusual. At the other end of the spectrum, if both partners have recently left long-term relationships, they often have emotional baggage to struggle with. It can take time to build up the courage to reopen a damaged heart, so the process naturally slows down.

Another situation involves people who have already known each other for many years. They mingle in the same circles, and one day happen to fall in love. This relationship has advanced to the *initial phase* very slowly (through friendship) into the *courting phase*, but has hovered there for a while – a long trial period. During this long courting phase, these two 'friends' have got to know many different sides of each other before a closeness develops between them and they're ready for the *dedication phase*. Cupid intervenes 😄 ♡ and gets the job done.

Why do we get stuck on the ladder?

So why do we get stuck on the ladder, just like the motley crew of Glass Half-empty, Over-doer, Grass-is-greener, Clingy, 1NS, The Other Woman, and No Self-confidence? All of these folks *want* to be with someone, it's just that they can't seem to make it work. Most claim that they just have trouble finding the right person – a common way of thinking. But the real problem is that we get stuck in certain phases on the ladder, because it's not always easy to open ourselves up to intimacy. Some people figure the initial phase out quickly, hopping up and down on the first rung repeatedly with multiple partners but never taking the next step. Others get stuck in the courting phase but are afraid to take that last step. Some folks try to skip phases and jump straight to the top of the stepladder, but there's a good chance that you'll fall if you do that. And a few poor souls spend all day studying the ladder, but never manage to find someone to step up with.

So how come some of us get stuck in one phase, while others seem to effortlessly strut up that ladder? The explanation is that human beings are all subject to different *internal* conditions affecting how we create intimacy. Via research studies, we understand now what causes these differences, and also how to remedy them. All of this knowledge has been collected into a psychological theory dubbed *attachment theory*, initiated by John Bowlby's work during the 1950s. This theory also explains why intimacy can sometimes make us feel bad. It explains the discrepancies in how different people experience infatuation and/or love, and the causes behind the 'unexplainable' magnetic attraction between certain individuals. It explains, as well, what happens when infatuation evolves into a serious relationship, and also why it occasionally snarls there.

Comprehending human nature is a daunting challenge, so it's no wonder that innumerable books have been written about us – our behaviours, driving motives, and relationship struggles. As individuals, we're fascinating and unique. Both you and I have separately collected an incredibly individualized wealth of experience, affecting how we feel, think, act, and react. Humans are innately social, and we're all interwoven into a complex social fabric. Our actions and decisions are highly influenced by the people around us and in our lives. If only that were all! Human beings are biological creatures too, affected by the environment we live in, not to mention that genetic roll of the dice that makes individuals physiologically unique. Current attachment theory is the result of over sixty years of research into how human relationships function. It charts out the various factors that affect our efforts to form emotional ties to one another. It's structured by dividing people into different groups, based on what sorts of problems we encounter in our relationships. Obviously we're simplifying the complexities of reality, but it provides us with an effective tool for aiding our understanding of ourselves.

Attachment theory also builds on the fact that we learn how to form relationships when we're very young. The relationships we grow up with imprint patterns on us that strongly influence us for the rest of our lives. When we meet someone we like, we normally employ the same behaviour for creating closeness (intimacy) with that person that we used with our parents when we were little. The result of this is that our early relationship with our parents will continue to play an important role for us even into adulthood. One implication of this is that there's nothing strange or faulty about your or my relationship model. On the contrary – according to what we learned as children, it's right on the money. Research also reveals that the nature of our relationship models isn't *exclusively* determined by how we were raised – genes have their role to play as well.[3]

In order to understand how it all fits together, we initially divide ourselves into two groups. The first consists of people who felt *secure attachments* in their relationships. The second group consists of people who felt *anxious attachments* in their relationships. Those of us in the secure-attachment group usually have a relatively easy time finding a partner. Those of us in the anxious-attachment group usually have a lot more difficulty managing our relationships. Glass Half-empty, Over-doer, Grass-is-greener, Clingy, 1NS, The Other Woman, and No Self-confidence all find themselves in the anxious-attachment group.

The anxious-attachment group is further divided into two subgroups: the *avoidant-anxious-attachment* group and the *ambivalent-anxious-attachment* group.

A fourth attachment pattern exists as well: *Fearful-avoidant* (disorganized-unresolved) *attachment*. Our attachment patterns are often passed down from one generation to the next. Fearful-avoidant attachment patterns may develop in families suffering from abuse and violence, where the caregiver often is both a source of security and a threat. In these instances, children learn to connect love with pain, leading to problems in their future relationships. They may even completely avoid relationships altogether. Because this attachment pattern is relatively infrequent and involves issues beyond the scope of this book, I will focus primarily on the three widespread patterns. We're more complex than these groupings alone, of course, and don't always fit neatly into one category.

Three attachment patterns, three relationship models

Depending on which group you find yourself in, your relationships will be affected in different ways. Your relationship model affects your attitudes and reactions regarding intimacy and togetherness, how you handle conflicts, your attitude towards sex, your ability to express your needs, and your expectations about your partners. In other words, your relationship model sticks its nose into everything, controlling most aspects of your relationships.

The tricky thing here is that, by having different relationship models, it's almost as if we're speaking different languages. It complicates our attempts to both meet and understand one another. And let's keep in mind that we live in the real world – there's no need to get concerned because you don't happen to fit neatly into one category.

The secure-attachment group. Folks in this group find it easy to get close to other people. They're not particularly worried about getting abandoned, and don't feel uncomfortable when others get close to them. The 'secures' are often untroubled about being dependent on others, or whether others are dependent on them. However, they usually don't mind being alone either. They don't feel threatened by isolation, even if they still prefer being in relationships. They are often warm, loving people who enter relationships fairly easily. They find it rather easy to express their needs, and often communicate in a straightforward, clear manner (they don't need to play games), which helps explain why they also tend to have long relationships. About 50 per cent of us belong to this lucky group.[4]

The avoidant-anxious attachment group. These folks tend to be socially fluent, and are often well liked by those around them. They're frequently attentive to their appearance and appreciate order. They're normally ambitious and tend to do very well in the workplace. Generally they don't feel comfortable getting close to other people. They often feel that other people want to get closer than they themselves enjoy. This causes them to distance themselves in relationships, and they get uncomfortable if things move quickly. Emotional intimacy is often equivalent to a loss of independence for this group, so many of their actions revolve around lessening how close they are to their partner. For instance, the 'avoidant' often likes to keep a Plan B (an exit strategy) in their back pocket, some reason why they can't be there for both weeks of the holiday – they need to 'catch up on work', or need to stay at home to finish the decorating. Perhaps they're working overtime because it helps solve their intimacy problem. They may 'withhold' sex from their partner, or *only* focus on sex, albeit with rules like no kissing during sex, no cuddling afterwards, or other strict demands. These are all strategies for creating distance. It's also a fact that the avoidant, as a group, have the least amount of sex with their partners. And let's not forget infidelity. Studies show that those of us with avoidant-anxious attachment are more likely to be unfaithful to our partners than those with secure or ambivalent-anxious attachment.[5]

If you date an avoidant, you might find that they're 'not ready to commit', yet are happy to go on dating nonetheless, possibly for years, while they 'see where things go'. They find faults in their partners: she doesn't speak well, he doesn't eat well, wrong job, wrong education . . . Their perspective about whatever their partner says or does is essentially warped. The avoidant harbour more negative views of their partners than folks in the other relationship models,[6] and these perceived defections make it easier for them to maintain a certain standoffishness. Unfortunately, day-to-day living as an avoidant's partner can be demoralizing or frustrating.

This can go beyond seeing their partners in a negative light – they also tend to show less aptitude at recognizing the thoughts and feelings of their partners. They may interpret their partner's worry or anxiety as anger, and they become easily defensive. One distancing strategy is referred to as the *Phantom-ex phenomenon*. It involves idealizing a previous boyfriend or girlfriend who they feel would have been the 'perfect partner' for them. This means that you'll always be second best. Some of the avoidant are flirters – a painful strategy for promoting uncertainty in their relationships. They avoid the phrase 'I love you', which implies that they don't have the feelings for you that you're looking for. The avoidant may pull away when things go really well, like after a great date when you've really connected . . . Suddenly they disappear for a few days, re-establishing distance. They may date unavailable people, such as someone who's already married. Or maybe they just mentally zone out while you're talking to them – getting distracted or ignoring you. They're often secretive, or never seem to finalize the details when you're trying to make mutual plans. Keeping physical distance is common here, such as not wanting to share a bed, avoiding sex, or even walking several paces ahead of you. All of this boils down to the avoidant making sure that the ones they love – or could love – can't impede their independence or autonomy. At the same time, the tools that put distance between them and their partners also put distance between them and their potential to find happiness in their relationships. They sometimes get told that they're 'too perfect', and they demand perfection in their partners as well. 'You're not perfect? Then I guess you're not good enough . . .'

Unfortunately, the anxious-avoidant often wake up to their own negative assessments of their partners only *after* the relationship (and the 'danger') is already over and the distance made permanent – *that's* when they feel love and longing for you. 'How could it end when we were so right for each other?' But only after the fact. Too little, too late . . . (Will you receive the honour of being their Phantom Ex? Who knows . . .)

When they meet someone, they often *think out* their responses instead of trusting their feelings; they supplant their emotions with their own logic. They defend their independence, and expect others to be independent too. If they find themselves coerced into a relationship nonetheless, often they would rather be alone. Isolation is a preferable comfort to the strain they feel from the demands of intimacy. They also tend to believe that they can solve crises better by themselves, rather than discussing them with someone else.

About 25 per cent of us belong to this group. Studies have also shown that this relationship model goes hand in hand with a unique variant of serotonin receptors. Perhaps it goes without saying that the avoidant are generally less happy when in relationships than when they're not?[7]

The ambivalent-anxious attachment group. These folks are often seen as creative, dynamic, and in touch with their feelings. They sometimes talk about the intimate details of their lives to strangers. Regarding relationships, in many ways they are the polar opposite of the avoidant-anxious attachment group – they *enjoy* getting close to other people. They want *more* intimacy than the other person is comfortable with. This powerful lust for intimacy often drives away potential partners. They supplant their logic with their emotions, responding only by how they *feel* about the relationship. They're demanding, often feel that something is missing when they're alone, and might worry about whether the other person loves them enough. And not just with partners, but during the earlier phases with dates or prospective dates as well. The ambivalent can easily become jealous or suspicious, because they get anxious and upset when their partner tries to take time to be alone. When they feel stressed about their relationship, they often want to stay in very close contact with the person they're dating. They might text and call too often, which, instead of strengthening the relationship, makes them seem clingy, lacking boundaries, or incapable of managing responsibilities on their own. At the same time, if they feel that they can't trust their partner, they might abruptly push them away through some form of protest behaviour. In these situations, they might become angry, distraught, or unpredictable. Their panic at the thought of abandonment can be overwhelming, eventually resulting in them avoiding relationships altogether: Why waste all that time building up yet another relationship, when you know the inevitable break-up will crush you?

About 20 per cent of us fall into this group, and here we find a genetic component as well. This gene regulates patterns in our dopamine receptors.[8] Two of the genes linked to our serotonin (avoidant-anxious attachment) and dopamine (ambivalent-anxious attachment) levels are both fundamentally related to our emotions, feelings of reward, attention spans, social behaviours, and tendencies in how we react in romantic relationships. But hold your horses! These genes explain a lot, but by no means everything. The environment we're raised in and our adult experiences of romantic relationships also affect our feelings of security. Bad experiences create one type of pattern, while loving, safe relationships create another. Secure individuals can, over time, become less secure (unfortunately), while anxious individuals can become more secure. This means that there are some people to whom we shouldn't give a third, fourth, or fifth chance to, because if you start losing a secure relationship model, you're losing one of your truly most valuable and sought-after characteristics. Set your boundaries for your own sake.

Find someone with the right relationship model

When you're dating, it's important to figure out which attachment pattern you have, as well as those of your dates. This is because your respective attachment patterns might well be at loggerheads. This will make it more difficult to form a relationship. Allow me to explain: if you've met an avoidant, they're going to spend a lot of energy on creating distance between you. It doesn't matter whether the subject at hand is which film you're going to see, how to raise your children, or where to go on holiday. Various dilemmas such as these get transformed into negotiations about independence and having enough space. The result of these 'negotiations'? You sacrifice your own desires because your partner will distance themself from you otherwise. And that's no fun.

Typically heard from the avoidant:

'You're too sensitive,' 'You're too needy,' or 'You're too weak.'

'What do you want from me? I haven't done anything.'

'Stop analysing everything!'

'Just give it a rest. I already told you I'm sorry.'

They may care about your needs to a certain extent, only to then ignore them again. They're also bad at picking up on verbal and non-verbal cues. Or maybe it's that they just don't care. Neither do they feel that it's their responsibility. Mixed signals are the avoidant's calling card. They prioritize independence, which often means devaluing both you and your needs. Keeping the relationship undefined suits their purposes – they want to have their cake and eat it too. To not be single, yet to remain independent. 'Friends with benefits' shows up here. Call it what you will, but if you've been dating someone for a while and they suddenly disappear or get cold feet, you may be dating an avoidant. Even when things have got more serious between you, you'll still be faced with question marks: *if* we're going away together, *if* we're going to decide to move in together, *if* we should . . . Get ready for answers like 'We'll see' and 'I don't know yet.'

Unfortunately, the avoidant are over-represented in the dating market, since they're quite simply the first ones to pull out of relationships and enter them unwillingly. This makes the odds of you meeting people with avoidant-anxious attachment pretty high. The secure attachment and ambivalent-anxious attachment types (who don't share the same fear of intimacy) are already in relationships, or don't hang out in the dating market nearly as long. And the avoidant seldom date each other, since they both lack the incentive and the 'glue' needed to hold relationships together.[9] Now, let's not throw the baby out with the bathwater: if your partner or date is an avoidant but is willing to actively try to change their relationship model, then you may wish to give them a chance. If not, then pack your bags, preferably before you get too involved. And make a mental note to yourself that it's nobody's place to make *you* feel like you're to blame. That you're too sensitive, too needy, or too weak.

The ambivalent-anxious types seek a lot of intimacy in their relationships, as mentioned earlier. The ambivalent are insecure, afraid of rejection, and dissatisfied when not in a relationship. We've actually witnessed this in MRI studies of the brain: the regions most connected to emotions react the most powerfully in the ambivalent.[10] They also find it the most difficult to consciously control themselves and calm down. If you find yourself in this group, try to learn to shift your focus from 'Will they like me?' to 'Is this someone I'd like to be emotionally invested in, someone capable of fulfilling my needs?' If you're dating an ambivalent, then it's important to be clear about where you stand regarding the relationship. Security and transparency are essential components of any relationship, of course, but maybe just a little bit more so in this case.

If you both have secure attachment models, as a rule you won't face the kind of issues around independence that occur with avoidants, since intimacy doesn't pose a threat to either of you. As I'm sure you've already guessed, the secure make the best partners. The secure are programmed to expect love. They react effectively to the needs of their partners. They're not particularly worried about losing their partner's love, are comfortable with intimacy, and find it easy to communicate their needs. The truth is, their world view is just plain rosier, and they anticipate more of the good things in life. In a perfect world, of course, we'd all be two secures who find each other. When that isn't the case, however, it's not always a bad scenario. When a secure starts a relationship with an avoidant or an ambivalent, their security can actually help alleviate some of their partner's anxiety or insecurities. The security of the secure throws a magical glow of security over the whole relationship.

And sometimes that's enough. Sometimes it isn't.

Attachment patterns that attract each other

Viktor, a friend of mine, is ambivalent-anxious. He often ends up dating avoidants. This may sound a bit weird, because it's a bad match. And yet this combination is quite common.

Paula Pietromonaco, at the University of Massachusetts, and Katherine Carnelley, University of Southampton, have studied attraction *between* the various attachment models.[11] They found that the avoidant often preferred the ambivalent. Another study showed that ambivalent women often date avoidant men. Doesn't quite add up, does it? That the people most protective of their independence should be drawn to the romantic partners most likely to try to erode this independence? Or that the folks looking for intimacy should be drawn to romantic partners who won't return their affections, but rather push them away? They won't hold your hand when you want them to, won't hug, and go on holidays with their friends instead of you. And they leave conflicts open, since open conflicts are a more effective way of maintaining distance than resolving them would be. Avoidant-anxious is in command, and everyone else better step into line. If things become 'too' intimate for an avoidant, it can even lead to him seeing his partner as his enemy. This predicament can be absolutely dreadful: your partner treats you like shit, while at the same time everyone else thinks he's the bee's knees. The impression he makes on other people (even strangers) is more important to him than the impression he makes on you – because he views you as a traitor. Your crime? Getting too close. And yet you never quite seem able to leave him . . .

Researchers hypothesize that these two attachment models actually complement one another, even if we might have the opposite impression at first glance. It has to do with how your way of attaching reinforces your self-image and role in relationships. I'll explain: the avoidant's self-image is that she or he is independent, autonomous, and strong – self-sufficient. These individuals idealize and even internalize this self-sufficiency as well. They need no one, and look down on those who do. When another person tries to coax them into a greater level of closeness than they're comfortable with, it confirms their self-image, and that person gets rejected.

And then we go through the same old motions, over and over again.

The sad thing is that we get used to it after a while. We get used to the distancing, to feeling unloved and unwanted. It's like a twisted relationship version of the game tag, with one partner backing away every time the other comes near. It can feel like they're masters at toying with our emotions, sensing exactly when we've got one foot out the door, only to reel us back in with a few strategically chosen words, a well-timed apology, or a thoughtful gesture.

Boom. Hooked again.

After we've experienced this long enough, we begin to equate the angst, the obsession, and those tiny little moments of happiness with *love*. But what you're really doing here is mistaking your currently active relationship model with *passion*. After you've danced this demonic dance enough times, you've rewired yourself to get attracted to exactly those individuals who are the least likely to give you what you want. And the thing is, you *will* be happy when you can find a safe *base* (how psychologists refer to it when discussing relationship models) that can provide you with strength and security. But to achieve this, your relationship model needs to be safe and calm. And safe and calm it is *not* when you're getting pushed away, belittled, or mocked. Under those circumstances, you need to remind your little active relationship model up there that what you're feeling *isn't* love. It's fool's gold, and your relationship model is tormenting you because it wants to take one more ride on the rollercoaster. True love won't systematically keep you at arm's length. True love means security and peace of mind.

From here on out, promise me that you'll evaluate your dates by whether or not they will try to meet *your* needs. Not whether *you're* good enough for *them*. Are you both able to freely express your needs together? Or do they make you feel uncertain about discussing them? Are they interested in trying to fulfil your needs?

No more ball and chain – why it's 'easier' to be single

When single, we can have a fulfilling, fun time with our friends. We're unencumbered by the relationship models explained by attachment theory. This is why we're often relaxed, happy, and satisfied with life *as long as we stay single*. When we unexpectedly meet a potential partner, however, that satisfaction can vanish in a heartbeat. Our relationship model kicks into gear the very second you see that twinkle in their eye. You're already shifting phases upwards – life is no longer a stroll in the park. The closer you get to this person, the more your relationship model starts calling the shots.

Its gears are already turning at the initial phase, but the intensity of your relationship model's command peaks during the courting phase, which is where we tend to have the most difficulty. By now we've grown quite close to our partner, and we'll lose intimacy if the relationship fails – the stakes have been raised. We also feel uncertainty more acutely at this phase. Once we reach the dedication phase, things quieten down. (Phew! Good news for once.) We usually feel secure in our relationship and don't have to worry about losing it. That being said, if the relationship becomes stressed, our relationship models kick back into gear.

Many singles think that if you just practise being alone long enough you'll find peace, which will carry over when you meet someone you want to be with. Unfortunately, that strategy is a mirage. No matter how safe, satisfied, and happy you feel when you're alone, you'll find yourself in a different position once your relationship model kicks in. Changing destructive relationship patterns requires meeting people: we *have* to let it kick in. If we want to be in a relationship, we have to keep dating.

Attachment patterns explain why staying single is so tempting to those out there with anxious attachment patterns. Love is more painful for these folks than it is for others. It makes it compelling for them – consciously or unconsciously – to avoid or sabotage long-term relationships. All creatures avoid pain, and we're no exception. In the short term, it's advantageous. Recent generations have been among the first people in history who have been given the opportunity to *learn* how to create intimate, romantic relationships. Of our own free will. Not that being alone would dramatically affect our species – we're survivors, and parents can both have and raise children without having to be a couple. But it's a shame to miss out on the relationships we truly desire because we're plagued by anxious-attachment issues from our childhoods. The fear of intimacy that pervades our culture is predicated on a misunderstanding of what freedom and independence are. Self-reliant people can react to situations or go to the shops by themselves – these are obviously practical abilities to have. But ask yourself this, my friend: is there any legitimate reason why someone who's so positively self-reliant shouldn't also be fully capable of becoming intimate with other people?

Why do we end up with a 'type'?

I've often heard my friends say that some guy is 'totally Angela's type' or that I'm 'exactly his type'. It's easy for us to assume that these comments refer to physical appearance. In reality, though, it has a lot more to do with the inner qualities (or traits) of the person in question, and I wish I didn't have to add this little detail, but – unfortunately – we're often drawn to negative qualities.

For example, if we're withdrawn and quiet, we might be attracted to people who are outgoing and ambitious. If we find intimacy uncomfortable, we might choose a partner who's distant and less available. If we tend to be controlling, we might seek out someone who's passive. We force the puzzle pieces together, not because we've found someone we actually sync with in a positive way, but because our *relationship models* and our *psychological defence mechanisms* sync up well. In the worst cases, we continue to create destructive patterns, the same patterns familiar to us from our childhoods, in accordance with our given relationship models.

Our self-image also affects who we're attracted to. If we have a negative self-image – we feel unattractive or unworthy of affection, for instance – we're easily drawn to people who confirm these conclusions. 'Better the devil you know . . .' says your reptilian brain. Escaping from negative relationship patterns involves becoming aware of the forces that are driving you. Is there a common thread among the people you've been attracted to? It may not jump out at you, but keep an eye out for the less obvious aspects. How did these people make you feel? Did you want to take care of them, or for them to take care of *you*? Do you withdraw when people get close to you? Our personal common threads might twist this way and that, but when seen together they reveal repeated patterns. Once you figure out what your patterns are, you can begin to connect the patterns in your adult relationships to your childhood attachment pattern. Is a picture forming?

Once you've become conscious of your patterns, you can begin to rethink your decisions when you're dating. You may have to date outside of your comfort zone, or take a chance on someone you previously would have walked away from. Old patterns can easily keep us going round in circles or lead us up the wrong path, letting our defence mechanisms do all the choosing for us. Is that what we really want?

Glass Half-empty, Clingy, and the rest of our motley crew

Let's revisit our old friends Glass Half-empty, Over-doer, Grass-is-greener, Clingy, 1NS, The Other Woman, and No Self-confidence. All these folks have different issues that disturb their ability to enjoy good relationships. Why do we have these problems, and where do they originate?

One Night Stand. 1NS earned his name for a reason. He can't hang out in the initial phase long enough for his relationships to get off the ground. 1NS has an avoidant-anxious attachment calling all his shots. His parents used nannies or babysitters and didn't allow their children to place demands on them. Routinely dismissed, he didn't get to feel close to his parents. As an adult, 1NS is well adjusted, socially competent, intelligent, and potential dates are attracted to him. Sexual encounters give him a taste of the intimacy he desires, yet it starts feeling dangerous by sunrise. He gets restless and needs to be alone. That first breath of fresh air comes as a relief, but days later he's already disappointed by how inaccessible a genuine relationship seems. As soon as 1NS hits the initial phase, his relationship model kicks in. He can stay in that phase long enough to get laid, but immediately afterwards retreats to the comfort of solid ground. 1NS hops up and down on the first rung, but with different people each time.

The Other Woman falls in love with married men, never single guys, and can date them for long periods of time. She has an ambivalent-anxious attachment, and doesn't believe that anyone will want to stay in a long-term relationship with her. As a mistress, she can create something like a long-term relationship without triggering her fear of disappointment. Since the man already *has* a long-term relationship, a genuine long-term relationship with her is implicitly unavailable – there's no shock treatment waiting at the end of the tunnel. The Other Woman steps up to the courting phase of relationships and can hang out there for years. She knows that this situation is bad for her and feels humiliated by it. But when it comes to single guys, she won't even climb the first step; these men don't trigger her desire. This is all rooted in The Other Woman's fear of abandonment. If her married boyfriend actually leaves his wife for her, her relationship model will cry foul: 'He might leave you now!' And then she once again retreats to the safety – and loneliness – of solid ground.

Clingy wants to hop straight up to the dedication phase. Clingy loves passionate relationships, but she's afraid of abandonment and gets easily anxious and stressed. She demands guarantees of commitment from her partners. Clingy has an ambivalent-anxious attachment, and this causes her to lose patience with the initial and courting phases of dating – why not leap to the top? It's the best, right? She experiences the uncertainty of the early stages as torture, and she's adamant about ascertaining whether it's true love from the very first date. This scares away those who are interested in her, who might look forward to a relationship if she gave them a little more time. And so, inevitably, she finds herself staring up the ladder.

No Self-confidence also has trouble handling the initial phase. When someone shows interest in him, No Self-confidence excuses himself and disappears. It's become so bad that he avoids parties and events where strangers will be present. No Self-confidence has an avoidant-anxious attachment and lives with the feeling that he's just not good enough. His childhood was characterized by an emphasis on success and achievement, and his parents and siblings are all over-achievers (or at least appear to be) academically and at work. His parents preached that a good career, good social standing, and a good income are the secrets to happiness. No Self-confidence went to a good school just like his siblings, but he didn't live up to every-one's expectations. When he meets a potential date, his relationship model argues that she'll reject him if he can't fulfil a long list of hidden requirements. No Self-confidence doubts his ability to live up to these expectations and feels ashamed about his failures. The fact that No Self-confidence feels this way isn't always easy for other people to detect, but it results in him having difficulty getting to the initial phase. His relationship model holds him back.

Glass Half-empty is the guy who always starts finding faults after a few dates (*Seinfeld* fans will recognize Jerry Seinfeld's character here), and all these 'flaws' turn out to be deal-breakers. Glass Half-empty has trouble revealing his true self, but he always shows up looking sharp. He has an avoidant-anxious attachment and for the first few dates can easily project a glamorized image of himself. After a few dates, he's getting to know the other person and a mutual interest has developed. The natural next step would be to start spending more time together: the courting phase. But this is where Glass Half-empty hits a wall. His relationship model prevents him from revealing to his partner that he needs someone. Negative observations and overly critical thoughts about his partner's attributes start hounding him. Does he even want to be in a relationship? All of these circumstances cause the relationship to get stuck in the courting phase. Glass Half-empty was a lot more comfortable back in the initial phase, when things weren't getting so serious. If his partner eventually gets tired of his slipshod, lackadaisical attitude, she'll jump ship and leave him back on the boat – all alone.

Over-doer is the woman who focuses exclusively on her partner. Her urge to adapt to her partner's wishes is so overwhelming that she essentially becomes invisible, which results in her relationships running out of steam. Over-doer has an avoidant-anxious attachment which makes her feel the most stable in the initial phase. She *pretends* to ascend to the courting phase, but it's an illusion. Intimacy is fairly shallow and noncommittal in the initial phase, and by being able to avoid revealing too much about herself she can master the art of making her man happy. Eventually, though, Over-doer's partner sees that it's time to enter the courting phase and they begin to meet up more often. Over-doer loves this idea! Unfortunately, although the relationship has technically ascended to the courting phase, Over-doer still acts like they barely know each other. She sticks to her guns as the ideal girlfriend, trying to fit her man like a glove. But by being who he wants her to be and not who she is, she slowly fades into the background and they never connect on a deeper level. As the months or years tick by, eventually her partner manages to see through her smoke and mirrors, and realizes that he has no idea who Over-doer really is – they might as well be on their first date. They break up, and Over-doer is on her own again. Tragically, Over-doer is going to try a little harder next time, instead of screwing it up like last time. Good luck with that.

Grass-is-greener also struggles during the courting phase. This guy's had quite a few relationships, and sits eternally on the fence regarding commitment. Grass-is-greener has an ambivalent-anxious attachment pattern, and it prevents him trusting his partners. He can handle the initial phase like a fish handles water, and he ascends fairly easy to the courting phase as well. But with this guy, the trial phase just never ends. He can stay in a relationship for a long time, trapped in constant emotional vacillation – 'Should I stay or should I go?' Eventually, Grass-is-greener's inability to commit to a relationship causes his partner to up sticks and move on.

Different relationship models, different problems

Our problems on the relationship stepladder are unique, depending on who we are individually. But the patterns are there. Sooner or later, our relationship models eventually compel us to take control over situations that threaten us with painful rejection. The nature of this control varies among individuals.

Folks with *avoidant-anxious attachment* struggle primarily with self-control. This can involve self-retreat, staying distant, or – contrarily – adapting to your partner's wishes. However this urge manifests itself, the result is that you never really get to know each other.

If you have an *ambivalent-anxious attachment*, you try to control your partner instead. You'll do whatever it takes to keep hold of this person, insisting on confirmation or guarantees, and reassurances of their devotion.

Whichever method of control these attachment patterns wield over us, they leave us stuck in a certain phase. If we want to establish an intimate and long-lasting romantic relationship, we need to do something to take control away from these patterns. Yet control, from a historical perspective, has aided the survival of our species. It's the reason we store food, water, or fuel, and why we prepare for winter or droughts. We have insurance, healthcare, a justice system, and other forms of social safety nets to alleviate our anxieties over future calamities and unexpected events. We possess the ability to predict potential threats. Generally speaking, control is a resource, not a problem. As infants, our biggest threat was being abandoned by our parents – we wouldn't have survived without them. It's the first threat we learned to react to. How did this express itself? Well, we studied our parents' behaviour, watching for signs that they might leave us, and our subsequent behaviour was the result of us trying to prevent that from happening. Either we tried to control ourselves or we tried to control our parents, and our attachment pattern developed accordingly. Attachment patterns helped us to maximize our closeness to our parents, which is why they're fundamentally connected to human survival. The challenge is that our childhood methods of gaining control get covertly baked into our relationship models. We carry on behaving the same way as adults, and the more anxiety we feel, the more we rely on the same old methods. When we find intimacy within reach, our relationship models create visions of abandonment. These visions trigger emotional responses in us, offering us a taste of what we fear abandonment will feel like. So how do we respond? We either tighten our grip or we push away, depending on our relationship model.

Change your relationship model, change your life

Entering a relationship involves the interaction of three systems: our emotions, our thoughts, and our actions. These are inter-dependent, affecting each other. But how they interact varies between individuals.

Let's take a closer look at our *actions*. Human problems are often caused by personal actions that have knocked us off track in life, steering us away from the lives we'd rather lead. We repeat certain actions until they become systematic mistakes that can dog us throughout our lives.

If you want to change your life, you have to change your actions. This isn't easy – old habits are hard to break. If you want to change your situation, you also need to develop a new approach to dealing with pain. Although our attachment patterns tell us otherwise, the feelings of anxiety or pain we get as we become closer to other people are *not* concrete threats of impending catastrophe. Those alarm bells mean that you're closing in on a meaningful relation-ship. If you want to get close to someone, to have a long-lasting relationship, then you need to recognize the occasions where you ought to resist the impulse to react against that pain. Remind your-self that you're not actually in danger. Recognize your situation for what it is: the price of admission for the experience of two hearts becoming one.

The first step towards meaningful change is to understand where your problems originate. What kind of emotional legacy has your childhood left you with?

Some of us feel so much pain when getting close to someone that we're overwhelmed, and we give up and return to previous, more familiar behaviours or situations. When our little motley crew (No Self-confidence, Clingy, and co) find themselves in emotionally challenging situations, they show how they earned their nicknames by abandoning or neglecting their relationships at the point when their pain reaches a certain threshold. For example, if Glass Half-empty wants to change his situation and enter into a serious relationship, he'll have to learn to handle his pain differently when he starts seeing flaws in his partner.

I certainly don't want to give the impression that relationships are nothing but a toxic cocktail of pain and suffering – of course they're not! But if we want to enjoy all the wonderful things that they have to offer, then we also have to accept the fact that creating and maintaining relationships involves dealing with burdensome emotions at times. And for some of us it's much more of an uphill battle than for others. Still, if we can't learn how to handle the storms of the heart, then it doesn't matter if we've waltzed into a relationship that's wonderful 99 per cent of the time. Our dilemma is that relationship models focus on those scattered painful moments, imagining threats and then holding us back. They're more than happy to suck us back into our previous patterns where we've been avoiding the pain again and again, and the price of this pain relief is not getting to experience the joys of deeper, more meaningful relationships. Although the short-term relief is always satisfying, as the process repeats itself, our loneliness and dissatis-faction continue to grow. Unfortunately, our psychological mechanisms aren't always designed to take in the big picture, and bad relationships from our past cause us to feel insecure, making it more difficult to create new relationships. But luckily we can turn this phenomenon on its head: we can face our dragons. If we want to experience true intimacy and the full richness of love, we can learn how to handle the painful emotions that our brains have linked to it, and then we'll begin to get constructive, positive results. By being brave and taking proactive steps, we can change our rela-tionship models, and that will result in feeling more secure about ourselves and our situations, making it easier to create genuine relationships in the future.

Tool 1: Do the opposite

Below are a pair of tools that can be useful when beginning new relationships and your old habits and doubts start to creep in. Here are just two, but there are many other methods available for helping you to change your behaviour. Try these and see how you get on.

First up is the *Do-the-opposite* method. This involves actively challenging your relationship model in given situations – doing the opposite of what would normally feel natural, logical, or safe from your perspective. It requires you to separate your *actions* from your thoughts and feelings. By planning your actions for a situation ahead of time, when that situation occurs, you can ignore your reactions or feelings and take the planned action. Try approaching the situation like this: you analyse it first – what usually happens when you're climbing the relationship ladder? Did you see yourself in our cast of characters perhaps? Focus on specific situations where you know that your behaviour or reaction has given you problems. When you've located a situation like this, you can break it down in a so-called *situation analysis*. I've given examples for Glass Half Empty and 1NS situations but you can use the same headings for your own situation. Go grab a pen and paper!

	Situation analysis	(Glass Half-empty)
1.	Problematic situation:	I always start finding faults with my dates, which bothers me.
2.	What are you thinking?	She's not right for me.
3.	What are you feeling?	Anxiety, stress.
4.	What do you do?	Break up.
5.	Short-term gain:	After breaking up I feel relief.
6.	Long-term consequences:	Missed another opportunity. Single again, maybe forever?

	Situation analysis	(One Night Stand)
1.	Problematic situation:	I get lots of sex, but I never get to know anybody – I can't even stay the night.
2.	What are you thinking?	I'm unusually picky.
3.	What are you feeling?	Huge relief as soon as I head home.
4.	What do you do?	I leave before dawn.
5.	Short-term gain:	I get sex. (But only sex.)
6.	Long-term consequences:	I stay single and nothing changes.

What is your Do-the-opposite situation? You've filled in the form and found at least one situation that you can work on. Look at the fourth question, where you've said how you react. The Do-the-opposite method means that you plan to do exactly the opposite of what you usually do. You don't have to change all your faults – at least not all at once! Take baby steps. (After all, didn't it start that way?) Start with something you can handle, and actively do the opposite when that problem occurs, ignoring those thoughts and feelings that arise. (And later on, after some experience with that, you can tackle your next issue.)

Here are a few examples:

Old behaviour: I talk non-stop.
New behaviour: I decide to shut up and listen to what my date is saying, and ask questions – even though listening silently is incredibly awkward for me.

Old behaviour: I'm so scared of rejection that I'm afraid to talk to people I like.
New behaviour: The next time I'm at a bar or a work party I'm

going to talk to five people before I leave. I don't care what we talk about and I know I'll feel scared, but I'm just going to do it.

Old behaviour: Everything has to be perfect on my date – I expect only the best of myself. It's exhausting, and I'm not having any fun dating.
New behaviour: I lower my standards. I don't overdress, and I don't go out of my way to choose a place or activity that's exceptional – we'll just grab a beer or something. I'm going to be myself, and instead of criticizing myself, I'm just going to go with the flow.

Old behaviour: I constantly oversell myself, bragging about my accomplishments.
New behaviour: Next time I'll talk about a personal memory that was particularly emotional.

Tool 2: The Long Drive

The Do-the-opposite method involves withstanding powerful emotional pressures, and it can take incredible effort at times. Progress often means two steps forward and one step back, and sometimes you might get exhausted and revert to old behaviours. When you're feeling like this, you can switch to the *Long-drive method* instead, which helps you handle the difficult thoughts and emotions that the dating process stirs up in you. When you're facing a situation where you know you ought to do the opposite, imagine that you're sitting in a car, about to go for a long drive. You're driving somewhere you've always wanted to go, and this time you've filled the tank, brought along some sandwiches, and your neighbour said she'd feed your cat and water the houseplants – nothing's stopping you today.

As your car drives down the road, signs are constantly swishing by. Some are telling you to stop, and billboards are trying to get you to veer away from your destination. But this symbolic journey is towards that wonderful place filled with exciting things that you've never seen or experienced! All these stupid signs are just the old thoughts and emotions that crop up each time you break your old control behaviours. Your mission is to keep your eyes on the road and ignore those signs. You still have to read them – it's not like you can close your eyes – but you're not going to do what they say.

Let's give it a go: Flavio is sitting in his car. He's started dating Felicia and they've gone out a few times. When they set up the next date he was into the idea, but as the day is nearing he starts getting cold feet. Is he up for this yet again? This is the point where Flavio usually starts wondering whether this woman is the right person for him and starts pulling away. But now Flavio also knows that he *has* to keep meeting people if he wants to see what's at the end of that road, so he swallows the bitter pill – he does the opposite and goes on more dates with Felicia, *despite* the fact that warning signs are screaming for him to turn his car around. He keeps his hands on the wheel and studies the horizon. 'You're a bad match.' 'She's not right for you.' 'This relationship is going to be terrible.' But he doesn't cancel the date this time. He sticks to his guns, focusing on his destination and not letting the signs affect him. The signs never give up, saying things like, 'You're not really attracted to her' and 'She's going to suffocate you.' Flavio's relationship model is merciless in its attempts to get him off the highway, but he goes on that next date and it's not too bad. When Flavio's little demons pester him, he focuses on his destination and ignores the road signs, letting them zip past. He makes the best of the situation. Maybe things eventually go so well that Flavio falls in love, who knows?

'This isn't working.' 'She's wrong for you.' 'It'll never work out.' These signs were posted by our relationship models, so don't let them sidetrack you – there's a reason why they're so pervasive. Usually, we see them because things are *right* – we're on the *right road*. Keep driving. 'I feel nothing for this person.' This sign seems to be telling you that there's something wrong with your prospective partner, but what it's actually trying to do is block you from the 'dangers' of intimacy, and thereby lessen your pain. It's not a genuine message meaning something is wrong with this (budding) relationship. The awkward distance that you're feeling might mean the opposite: that in your heart, you feel something for this person. Your only solution is to expose yourself to that closeness or intimacy. The stupid signs probably aren't going anywhere anytime soon, but don't let them take the wheel from you.

Another common sign says, 'Wait for the right one.' This sign is telling you that you're not dating who you ought to be dating – what if your dream date suddenly shows up? A lot of us have been deeply affected by the 'soulmate' idea, but unfortunately, those kinds of thoughts are often our control mechanisms throwing a spanner in the works in a misguided effort to protect us. Those signs will still appear even when you *do* meet the 'right' person, because – in truth – that idealized five-star lover doesn't exist in reality. We expect our future partner to behave exactly like this or that, to look exactly like this or that, or to have this or that kind of life.

Now let's get one thing straight: you can't just expect to build a serious relationship with any old stranger you stumble across. And of course you should never put up with someone who humiliates you, ignores your needs, belittles you, or mistreats you. (And there is zero room for violence in a relationship.) But I've got my own little test for you that usually tells you whether you've got a good potential candidate on your hands. Ask yourself this: *Would I be friends with this person?* If the answer is yes, then I'd say you're looking at a potential partner right there. If the answer is no, then it's time to move on. Treat the other questions floating around in your head with a heavy dose of scepticism. You might fit together like puzzle pieces or you might match up like cats and dogs – the point is that you won't *know* until you can climb the next step on your relationship ladder. Do that first, and then you can make a more realistic evaluation of your situation. The catch-22 is: the better you and your prospect match up, the *more* your control system will start screaming bloody hell. Remember that, while your knee-jerk mental reflexes are telling you the opposite, you might actually be dating the most wonderful person you'll ever encounter.

Getting misled by illusions of danger

After everything we've just talked about, you must feel like you're about to walk into an emotional tornado.

You are.

But here's the thing: there *is* no tornado. It's all in your head – this storm is a risk scenario invented by your relationship model. It's a product of your childhood (and a gene or two) and as a way of handling adult relationships, it's also been completely misappropriated. Those old childhood patterns and mechanisms don't address any *genuine* risks of getting abandoned to the wolves. They're only protecting you from the *emotions* you feel from an *expectation* of getting abandoned. That just isn't based in reality, and these feelings are only harmful when you react to them. The problem is that if we reflexively act on these old impulses we create a genuine threat – the threat of being all alone. I'm talking about destructive behaviours such as controlling our partner's every move, only dating new people all the time, having only sexual encounters, playing hard-to-get, or constantly breaking off new relationships the second it feels like things are getting boring (which might be a sign that things are getting interesting – what that particular relationship model fights). To only ever be someone's bit on the side is a bad strategy, while some folks only start relationships when on holiday, knowing (consciously or unconsciously) that these will never lead anywhere. Some people constantly fret over whether the person they're dating is right or not, or inevitably choose long-distance relationships (which means being stalled endlessly in the courting phase and never truly accepting each other), or break up with partners who can't live up to their unrealistic expectations. Or maybe we keep dating other people or flirting with exes after we've entered a relationship.

These are all effective ways of preventing healthy, deep, and fulfilling relationships from forming. You can't expect to enter a relationship without occasionally having to face up to negative emotions such as anxiety or sorrow. The more we try to avoid these feelings, the more control they have over us. When we let our control mechanisms rampage through our love lives, what ought to be the unfolding of an exciting adventure sours into a dismal tramp through the mud. Seriously, if you've been stuck in negative trajectories, repeating over and over, then I don't blame you if you're tired of meeting new people – it's exhausting when it always ends like that! This can easily make us resistant to even the *idea* of relationships, causing us to only hang out with our friends or avoid situations where we might meet people we know we'd like. You dig a hidey-hole, deciding that the single life is the life for you – it's purgatory, life on pause. Maybe the right person will eventually come along, right? Someone who doesn't scare you with all those nasty feelings . . . They won't. That's not a reality you'll ever get to experience. Avoiding pain works in the short term, but it also keeps relationships locked away out of reach.

And hey, single life ain't half-bad. You certainly don't need a partner to feel like a fully fledged, complete human being. Society serves us up an image of what we're supposed to consider 'normal', and current generations have been fed an idea that 'normal' means being part of a couple, with single folks often coerced by this bias into feeling like unwanted leftovers. And that's usually about as far off the mark as you can get. You're most likely single because you've *chosen* against a relationship, not because there's no one out there who wants you. So wear your singlehood as a badge of honour. Plenty of singles aren't looking for anybody and are completely satisfied with the way things are. As I mentioned previously, up here in Sweden single households are the most common living arrangement (not that everyone who lives alone is necessarily single, of course). Living *alone* is actually the norm. I know plenty of people who have been single for ages, and some of them don't date at all. Others go on dates, but just haven't found a good candidate yet. Finding the right sweetheart is a heck of a challenge, but that's no reason why you should settle for second best. All that being said, if you *do* want a relationship, then you need to get out there and do the legwork. Don't let your relationship model hold you back from getting to that place you'd like to be with that person you'd love to love.

Up until now, you've probably been passively responding to whatever whims your relationship model has had in store for you, most likely without knowing it. It's determined how you've shaped your life, conforming it to what *it* thinks your world ought to look like. These are still defence mechanisms that serve a useful purpose in our lives – they *should* be there. But you need to take control over the control. Learn to use your capacity for control as a way to *increase* your odds of discovering intimacy. That will bring you one step closer to a satisfying romantic relationship.

Many of us need time to adjust to a new prospective partner. Don't force commitment too early. Continue to meet more often, and if all your ducks fall in a row they'll be happy to get closer to you all on their own. Be your best, most authentic YOU. Have genuine meetups, and make sure that you can be vulnerable in each other's company. If commitment still seems elusive, find out where the other person stands on things, how they feel about it. (You might be dating Grass-is-greener, who knows?) Perhaps they're really interested in you but are wrestling their *own* attachment-pattern monsters. If they're willing to work on taking control over their relationship model, then why not give them a chance? If they're not, then move on.

Walking into your emotional tornado is how you find the end of your rainbow!

Love conquers all, right?

So . . . Is love enough?

We both know the answer to that question: nope. Love is magnificent, but it doesn't conquer everything. You might be swimming up to your gills in love, but relationship models and personalities can still muddy the waters enough to prevent the two of you from becoming a pair. Perhaps love makes one or even both of you unhappy, draining your energy away in a destructive relationship.

True love means getting our emotional needs met. It means feeling safe, secure, supported, and loved. This makes us strong. We can shift our attention outwards, to focus on the things we want and need. It lays the world at our feet, opening up our creativity and allowing us to take risks because we sense that life is out there waiting to be lived. Our relationship and the time we spend together become both a stable base and a source of energy. To drive my point home, I'm going to ask you to imagine this: a small child is within sight of her caregiver. Her caregiver is a happy source of security, always there when the child needs them. Only then can this child explore her world with curiosity and enthusiasm. Now, imagine that this caregiver is absent or fails to fulfil the child's need for security. This results in the child feeling stressed and unhappy instead, and shifts her focus towards her caregiver, or even just *finding* her caregiver. In other words, a feeling that's anything other than 'Watch out world, here I come!' As adults, we're no different. When our partner fails to fulfil our base needs, we feel a chronic sense of worry and anxiety. We fail to thrive. At the bottom of it all, we humans are only as 'needy' as our unfulfilled needs. It's that simple, and don't let anyone tell you otherwise.

There is an effective method for figuring out whether your (prospective) partner is up to scratch. Sniff out some tell-tale signs of his or her relationship model, which you can do by expressing your needs, clearly and openly, with all the strength, warmth, and dignity you can muster – as your most authentic you. What you're doing here is turning your weaknesses into your strengths. Are you afraid that she's going to leave you? Tell her that. Is something else bothering you? Pluck up the courage and tell him that. You'll come out a winner no matter the results. The reaction you receive will provide you with useful information on what to do next. Either they'll meet you halfway (the right reaction) or else they won't (the wrong reaction). Pay attention. Is she there for you? Are your needs important to him? Either reaction will give you insight into who you're dealing with, which will be your compass on your quest for happiness. Stay here, or move on? People spread clues about their relationship models all around them via their words, their actions, and their decisions.

I once heard someone say, 'You're only as troubled as the relationship you're in.'

I couldn't have said it better myself.

22: You and I – forever and ever

Some relationships have a short shelf life. Some last for years, and others continue for the rest of our lives. What is it that determines how your relationship will work out?

We've spent some time taking a hard look at how our childhood relationships with our parents exert influence over our adult romantic relationships, particularly in their early stages, as we're gradually getting close to one another. It's time to take a look at the tail end of this equation, and this might take a while – the answers aren't straightforward here either. That being said, the research world loves a challenge, and for over half a century they've been studying which factors contribute to long-lasting relationships.[1]

A familiar challenge for most couples is bridging that gap between passionate infatuation and the deeper connections needed for committed relationships. In this chapter, we'll look at which factors can move your relationship in a rewarding direction, and what *you* can do to nourish and encourage those factors.

Together till the end of time

'And they lived happily ever after.' Fairy tales paint a pretty picture. Research, however, paints a different picture. American and European researchers tracked 1,761 couples who remained married over the 15 years that the study was carried out. The patterns that emerged showed that the initial period of infatuation – when we're walking on air – lasts on average for around two years. After the euphoric trance of new love wears off, though, we find ourselves, at least happiness-wise, in the same place we were *before* the relationship started.[2]

When we're in love, we're basically happy all the time. (Isn't that the appeal?) We could be doing just about anything – driving in rush-hour traffic, loading the dishwasher, brushing our teeth – and happy little feelings of love can wash over us out of nowhere. Researchers refer to this as *passionate love*. Common characteristics are sexual lust, intense longing, and powerful attraction. After about two years (on average) have passed, we experience what the guys and gals in lab coats refer to as *companionate love* ('friendly', 'platonic', or 'non-romantic' love). This is a more relaxed state of affairs, but the bonds you share are probably stronger now. If you accept the fact that your passion isn't burning holes in your clothes like it was at the start, then you know that nothing is wrong. Things are the way they are meant to be. And passion will also probably rekindle later on in your relationship. For couples with children, this often occurs after the kids have finally moved out. Generally, and according to research, the couples who didn't divorce were also the couples who were most 'satisfied' at the outset of the relationship. But for couples who have only stayed together for the sake of their kids . . . Well, the time after your little ones have flown the nest is frequently when suppressed conflicts bubble up to the surface.

Passion – can we keep it burning?

Yup. Well, sort of. It's a little more complicated. To help you understand it, I'm going to tell you about different kinds of love. Because not all love is the same, of course – we can feel love for our family and love for our friends, and we can feel romantic love. Romantic love carries different strains of closeness and intimacy, and can even have a sense of destiny about it. 'It was meant to be,' as they say – romantic love is a *story*. You have 'your song' and that now-famous place where you first met. Maybe you remember the first time you locked eyes. You mark dates on your calendar, celebrating anniversaries of when it all went down. There was a twinkle in your eye, a fleeting moment of tenderness, a mutual understanding, and boundaries fell as two merged into one. Yet this union is made up of two lovers, each celebrating the wonder of the other. Two bodies, living life together . . . Erotic or not, this feeling of union is so powerful that it changes our lives.

Romantic love also comes in different flavours. For the sake of simplicity, I'm going to stick with the least complicated way of dividing it, which is into the two types I've already mentioned: *passionate love* and *companionate love*.[3]

Have you ever wondered why passion even exists in the first place? Or why it fades away? Passionate love has been defined as a strong attraction and intense longing between individuals.[4] It can even express itself as a form of obsession. In their study *Passion, Intimacy, Time*, researchers Baumeister and Bratslavsky suggest that passion is a result of the great amount of activity that happens when relationships begin.[5] Intimate feelings grow quickly at the beginning of a relationship, and everything can seem surprising. Do you like the same things? What is her family like? Do you enjoy the same type of food? Later on, once we've got to know our partner better, there are fewer novelties to discover. According to Baumeister and Bratslavsky's hypothesis, it's this gradual decrease of exciting new revelations that contributes to the decline of passion.

Falling in love affects our neurochemistry, unleashing a cocktail of chemicals into our brains. *Dopamine* gets triggered by the 'hunting' aspect of love – when we find 'the right one' (again), we get high on it. *Oxytocin* gets released through physical touching and trust. Serotonin is stimulated by our new sense of heightened status. Being liked by certain people gives us pride, particularly if we attribute a particular status to them. *Endorphins* get triggered by pain, but also by crying and laughter – everyone has seen couples in love who laugh all the time. *Cortisol* makes us feel bad when our romantic connections are severed, but also helps us get over those feelings. After all, if we'd stayed hung up on someone who would be unavailable for the rest of our lives, it wouldn't have benefited the survival of our ancestors, and therefore our species. As long as we're still newly infatuated, though, we trip through life effortlessly, without a care in the world.

And then that fateful day comes, the day your euphoric joyride on the love express comes to an end, and old dopamine and his friends decide that you've had enough. It's the day you wake up thinking, 'WTF – this isn't what I signed up for!' You might blame your partner – maybe you feel that they've changed, that you no longer see the same person you fell in love with. Maybe you think that you've sold yourself short, that you've settled. Maybe you even switch partners, hoping things will work out better this time. But this decrease in passion ought to be expected – dipping back down to where we started is a normal part of how romantic love develops. The next time it happens to you, keep in mind that this day was coming. A new partner might solve this problem temporarily, but sooner or later you'll end up back at where you are now. You're just rewinding the movie instead of seeing how it ends.

Companionate love is inherently different from romantic love. It involves feeling a deeper devotion to the person we've woven our life together with.[6] It's the love felt between best friends, the feeling of knowing that someone else cares about us.[7] This love contains closeness and trust. Whereas passionate love is heated and erotic by nature, companionate love is warm and encompassing – it's the glow of the embers after the fire has died down. As I've stated, passion generally has a shelf life of around 24 months.

Although . . . *Some* researchers regard the decline of passion as a result of specific developments in a relationship, not merely an inevitable injustice unleashed by the relentless ticking of the clock.

The triangular theory of love

Earlier in this chapter, we divided love into two categories: passionate and companionate. We're now going to develop this into a triangular theory of love. This theory allows us to evaluate the status of any relationship, and at any time.[8]

The three points of this triangle are: 1) passion, 2) intimacy, and 3) commitment (promising to be there for each other, to belong to one another). A relationship that ranks high in all three categories can be considered complete, or fully developed. You love your partner and feel close to them in a committed relationship. Commitment without passion and intimacy is . . . Only commitment (an emotionally empty connection without the right feelings). Passion on its own is *blind* passion (no commitment and no emotional closeness). Intimacy without passion and commitment is more of a friendly kind of liking (camaraderie). These three extremes combine in endless ways, and relationships can swing between *passionate* phases, *intimate* phases, or even *commitment* phases (so-called 'low periods'). An ideal relationship is strong in all three as often as possible.

We've looked at why passion subsides, and whether it's inevitable or not. But there's no need to panic, because the ebbing of passion can be balanced against other components such as friendship and common values, which often outweigh the more evasive passion. These are also the uniting factors that help us stay together in the long run. Seeking balance is the key to a successful strategy; it's balance that brings us long-term satisfaction.

23: Passion: from tragic to magic

It's time to examine the relationship between passion and expectations. Is it better to get struck by a love-bolt and for your relationship to start with an explosive jolt, or is it better to take a more thoughtful (and boring) approach when searching for love?

Patience is a virtue

Are you looking for a long-term relationship? If so, be patient with the dating process; let it take time.

'Be slow in choosing a friend, slower in changing,' advised Benjamin Franklin. If you move too quickly, you'll fail to see whether your values and goals are compatible, or whether you sync emotionally. Moving too quickly also hinders your ability to objectively assess the risks of your relationship becoming unstable, short-lived, or simply unfulfilling. The researcher Susan Krauss Whitborne discusses what she calls the *cohabitation effect*.[1] This refers to how couples sometimes begin relationships too quickly, or move in together or get married too early, and struggle – not because they're a bad fit but because the process was too fast. And sharing common values is crucial. W. Bradford Wilcox, professor at the University of Virginia, has stated that 'People should go slowly into a relationship, and be deliberate about them.'

Imagine you've begun dating someone and things feel positive – you seem to share similar values, and you can see a potential future with this person. If this happens, keep dating – enjoy their company, get to know them, and absorb being with them for a bit. See if that steers you towards starting a relationship, or whether it's time to move on. And if you sense that something's missing from the picture or your instincts tell you something's off, interpret these signals wisely and check in with your relationship model.

Keeping things moving

Novelty packs a real punch. When new things grab our attention, we notice and remember the circumstances around them. When our relationships shift from exciting or surprising over to predictable or run-of-the-mill, our passionate feelings subside. We don't continue to feel this passion for the rest of our lives because it isn't particularly productive. Even if passion didn't abate, we have an innate ability to habituate to circumstances nonetheless. We take that new job, our new house, or our new partner for granted after a while, letting the familiar breed indifference. The ebbing of passion plays an evolutionary role too: if we never lost our rose-tinted glasses – shutting the blinds a dozen times a day to roll around on the bed – we'd never get anything else done. We'd have a hard time focusing on work, we'd neglect our kids, and our friends would get pretty tired of us. In fact, infatuation shares some common characteristics with substance abuse and narcissism. So when you consider all that, how come we view the shift from passionate love to companionate love as such a downgrade?

Being in a state of passion affects our brains like a drug. Obviously, coming down off your high and feeling that inspiration fade is a drag. As it turns out, we're programmed to seek out *variation*, which also affects our brains like a drug (with dopamine playing the lead role). It's believed that we adapted a drive for sexual variation because it prevented inbreeding among our prehistoric ancestors. In other words, when your partner starts to feel as familiar as a family member, sexual attraction fades away. I think we all know that the flames of eroticism just don't burn as brightly later on in a long relationship as they did in the beginning. A natural mistake is to misinterpret the natural shift that occurs around the two-year mark as a sign that we're not a good match, or that something has gone wrong with the relationship. And all the while we're also haunted by thoughts that things could be different – more exciting, rewarding, profound, satisfying, better – with *someone else*. That greener grass on the other side . . .

But don't lose hope just yet! There's a lot more to this picture. Long relationships need to renew themselves again and again. Like a house, they need frequent maintenance – at some point you'll have to fix the wiring, mend a leak in the basement, renovate the kitchen, even replace the roof. There are voices in the research community who say we need to keep the passion flickering in our relationships, long after those lovely fireworks in the earlier phases have died down.[2] And they've found out how we can do it too.

Unknown elements

In a classic experiment, Arthur Aron gave a handful of couples a list of activities that both partners found 'pleasant' (watching movies, visiting friends, cooking, and so on).[3] A second group of couples was given a list of 'exciting' activities (dancing, going to a concert, skiing) that they hadn't done in a long time. The researchers asked the couples in each group to choose *one* activity to do. They were instructed to do this activity together for 90 minutes once a week, over a span of 10 weeks. Afterwards, the couples who had participated in the exciting activities reported greater satisfaction in their marriages than those who participated in the pleasant activities. In other words, developing your skills together (doing things that are exciting) leads to greater fulfilment (and a more passionate love life) in relationships. Working out, learning, or doing projects together helps your love grow – particularly if your relationship has hit a dry patch.[4] According to a study entitled *Marital Boredom Now Predicts Less Satisfaction 9 Years Later*, boredom should be keenly avoided in relationships.[5]

There's another study supporting the theory that passionate love can be kept alive over a long relationship. In this study, 40 per cent of the married couples involved reported that they still felt an intense love for their partner long after the passion was supposed to have died out.[6] Brain scans have also confirmed that passion can survive in a relationship, even as the years roll by.[7] So what's the secret?

Strong emotions are an influential factor. If our relationship continues to induce powerful emotions in us, it amplifies our passion – we don't just take it for granted. If there's a little uncertainty in the air, it enhances the satisfaction we feel from positive circumstances. According to a series of studies conducted by Harvard and the University of Virginia, if someone was the recipient of a kind gesture but also *uncertain* about who was behind that gesture, they experienced a longer rush of happiness. The study participants were offered drinks. When they didn't know what drink they'd be offered, their brains showed greater activity in the area where we register positive emotions. This most likely provides part of the explanation as to why the couples who participated in more exciting activities experienced greater feelings of passion and fulfilment in their relationships.

Interestingly enough, the unexpected seems to satisfy us more than stability and predictability. Esther Perel addresses this in her book *Lust*.[8] Lust is contingent on a certain level of uncertainty. Perel also discusses a sense of mystique: 'The long-term maintenance of desire involves bringing unknown elements into an otherwise familiar routine.' We can do this by seeing our partner in a new light – as if they're someone we don't really know. In that way, we re-experience a sense of mystique about them.

Seeking out the safe and familiar puts us in a sticky predicament: we need to feel control, yet we also want to feel desire for our partners. These contradictory needs for desire and stability are at loggerheads.

The thing is, the passion that we feel for *activities* (hobbies, say) is remarkably similar to the passion we feel for our partners.[9] In fact, enjoying activities related to personal development (or self-expansion) leads to better-quality relationships.[10] Passion in relationships can get a boost when we develop *our own* interests and abilities (for instance, through exciting new experiences), because we harbour more positive attitudes towards our partners.[11] In other words, exciting or enriching activities boost your passion for life, which boosts your passion for your lover. And a quick word to clarify what 'passion for life' entails: it's defined as an urge to pursue activities we love and value. Passion can be for an *activity* (playing the piano, soccer), a *person* (our lover), or for *objects* (collecting Bobbleheads). In order to reap positive benefits in our relationships, however, we need to invest our energy in what's called *harmonic passion*, not *obsessive passion*.[12] When we're focused on activities with harmonic passion, we have control over how much time we spend on them – they're well integrated into our lives. We experience positive effects not only *while* we're doing them (positive emotions, concentration, flow), but afterwards too. When our passion for an activity is obsessive, however, our desire to take part in it overwhelms our identity. We experience a loss of control, which can cause feelings of anxiety. It can be difficult to integrate it into our lives, including our relationships – resulting in negative emotions.

Both are forms of passion, so stick to the one that lets you reap the positive benefits![13]

Should we lower our expectations?

In his book *Why You Will Marry the Wrong Person*, the philosopher Alain de Botton writes that contemporary relationships struggle from unrealistic expectations.[14] Another factor that can contribute to us falling for the wrong person is if we experience being single as unbearable – rushing to escape singlehood like we're breaking out of jail turns us into terrible decision-makers. According to de Botton, we need to be reasonably choosy before starting a relationship with someone. In order to succeed, first see to it that you can handle life *without* a relationship.

Besides that, argues de Botton, one person alone isn't going to fulfil *all* of our needs and desires. This might not be big news, but he presents the quandary from a somewhat different perspective: if we accept that every person who stays in our life for a long period of time is going to upset, frustrate, irritate, and disappoint us, then our best move is to choose the 'least wrong' person. Sounds a bit like a consolation prize, right?

We're not always aware of the motivations behind our actions and decision-making. As we discussed in the chapter 'Your relationship toolkit', we've got plenty of baggage from childhood running the show from backstage. According to de Botton, divorce and emotionally driven marriages come hand in hand, leading to familiar, problematic patterns crisscrossing our lives. For those who've worn out a few rings, second and third marriages are seldom better than the first; we can become convinced that we're getting what we deserve, or maybe we try to compensate for issues from our childhood. If your parents were passive, for instance, you might choose a dominant partner. If you had dominant parents, you might land an authoritarian partner you can rebel against, or perhaps you choose obedient partners. Another example is when you feel you have to 'pay off a debt' you think you owe your family. If one of your parents was in poor health, perhaps you feel most comfortable taking care of a sick or needy partner.[15]

And then we have to deal with that pesky 'soulmate' concept, which suggests that your perfect match is just waiting for you out there (a belief shared by 73 per cent of Americans).[16] Flirty pics of kissing couples scattered across Instagram also play up these beliefs. When examining this phenomenon, the researchers Eidelson and Epstein found that highly romanticized ideas about love might sound all well and good, but they can also trip up our ambitions; these beliefs are actually linked to dysfunctional relationships.[17] The concept that we have a soulmate, referred to as *soulmate beliefs* (believing in fate, that a relationship is 'meant to be'), implies that you can find someone you'll never have problems with, skating merrily along to the tune of love, without a care in the world. And when you experience problems? Whoops, I guess he wasn't your soulmate after all . . . A moment of reflection about these expectations inevitably brings us to the realization that relationships without problems are a mirage. Those harbouring soulmate beliefs jump overboard from relationships more quickly, too, when problems arise.[18] Unfortunately, you'll also find a few revenge seekers in here, triggered by their insecurities over relationships.[19]

On the other hand, having *work-it-out beliefs* is a wonderfully beneficial attitude to have, and can help relationships to overcome or withstand problems.

To sum up: some expectations benefit you; some don't. Try to aim towards those that are helpful for both you and your relationships. The results of all this research reveal that you can feather your nest for a dream relationship before you move past the cooing and wooing by enjoying the single life, improving your self-image, and letting the dating process (of getting to know each other) take its time.

Bad relationships are bad for your health

When we're faced with three alternatives: a good relationship, a bad relationship, or no relationship at all, only two of these options are worth considering, because bad relationships are *literally* bad for your health.

Studies have revealed that the consequences of living in a bad relationship can be depression, worsened physical health, and of course the increased risk of the relationship failing. The cells in our body contain *telomeres*. Each time a cell divides, these telomeres get shortened. The shorter our telomeres, the more our bodies physically age – regardless of our numerical age. So we want our telomeres to stay nice and long, and there's no need to see them getting chopped down prematurely. Stress and smoking shorten telomeres, and so do destructive relationships. Depending on their relationship histories, the biological ages of identical twins can differ by almost ten years, according to the studies.[20]

24: Be an optimist – or at least find an optimist

What can you do to be happy? Or at least feel happier? Do you need to take more after-dinner walks, go dancing now and then, see a therapist twice a month, sign up for an art class, or maybe get your black belt in karate?

Find something fun to sink your teeth into that makes you feel your best – for your own sake. And eventually for your relationship's sake, because people who radiate well-being naturally cheer their partners up too.

Honey vs vinegar

According to one study, *Optimism in close relationships: How seeing things in a positive light makes them so*, optimists express greater satisfaction about their relationships.[1] It's believed that this occurs because optimists pay greater attention to their partner's support. That particular characteristic – the feeling that you have your partner's support – holds a slew of positive side-effects for your relationship. For instance, optimists more constructively view how they and their partner respond to a conflict. Due to their positive attitude, a week later they're also more likely to feel that the conflict led to an improvement. Optimists tend to be more satisfied romantically, and their relationships enjoy lower risks of break-up.[2] In layman's terms: who wants to walk away from a good thing?

Life works out better for optimists in many other ways as well. They handle daily life more effectively and enjoy positive mental and physical health benefits,[3] giving them a leg up in life. They function better socially,[4] their friendships last longer,[5] and they're more popular as well.[6] This is most likely due to their overall contentment, happiness, and positive outlook – they're simply easier to be around or deal with.

So what are optimists made of? If those are the shoes you're hoping to fill, it's probably good to know. One definition of optimism is 'the cognitive disposition to expect positive outcomes',[7] and the decisive factor here is that optimists *interpret* others' intentions differently: they see the glass as half-full.

Life has the meaning you give it

Certain individuals feel that there is a meaning behind what happens to them, and these same people tend to interpret experiences more positively than others tend to do. This optimistic tendency benefits romantic relationships as well.[8] So the next time that things aren't quite going your way, see if you can't find a positive spin on the situation that makes it feel worthwhile. If you want to make an omelette, you've got to break a few eggs, so give it your best.

Happiness: your golden ticket

A longer life expectancy, fewer illnesses, longer marriages, and less criminality. More creativity, a stronger work ethic and better job performance, higher income, and an enhanced ability to assist others.[9]

What's the secret to all of these wonderful life benefits?

Happiness is the key. Happy people are more successful at achieving their goals, and happiness steers us towards seeking out and developing relationships, thinking more creatively, and being more curious and interested in new activities. Happiness is good for you, and for those around you.

So what exactly *is* happiness? Fundamentally, happiness is the feeling that life is *good*, that it's meaningful, enjoyable, and rewarding. You've likely heard some version of this sentiment before: your happiness hinges on your attitude towards your circumstances. Positive emotions expand and deepen our personal resources. A good mood improves your life in all sorts of ways. Staying in touch with your smile makes life's difficulties more bearable, and the bad times feel shorter while the good times feel longer. We do a better job at almost everything when we're happy. Happiness improves your health and life expectancy, and reduces how often you catch colds. One study investigated the emotional lives of 180 nuns and the effect on their general health.[10] The researchers examined personal documents that the nuns had written at the age of 22, seeking out words and phrasing that indicated either positive or negative emotions. By correlating these letters, written by the nuns at the age of 22, with letters written near their deaths at the ages of 75 to 95, and comparing whether they had exhibited either more or less positive attitudes, the scientists were able to determine how a positive attitude affects life expectancy. When the 25 per cent of nuns with the most positive attitudes were compared to the 25 per cent with the most negative attitudes, the happy-go-lucky nuns lived on average 10 years longer. Similar studies on other groups of people have shown similar results. Laughter really *is* the best medicine: when they say that it extends your life expectancy, they're not just joking around . . .

In their book *Happiness*, researchers Ed Diener and Robert Biswas-Diener describe three aspects of what the 'psychological wealth' of happiness is all about.[11] These are health, relationships, and meaningful activity, and all three are directly related to our feeling of happiness – or lack thereof. These three aspects can build a positive feedback loop – happiness makes us more successful in these three areas of our life, which make us happier, which makes us more successful, which makes us happier . . .

And the feather in your cap is that you'll make a better partner.

The Pleasure Purpose Principle – key components

If you're looking for happiness, put your energy into activities that bring you *pleasurable enjoyment* and a sense of *meaningful purpose*.[12] Likewise, you should avoid things that feel meaningless or cause you pain (unless you're confronting your relationship model, that is). It's simple maths: if you can take pleasure in purposeful activities, your happiness will grow. The term for this is the *Pleasure-Purpose Principle* (PPP). According to this principle, established by Paul Dolan, author of *Happiness by Design*, our active decision-making, choices, activities, how we direct our focus, and our ability to be present with others all contribute to our happiness. According to Dolan, we are what we pay attention to,[13] and so we ought to shift our focus to the things that bring us happiness.

In other words, happiness is about finding both pleasurable enjoyment *and* meaningful purpose in our everyday lives.

25: Compliments, criticism and saying *I'm sorry*

Finding someone to start a serious relationship with takes a little time, and coupledom – as many of us can attest – isn't always a waltz on rose petals. The important thing is doing your best to maintain a positive atmosphere. In this and the next chapter I'll offer a few tips to help you keep your dating journey on the sunny side of the street.

Compliments

Imagine a situation in which you feel unappreciated by your partner. You do nice things for them and try to make them happy, yet they never say a single word to acknowledge the effort you put in. Would that feel OK? Would you continue to feel motivated to do all those little – or even big – favours for this person?

The Journal of Personality and Social Psychology published a study which showed that (honest) compliments increase the satisfaction of couples in relationships.[1] And this doesn't mean that you have to build a Taj Mahal every time your lover brings you a cup of morning coffee – a simple text showing your appreciation for that or thanking them for washing that stain out of your jacket also shows that you notice them. IRL, over the phone, in a text – by passing along compliments, we reveal that this person is in our thoughts, whether they're physically present or not. Here are examples of the kinds of things you can write or say: 'Latisha, I love playing chess with you' or 'Thanks for that incredible meal last night – you really know how to set the atmosphere!' or 'Jeanette, I know I sometimes forget to show it, but I do appreciate everything you do for me. It really means a lot.' You can compliment them on their ideas, appearance, motivation, attitude, how they focus on their goals, or – what the heck? – that little thing they do in the bedroom that makes you feel so good. That you speak from the heart is all that matters, so be genuine and try to offer unique compliments. For example, if they get complimented on their broad shoulders every day, maybe you should point out how much you love that smile instead. Pay attention to the details. We all enjoy hearing that we're attractive, but hearing *why* is more flattering. If showing appreciation doesn't come naturally to you, make an effort to express your feelings. Tell him that it felt really good to meet him the last time you went out. Did you miss her? If you did, tell her. Work on being more open with your feelings, and eventually even other feelings beyond just the light-hearted, happy ones.

Empathy – one trait to rule them all?

Empathy might be the greatest tool in your kit. If you find a partner who's empathetic, you'll improve your odds for a good relationship, and perhaps for a long time too. It's even better if *both* of you have well-developed empathy – then your relationship stands an even greater chance of earning a gold-star rating.[2]

So what exactly *is* empathy, anyway?

Empathy is conventionally defined as 'an other-oriented emotional response congruent with the perceived welfare of another that results from adopting the perspective (i.e. imagining the thoughts and feelings) of a person in clear need.'[3] Expressed more simply, it's your ability to feel what someone else feels.

Empathy is thought to cause us to help others in need and to make us more sociable as human beings.[4] Researchers believe that we developed empathy primarily because it motivates us to pay attention to our children and focus on *their* needs. If human beings hadn't been interested in protecting and watching after their young, we wouldn't have survived at all. Due to a mental ability we possess called *cognitive generalization*, our empathy – the emotional trait that causes us to feel connected to our children – extends to how we react to other people and also to animals.[5] Other social species also exhibit certain levels of empathy. Elephants, for instance, mourn their dead for long periods of time.[6]

Empathy is a trait that has a powerful effect on our romantic relationships.[7] When these relationships have empathy we feel emotional support, which makes us feel even more satisfied.[8] Remember that we need to communicate our feelings for our relationship to reach any kind of depth. Otherwise, you'll get stuck on the lower rungs of the relationship ladder, and miss out on the true intimacy that can be so wonderful to experience.

What you say and what you do

One study asked participants to name the *best compliment* they'd ever received.[9] Out of 132 people, only 12 mentioned a compliment about their appearance. The majority of the participants' favourite compliments – for men and women alike – were regarding their *emotions* (usually linked to a relationship and the strength of their emotional ties to partners), followed by their *personalities*.

All that being said, watch out for people who expect you to do something in return because they've complimented you or done you a favour like inviting you to go to the movies. And then, afterwards, they suddenly say something like, 'What? Don't I even get a smile?' You should also be on your guard if your date has a 'my way or the highway' attitude and wants you to keep in line, forever at his beck and call. It's also unfair if your date always expects you to be 100 per cent independent, or doesn't want to be there for you: 'That's not my problem, you need to sort it out yourself.' We need someone who listens to us, never someone who mocks us for needing support, comfort, or compassion.

People who flip-flop back and forth between distance and getting close to someone create unhealthy relationships. People who are hot one day and cold the next act this way to maintain distance, perhaps even telling you they're 'not really a relationship kind of person'. You'll never know where you are with this person, which leaves you living with continual uncertainty and insecurity. And please, avoid people who haven't 'cut the cord' in a healthy way with their ex – even if it seems that they're on their way out. Remember the strategies which 'avoidants' employ to keep distance between you. Another bad egg is someone who seems disconnected from any purpose in life, who seems to lack goals – this will eventually frustrate your relationship. This also applies to people who seem out of touch with their feelings; they can also be difficult to live with.

'Could you help me with something?'

If you want someone to like you that little bit more, it might seem logical that you should treat them to a small gift or a kind gesture – not the other way around. Many times, however, *asking* someone for something has a greater effect on them than *giving* them something. Called the *Benjamin Franklin effect*, this phenomenon addresses how others' attitudes towards you are formed by how they behave towards you, as well as our habit of liking people more after we've been nice to them.[10] On top of all that, it's also a sign of respect: you flatter the other person by humbly acknowledging that their skills and experience are greater than your own. Keep in mind that your requests should be small gestures, ones that are easy for them to provide. Don't go asking them to drag your old piano from your childhood home in northern Sweden to your new fourth-floor flat with no lift and nowhere to park in downtown Stockholm.

Criticism

If compliments are so great, then it's no big shock: criticism has the opposite effect.[11]

A study conducted on 65 married couples investigated the effects of compliments and criticism. The first thing researchers noticed was that not all criticism resulted in equally negative consequences – *how* criticism was delivered proved to be the biggest factor. The couples in better relationships 1) gave criticism with less negativity, 2) used more eye contact, and 3) allowed each other equal room to speak. Pay attention to and apply these important tips, because giving in to your negative tendencies (towards drama or rage, for instance) damages your relationships, especially if there's a risk that your intensity might spiral out of control – that you'll sprinkle too much chilli on those little morsels of truth you're about to dish out.[12]

According to John Gottman, the appearance of negative criticism (such as an attack against someone's character) early on in a relationship should be taken as a warning sign, because hard criticism can lead to a feedback loop of shame and hurt feelings. Reacting defensively by throwing a temper tantrum helps no one involved – negative criticism delivered with contempt, hostility, or as provocation has been shown to push relationships into downward spirals.[13] At the same time, even if the process isn't all fun and games, giving critical advice isn't *always* bad – in the long run, venting a little frustration by talking about it now and again is good for your relationship.[14] If you're feeling unhappy and need something to change, dare to discuss what's upsetting you. If you don't, you'll carry on with a chip on your shoulder either forever or only until the bubble bursts and you break up. Voicing your concerns – while still keeping your cool – strengthens your relationship, because your relationship should be rewarding for *each* of you.

The important thing to remember is that positive attitudes should dominate your relationship; positivity makes them stabler and happier[15] and helps everything to go a bit more smoothly when life's heavier topics arise.[16] Maintaining a positive attitude – ideally from both partners – prevents the escalation of negative feedback loops while you're discussing the tough stuff.

Two things that differentiate couples who are happy with their relationships from those who aren't[17] are their use of *eye contact* and *positive conversation*.[18] These signal engagement and interest, and help to maintain intimacy and a sense of closeness.[19] The more assurances we provide our partner (in the form of support and comfort), the more pleased and content we feel as a couple. Talking is important.

Avoiding stress is also important. Stress encourages negative attitudes and leads to a greater number of negative interactions between partners. The more stress we're under (imagine you're late for an important monthly client meeting, or your toddler is throwing a tantrum in the supermarket), the more frequently negative behaviour expresses itself.[20] We become quick to criticize, get angry more easily, and waste more time on disagreements.[21] Stress can sour your outlook on your relationship,[22] which in turn can create distance between you and your partner.[23] And if all that wasn't bad enough, it increases the risk of infidelity.[24]

One bad thing leads to another, but one good thing does as well, so in order to optimize your chances of keeping a positive vibe going, try to plan any critical conversations for when you have time to talk things out after you've both had a proper meal and a good night's sleep.

I'm sorry!

Irritation and hurt feelings eventually show up in most relationships, so this astute observation by the American journalist and early twentieth century humorist Robert Quillen might not sound so surprising: 'A happy union is a marriage of two forgivers.' The research backs up his observation. According to a study conducted over a 20-year timespan, the factors which led to flourishing relationships were the ability to *ask for forgiveness* and the ability to *forgive*.[25]

Imagine a situation in which you've made your partner upset, hurt, or angry – you fucked up, in other words. The natural thing to do in this case is ask for forgiveness,[26] which will help you and your partner overcome the conflict.[27] So what are the right ingredients for an apology? It should take into account the following factors:

- The more committed the two of you are, the easier it will be for your partner to forgive you.[28]
- Showing satisfaction will also make redemption more likely.[29]
- It's much better if what happened wasn't done on purpose.[30]
- A successful apology must be genuine; it must come from the heart.[31] Only an authentic apology will get the job done and help to repair (or even improve) your relationship. This explains why brief apologies rarely suffice. You've quite simply got some serious explaining to do, and the effort you make will reveal your sincerity.

An extensive study concluded that there are eight important ingredients in a good apology:[32]

1. *'I'm sorry.'*
2. *Showing regret*: 'I wish I hadn't done/said that.'
3. *Accepting that you're at fault*: 'It's my fault.'

4. *Confirming that you hurt the other person*: 'I realize that I hurt your feelings.'

5. *Promising that you'll improve*: 'I won't do it again' or 'I now realize that you get upset when I say things like that, and I won't speak to you like that again.'

6. *Expressing that the other person's forgiveness is important to you*: 'Can you forgive me?' or 'I get so angry with myself when I've hurt you like that.'

7. *Showing a desire to repair the relationship*: 'I'd like to make it up to you' or 'Would it be OK if I buy you dinner so we can talk more about this?'

8. *Offering an explanation*: 'I was angry with my boss and answered the phone when I was still upset, so I snapped at you instead' or 'I'm running late because there was an accident on the motorway.'

26: How to fight right

Although we sometimes miss what's right in front of our face, we usually have a pretty good idea whether we're in a good relationship or not. If things aren't going well, reflect on the following: does positivity outweigh negativity between the two of you?

Five to one: keeping things positive

Not all negativity is equally consequential or destructive. Generally speaking, the balance of positive to negative in a relationship should be about 5 to 1: for every negative interaction we should have at least five positive interactions, and for every negative statement we should say at least five positive things. This is based on the *Gottman principle*, established by John Gottman and Robert Levenson from their studies of couples in the 1970s.[1] Gottman and Levenson asked the couples to resolve an argument within fifteen minutes. Then they grabbed their notebooks and observed. After collecting and reviewing analysis for over nine years, from these fifteen-minute interactions they were able to predict – with 94 per cent accuracy – whether or not a couple would get divorced.

So how could they tell?

The difference between the happy and unhappy couples hung on the balance between their positive and negative interactions during the argument. The magical ratio that predicted whether a couple's love would stand the test of time was 5 to 1. The successful couples laughed more often, had positive attitudes, and were more playful. If there was a 1-to-1 balance between the positive and the negative, riptides and crosswinds lay ahead. But just because alarm bells are going off doesn't automatically mean that a relationship is headed for the rocks. Some couples stay together throughout their lives despite being miserable. But 5 to 1 isn't an exact ratio for every single romantic relationship – and other kinds of relationships carry different demands. Parents should have more of a 3 to 1 ratio with their (non-adult) children, for instance. Bosses to employees? 4 to 1. Friends? 8 to 1.

As a general rule of thumb, negativity poisons the well and it takes a lot of positivity to dilute it. Hence 5 to 1. Empathy and validation (making sure that your partner feels heard, understood, and affirmed) are the keys to repairing the damage caused by conflicts.

And here's the part where I tell you that anger in a relationship isn't as bad as it sounds – it's *how* we express anger that matters. The behaviours that poison relationships the most are emotional rejection, criticism, and defensiveness. You can get angry without being mean, rude, or unfair. Psychologist Esther Perel says it's all about the making up, not the breakdown. How do we restore harmony in our relationships? According to Perel,[2] relationships go in cycles of harmony, disharmony, and reparation. Or, you could say, connection, disillusion, and reconnection, where we drift apart but then find each other again. Perel maintains that the most important thing is our ability to *reconnect* to the love we felt before. Exactly how we argue or disagree isn't as critical.

The people we spend time with affects who we are too, and we *become* different people when we're *with* different people. You may discover that you're really quiet in a new relationship, for instance, which you've never been before. Or perhaps you're normally reserved, but in a new relationship you become downright chatty. We're not static as individuals, and we change from one relationship to the next.

Have you considered that conflicts can be seen as a kind of balance of energy? The higher one's level of irritation rises, the more the other is forced to back off – a sort of power balance.

According to Gottman and Levenson's research, the periods (on average) showing the greatest risk for separation are at the seven-year-itch stage and when a couple's first child (assuming they have one) is around 14 years old – a documented low point of satisfaction in many relationships.[3] The study also predicts break-up or divorce if a couple have many conflicts, or express negative attitudes while arguing during the early stages of a relationship, although these proved less harmful when they occurred later on. It predicts poor outcomes for couples who lack positivity in their daily interactions, although this is also less dangerous down the line. To sum things up, it's in your best interests to keep your interactions on the positive side of things regardless of how things are, or the relationship in question. Stay positive, and speak kind words from the heart. If you feel compelled to say *something* critical, remember to criticize someone's behaviour, never their personality.

The beautiful thing about relationships and happiness is that they're part of a feedback loop, enhancing and assisting each other. Happy people enjoy better relationships, and good relationships make us happy. So, the more positivity you can create in your actions and emotions in your relationship, the happier and more stable your relationship will become. You'll be happier, your relationship stronger, and your partner more satisfied – win-win!

Communicative behaviour in romantic relationships

Most behaviour can be expressed IRL, over the phone, or through texts. It's important to keep in mind that what you text or say when calling affects your relationship just like it does IRL. [4]

Positive behaviours/factors

- Sending clearly understandable messages[5]
- Showing empathy for your partner by listening to them[6]
- Being respectful during conversations[7]
- Showing devotion[8]

Negative behaviours/factors

- Criticism[9]
- Withdrawing, avoiding, or ignoring your partner[10]
- General negativity[11]
- Lacking a sense of togetherness[12]
- Showing disappointment over your relationship[13]

Keep your voice down

Couples in flourishing relationships handle conflict differently from couples in stagnating relationships. To begin with, they open their arguments on a softer note. They also frequently tend to the well-being of their relationship in both large and small ways by emphasizing the positive side of things. Some ways to do this are:

- *Show interest*: ask open-ended questions and nod.
- *Express your devotion.*
- *Demonstrate that your partner is important.* Keep those kind gestures flowing and you'll quietly build up a buffer of positivity.
- *Show appreciation.* Focus on your partner's positive qualities, their positive accomplishments, and on the positive moments that you've shared.

In an argument, it's useful to find the points you can agree on, to show empathy, to ask for forgiveness, to accept the validity of your partner's point of view, and (seriously) to joke a little. Playfulness is a plus, and it doesn't matter how silly you get, either – just be careful to stay respectful of your partner and make sure to joke about something that you *both* can laugh at. The best tool you have for breaking the tension of a heated argument is your sense of humour.

According to communication psychologist Haim Ginott, there is a model (the *XYZ-formula*) that you can use to deliver criticism without provoking defensiveness or aggression from your partner. It should sound like this:

'When you did X, it made me feel like Y, and I would much rather you had done Z.'

A concrete example:

'When you didn't call me to let me know you'd be late for dinner, I felt like you were taking me for granted. In future, I would appreciate it if you'd call me and tell me when you know you're going to be late, please.'

By phrasing our statements carefully like this, we don't accuse the person of disappointing us, but rather their *behaviour*. Saying how you *feel* instead of how *they are* is the difference between an explanation and an accusation. Accusations make people defensive, while explanations are a considerate way to get your point across. Also, notice that we asked for the person's cooperation – we didn't demand their compliance.

If you considerately explain your disappointment using this formula and yet your partner responds negatively anyway, like: 'I didn't know you feel Y when I do X, but actually I don't really care', then you've certainly discovered some relevant information.

27: Love *should* be blind – at least a wee bit

When we're in love, we often see our heart's desire through rose-tinted glasses – doesn't this seem just a tiny bit naive?

According to the research, it's not such a bad idea. A little soft focus actually tends to improve the outcome of your relationships.

Showing your good side

In the early stages of relationships, we work harder at showing our good side, and we usually focus on each other's positive traits.[1] In those early days, you both float along in a haze, dancing with idealized versions of one another. We make an effort to have a good time on dates, and paint ourselves a positive portrait of the other person's personality.[2] This increases our feelings for one another, upping the odds that we'll think we've discovered 'The One.'[3]

Then a little time goes by, a relationship develops, and things are getting serious. As we let our guard down a few cracks begin to show – we're making less of an effort on *impression management*. Our partner's negative sides begin to reveal themselves at the same time, but we're often so invested in the relationship by then that we're hesitant to back out. This might sound like a bad deal, but it can actually be a good thing. A study at the University of Groningen, in the Netherlands, evaluated over 500 couples regarding compatibility and established that the couples who held *positive illusions* about each other enjoyed more successful relationships. They continued to see their partner as good-looking, kind, and intelligent – as a real 'catch'.[4] They emphasized the other's strengths and paid less attention to their weaknesses, and enjoyed better relationships over time in a variety of ways. The fascinating thing is how people began living up to their partner's image of who they were. Hand in hand with positive illusions come self-fulfilling prophecies.

The rose-coloured-glasses effect has a great deal to do with how we speak about each other, how we interact with one another, and how we view each other's qualities and behaviours. It even causes us to primarily remember the good times over the bad. And how we remember the past affects how we treat each other in the present.[5] Partners who are very satisfied with their relationship can remember more positive events than have actually taken place, affecting where they place their partner on a positive–negative spectrum. I'm sure it's no surprise, but the more we tip the scales, the more satisfied we are. And our relationships last longer too.

Seeing our partners more positively than they see themselves is a phenomenon researchers call the *love-is-blind bias*.[6] It appears likely that it shares a connection with the psychological phenomenon of *confirmation bias*, when we reinforce our first impressions by only selecting the evidence that supports how we initially decided to see someone or something.

Benefits of holding positive illusions about your partner's qualities

- Greater satisfaction with the relationship
- Love!
- Commitment
- Trust
- Fewer conflicts and less ambivalence[7]

When the fire of love needs a little stoking

OK folks, let's ride our time machine into the future, after your prospect became your date and your date has become your partner. One morning you wake up and the thought hits you: 'Back in the old days, we used to have a lot of fun together . . .' Your partner used to surprise you with romantic gestures or exciting adventures, but lately it seems like you're doing all that fun stuff less and less often. Neither of you is really giving it your all, like you used to. The magic is gone, taking the stomach butterflies along with it. Losing that loving feeling hurts; it's a painful thing to realize that it's happening while your relationship is becoming more comfortable – but predictably routine – at the same time. And I'm not just talking about physical attraction or making whoopee; there's a larger picture here: your *emotional attraction* has gone into decline. It's *this* that first caused us to open up, to lie awake all night making pillow talk or to feel those powerful bonds of connection.

'I love you, but I'm no longer *in* love with you' or 'I used to feel physically and emotionally attracted to you, but the way things have gone with our relationship at this point, I no longer feel that way.' Nobody wants to say or hear either of those sentences. Here are three steps to try instead:

1) Focus on what's working, not on what isn't.
Where you put your energy is usually where you'll get results, so tell your partner everything you appreciate about them and everything you like about your relationship. This is especially good to keep in mind during periods of conflict, when we can easily get tunnel vision and forget about our partner's good qualities. Take a moment to broaden your perspective and look at the big picture, your whole relationship. What keeps you together? Whatever that is, *that's* where you want to put your energy and awareness. *That's* what you need to appreciate together. Your thoughts have the power

to affect your emotions, and your emotions have the power to affect your surroundings. In other words, focus on those thoughts and feelings that get your life juices flowing. This in turn will inspire your partner to get closer to you again.

2) Give yourselves some space.
If one of you needs a little space, there are two ways to react. You can cling more tightly, which usually causes them to push you away. The other thing to do is give your partner more breathing room, and if you concentrate on your own space, then something really good will probably happen: you'll manage to zoom out and give your energy a boost. You can collect your feelings so that they don't catch you off-guard later on, and whether it's been hours or days, this pause should also give your partner the time they need to process their own thoughts or doubts.

3) Create attraction and reconnect.
OK, so your relationship is on the fence right now, but here's the good news: if you've ever felt attraction towards each other, then you can feel it again. You've already got the ingredients to give your relationship a new kick-start.

Hold on a sec, Angela – we do?

You do! Hear me out. Relationships require a little novelty and unpredictability: it's time to try some new activities together. Do you remember the study that showed how couples had better relationships when they tried exciting new activities together (as opposed to pleasant ones)? Well, it's your turn now. Change your weekend routine, for starters. Try doing something neither of you has done before, whether it's field hockey, samba lessons, museum visits, just visiting other friends or even going on holiday to a new destination together. And if you've been joined at the hip lately, then maybe it's time to do things *separately* for a change. Do whatever it takes to pull the rug out from under that old routine. Find unexplored territory, get your curiosity fired up, and experience the unpredictable.

Get close quick: a how-to guide

Arthur Aron, a researcher at the International Relationships Lab at Stony Brook University, NY, has studied what happens to us internally when we fall in love. Besides that, he's developed a quiz for 'generating interpersonal closeness', a series of 36 questions that can speed up the falling-in-love process by quickly increasing the emotional intimacy in your relationship. These questions have a positive spin so you can go through them with friends, family, or even close colleagues. The process usually takes about 45 minutes, and almost always helps us to get to know each other better, often making us more eager to meet up again. Pay attention to this rule: you both need to answer the first question before you advance to the second question, then you both need to answer that question before advancing to the next one, and so on.

Feel free to bring these questions along the next time you meet your date or partner:

1. Given the choice of anyone in the world, who would you want as a dinner party guest?
2. Would you like to be famous? In what way?
3. Before making a phone call, do you ever rehearse what you're going to say? Why?
4. What would constitute a perfect day for you?
5. When did you last sing to yourself? To someone else?
6. If you were able to live to the age of 90 and retain either the mind or body of a 30-year-old for the last 60 years of your life, which would you choose?
7. Do you have a secret hunch about how you will die?
8. Name three things you both appear to have in common.
9. For what in your life do you feel most grateful?

10. If you could change anything about the way you were brought up, what would it be?

11. Take four minutes and tell your partner your life story in as much detail as possible.

12. If you could wake up tomorrow having gained one quality or ability, what would it be?

13. If a crystal ball could tell you the truth about yourself, your life, the future, or anything else, what would you want to know?

14. Is there something that you've dreamt of doing for a long time? Why haven't you done it?

15. What is the greatest accomplishment of your life?

16. What do you value most in a friendship?

17. What is your most treasured memory?

18. What is your most terrible memory?

19. If you knew that in one year you would die suddenly, would you change anything about the way you are now living? Why?

20. What does friendship mean to you?

21. What roles do love and affection play in your life?

22. Alternate sharing something you consider a positive characteristic of your partner. Share a total of five items.

23. How close and warm is your family? Do you feel your childhood was happier than most other people's?

24. How do you feel about your relationship with your mother?

25. Make three true 'we' statements each. For instance, 'We are both in this room feeling . . .'

26. Complete this sentence: 'I wish I had someone with whom I could share . . .'

27. If you were going to become a close friend with your partner, what would be important for them to know?

28. Tell your partner what you like about them: be honest, saying things that you might not say to someone you'd just met.

29. Share an embarrassing moment in your life.

30. When did you last cry in front of another person? By yourself?

31. Tell your partner something that you like about them.

32. What, if anything, is too serious to be joked about?

33. If you were to die this evening with no opportunity to communicate with anyone, what would you most regret not having told someone? Why haven't you told them yet?

34. Your house, containing everything you own, catches fire. After saving your loved ones and pets, you have time to safely make a final dash to save any one item. What would it be? Why?

35. Of all the people in your family, whose death would you find most upsetting? Why?

36. Share a personal problem and ask your partner's advice on how they might handle it. Also, ask them to reflect back to you how you seem to be feeling about the problem you have chosen.

Work smarter, not harder

Whether at work or with our friends or families, we take on different roles, and we do this in our romantic relationships too, of course. Which roles we play affect how much responsibility we accept, and these are influenced by our stance towards gender norms, our birth rank compared to our siblings, and which roles we've played in previous relationships as well – we tend to seek comfort in the familiar.

Are you always the one taking charge of things, getting meals planned, or keeping up contact with your friends and family? And in your relationships, are you always the *persuader*? By that, I mean, are you always telling your partner how well you two click or how you're so passionate together, or how you're soulmates? Do you try to persuade him to feel a certain way towards you? Unfortunately, as a rule of thumb, this strategy usually has the opposite effect, causing him to feel *less* for you, not more. This is because our partners tend to take on opposing roles – that's just the way these things work. When someone tries to persuade us, sensing that we're being pushed in a certain direction can automatically make us feel suspicious, and so when you become the persuader, your partner will often resist.

Instead of being persuasive, you should aspire to be *inspiring*; it's important to distinguish between these two. When you inspire, you do things so that *you'll* feel better. Do things you've been waiting to do, plan things that you know you'll enjoy. As you enjoy these things, your partner will be inspired to make you happier and to feel passion for you. But if your situation becomes more that you're planning fun activities and trying to make your relationship fulfilling for both of you, but he's not dancing to the same tune, have a think as to whether you're in a relationship that's right for you.

Factors for a passionate relationship

Give your new love a proper boost or rekindle the romance with your long-term partner – no matter how far down the line the love train has carried you, here are some factors that can help you fall more in love with your love:[8]

Think positively about your partner.[9] Stay focused on the good things, not the bad things. This is assuming that your partner is a nice person, of course – don't turn a blind eye if she isn't.

Remember the good times[10] *and stay focused on the positive ones.*[11] No matter how boring it might seem today, there were fun times in the past worth remembering. Research shows that couples who recall joyful occasions are more satisfied with their relationships. There are multiple ways of keeping these feelings alive, such as through text messages, or daring to be funnier or more romantic.

Think about your partner, when apart.[12] After you've said goodbye in the morning or go away for a few days, is your partner still present in your mind? If not, it may be a sign that you don't feel strongly about this person. I'm not saying that you should walk around with a portrait of your partner taped to the inside of your glasses, but they should at least pop up reasonably often in your day-to-day thoughts.

Novel and challenging activities.[13] Of course it's important to spend time together, but how you spend time together also affects your relationship. Taking on new and exciting activities can enhance your feelings for each other. The simple truth is that sharing positive experiences with your partner is a wonderful balm for your relationship.[14]

Time in joint activities.[15] It doesn't have to be anything more extravagant than cooking, tidying up, or cleaning out the attic together.

Time spent together. The more time spent together, the more feelings arise. Pottering about the house, gardening, or watching a movie together are all good ways of letting emotions grow – 'together' is the key word here.

Physical affection. A little kiss on the cheek or a pat on the shoulder when passing by can do the trick.

Eye contact.[16]

Give compliments[17] *and positive feedback.*

Gratitude.[18] Relationships are often maintained by 'little' situations, behaviours, or comments. Gratitude finds its place here. Appreciate the good things your partner has done; it's how we create the right atmosphere. Thankfulness improves your romantic satisfaction, inspiring further positive gestures – a positive feed-back loop.[19]

Practise responsiveness.[20] Responsiveness towards your partner's signals and needs reduces their stress,[21] and is easily expressed by giving them your full attention. Show that you care by listening attentively, and offering comfort and support when your partner needs it.[22]

Emotional contact.[23] Be open about your thoughts and feelings.[24] When was the last time you talked about your fears, dreams, or ambitions? Research confirms that conversations like these (as opposed to everyday chit-chat) deepen the level of intimacy in your relationship.

Make sacrifices.[25] Investing in your relationship signals that you value and prioritize it.

Reassurance.[26] This can be in the form of presents, flowers, cards[27] – anything that reaffirms your commitment to your partner. You can also tell her how much you appreciate her,[28] or how considerate you think she is.[29] These little gestures show your desire to be in the relationship[30] and that you're happy with it.[31] This increases your partner's satisfaction, engagement, and love[32] – all important factors for keeping your house of love warm, dry, and looking good.[33]

Phone control.[34] Sadly, many of us today are so distracted by our phones that our relationships suffer as a result. As I mentioned previously, though, using your phone to send sweet little texts when you're not together will improve your relationship.[35]

Body response to partner. When your partner touches you it shouldn't just make you feel affection – it should make you tingle a little too.

Sexual intercourse.[36] Having sex is a positive way of expressing the intensity of your love. We have more sex when we first fall in love, and happy couples have more sex than others. Regardless of why you're having sex, eroticism helps those tender feelings stand the test of time. If the other pieces of your relationship aren't in place, however, sex will not miraculously cure your romantic troubles.

Wanting to know the whereabouts of your partner.[37] It sounds a little stalkerish, true, but if we ignore cases of extreme behaviour, it's a signal that your partner is ever-present in your thoughts. Just remember that *wanting* to know is one thing, but actually trying to track your partner's every move is taking things too far. If you've met someone who demands to know what you're doing, where you are, and who you're with, take a step back.

General life happiness,[38] Cheerful people tend to feel stronger feelings for their partners (whether it's the chicken or egg here is unclear), while stubbornness, angst, or general dissatisfaction can slowly poison relationships. Let optimism or a sunny disposition nourish the feedback loops that interlink your general life happiness and the quality of your relationships, which offer mutual benefits on multiple levels.

Getting fired up about issues.[39] People who are passionate about life are usually passionate in their relationships too. If you want more passion in your relationship, put some of your emotional energy into your interests and pastimes. When you're fired up over something like a hobby or a political cause, your brain's reward centre reacts in the same way as it does when you're in love. Those feelings spill over.

Equal investment in your relationship.[40] One of the greatest risk factors for breaking up is when partners are unequally invested in the relationship. And it's not uncommon to see the partner who's putting in all the effort pull the plug, not the partner coasting along. Relationships need a certain measure of reciprocity, a little give and take.

May all of this knowledge lead you to a happier life in a healthier relationship. Love is special – let's try to keep it that way!

Afterword

I've just got home from a conference in Sopot, Poland, where I was a keynote speaker for a large Swedish company. It was held at the impressively nice Hotel Sheraton, and my hotel window looked out over the ocean and a beach that seemed to stretch on forever. This entire trip has been intensely exciting, with dinners, parties, sight-seeing, and even a visit to the spa. Last night, on my flight home, I was struck by the thought that single life feels a bit like being an atom. Like atoms, we bounce into each other. Certain people repel us – perhaps we sense from the start that our personalities don't click. We share an orbit for a while with other folks, and with a few of them that orbit stabilizes. And then, if love slams into us, we find ourselves forming a new molecule with that special someone – two hearts bind together on a new trajectory.

My first post-separation date took place on the island of Söder in Stockholm, with 'Kent'. We had matched earlier that afternoon, and he worked as a chef at a nice establishment in the city. We arranged to meet near the park at Mariatorget, and he was already there when I showed up. He was casually good-looking, and had proposed that we visit a restaurant where he used to work extra shifts. He was polite and it was a nice date, and yes, a few more dates followed.

That first date whetted my appetite. Little did I know that a year and a half later I'd have been on over 100 dates. I met plenty of Emils, Antons, Martins, and Alexes – the four most common names among my scores of dates. I met most of them in Stockholm, near to where I live. Around 1 out of 7 dates led to second dates, while only 1 out of 10 led to third dates. I set the age parameter from 18 to 100 – I wanted to see as much of the dating market as I could. I right-swiped 17 per cent of the time, and I've dated outside Sweden as well. I stared deep into a young hunk's eyes in Ockelbo, kissed divorced dads in my car, hit on men and got hit on at nightclubs, on party cruises, and in bars in Helsinki, Copenhagen, and also in backwater towns you'd never have heard of. I've been ghosted, ghostbusted, catfished, slow-faded, breadcrumbed, and zombied. And I've friend-zoned dates once or twice.

I even managed to get dumped *before* a date – the guy got cold feet, turned his car around, and texted me. I've laughed my ass off with some of the funniest people you can imagine. I danced to *dansband* music in my living room with a guy from Gotland, even though neither of us was really into *dansband* (a form of Swedish music that combines elements of polka, country, and rock). I got contacted by a previous date's girlfriend, who demanded to hear *exactly* what had happened – despite the fact that this was long after I'd dated the dude. I've been on pleasant strolls in Stockholm, inner-city coffee dates, lunch dates, bar dates, picnics, and several dates on piers. I managed to book two dates that accidentally over-lapped – at the same place – so that I went from one straight into the next. Believe me, that was embarrassing! And don't even mention all the dick pics I've had to see, despite never requesting a single one.

Over the course of these one hundred dates, I've run through a whole gamut of emotions. On some dates, I felt friendship. I felt the flicker of little flames on some, and on others I've sensed a deep connection. You name it, I've seen it on one of these dates, and it's been an interesting, informative, and exciting adventure, to say the least. Going on those dates was certainly a prerequisite for writing this book, but this dating experiment has also sent me on my own journey. In fact, it's been one of the most intensive periods of personal development in my life, a time that has fundamentally changed me.

So what drew me into this revolutionary internal process? One motivation was to rediscover my identity after my separation. My dates helped with this as well – each person I met brought me one step closer to understanding who I am as a person. At first I was sensitive and uncertain, but today I'm self-confident and know what I want. When I find it, *if* I find it, maybe there'll be something there. But until then, I'm continuing to enjoy my life just the way it is.

Being single wasn't as tough later on as it was in the beginning. At first, I was a lot more pumped-up about going on dates, but after a while I felt more relaxed, more demanding, and less prone to enthusiasm. More like: 'What do *you* have to offer that will make my life better?' My expectations, my instincts, and even my will-power all changed for the better.

In good relationships, 1 + 1 should equal 3. The whole should feel greater than the sum of its parts. *You* should have a better time in life, and *they* should have a better time in life. But I also believe you should enjoy being single, whether or not you're out there looking for love.

Here are five bits of advice that I've found helpful:

1) *Enjoy your single life.*
What if you're never single again? Don't feel angst over being single just because your friends aren't. Being single doesn't mean there's anything wrong with you – you're single because you're willing to wait for something truly special. Enjoy your life for what it is. A lot of people might be a little envious of your freedom: you can go where you want, do what you want, and meet who you want. You're free to fly above the nesters from one treetop to the next, meeting anybody you'd like to meet. Keep your eyes out for your dream partner, sure, but don't let your life get stuck in a holding pattern.

2) *Have a little fun.*

Laugh, be happy, and focus on the things that bring you joy. Being joyful and at peace with yourself makes you more attractive to others too. Try out new activities that seem exciting or new – for *your* sake. Go on that road trip with your sister's colleagues, throw a barbecue for your childhood friends, and just start saying *yes* to life and getting out there. (Bring a book, though, just in case.) One bonus side effect of an active lifestyle is that you up your odds of bumping into someone new . . .

3) *Discover who you are.*

Meeting people is one way to do this, because you discover what you like through these interactions. Let's not forget: *be yourself.* Don't get all twisted up trying to live up to the expectations of others. Figure out who you are and what you're looking for, and don't be afraid to put your foot down, saying something like, 'No, thank you, we're not a good match because . . .' or 'You seem like a great person, but we're looking for different things. Good luck to you!' Give yourself some love and a little credit: appreciate your own sense of humour, your ideas, your interests, and even something about your appearance. (Believe me, one day you'll look back at a photo from today and miss being the striking young beauty that you are, so go ahead and see yourself that way today!) Develop a sense of self-acceptance, and in the emotionally turbulent world of dating, try to see your reactions objectively, as an outsider would. This will make dating less stressful and more fun. If you've texted and it takes forever to get an answer, think: 'OK, they're obviously not going to answer me right away. This is freaking me out a bit. It makes me doubt myself, or whether I've written my text the right way. That really irritates me. But it's interesting too.' Take note of your highs and lows, and also realize that you're just dealing with the same stuff we all are. It's tough, it's fun, it's exciting, and it's nerve-wracking. Don't handle these pressures by misrepresenting who you are, or you'll set your date up for future disappointment. Instead, when it's time to meet up, be your best version of yourself!

Create a life for yourself that you already want to live – I can't stress that enough. Do you long for a warm, colourful, cosy home filled with scented candles and soft lighting? Go for it. Do you want to live in a white, minimalist, empty box? You have my permission. Whatever it is, create that. You've got no one you need to compromise with (except your kids, if you have any), so take advantage of your freedom. Changing your physical environment and finding yourself also go hand in hand.

4) *Stay active.*
Earlier we talked about how salespeople use the term *the numbers game*, meaning you won't get sales from every customer, but the more customers you approach, the more sales you'll get. Dating works this way too. If you go on 30 dates, you can expect about half a dozen of them to feel like a waste of time. About half will be OK, but only about ten will really be *good* dates, and I suspect that you'll only feel a genuine connection on perhaps *one* of those dates. These aren't statistically accurate numbers, but my point is that going on only one date isn't going to tell you much. In my own experience, my one hundred dates resulted in eight great dates, five terrible dates, and the rest landed somewhere in between. In other words, it's statistically unlikely that you're going to meet your fated heart-throb on your first and only date. Staying active is the key here, and going on numerous dates means that you're taking charge. If you're in a hurry to meet someone, go on dates more frequently and let the numbers do their work.

5) *Don't settle.*
Hooray, you've met someone! Sure, something feels a little off, but that's just life, right? Isn't flawed beauty just a poetic reality? Wrong! Walk away. There are things worth fighting for in this life, and even relationships worth fighting for, but is this fledgling relationship

really one of them? If something's telling you to hold back, take a second to reflect on why that might be. Remember that bad relationships make us miserable. Don't be fooled into wishful thinking – you shouldn't try to round a 5 up to a 10. (That's for 8s and 9s.) When you're dating and getting to know each other better, it takes time to learn to see all the signals, or at least enough of them. (We can never be *completely* prepared for anything, after all.)

There are great matches for you out there, so don't settle for less. A few years ago at a wedding in Nacka here in Stockholm, the priest uttered these words, 'If it seems easy and light, it's probably right.' What she meant is that things shouldn't feel overly complicated. You shouldn't have to fight to make things work, or at least not when they've only just begun. Long relationships will hit patches of turbulence, sure, but hitting big bumps when you're still on the runway is a sign that you're not in the best of hands. If things don't sit right before you've committed to a relationship, just move on.

Use the time you have while single to discover what it is you're looking for in a partner. If you need help figuring out what that is, here's a little exercise: get out a sheet of paper and divide it into two columns. On the left-hand side, write down five *musts*, qualities that your next partner needs to have. Are age and appearance important? Or is it being with someone who seems familiar, understanding, empathetic, adventurous, optimistic, or smart? On the right-hand side, write down five *deal-breakers*, things you can't live with, no matter what. Arrogance? Emotional distance? Rudeness? Addiction? Being judgemental, or financially irresponsible? Only you know what to write in your columns. Later on, when you're out there dating, you can refer to your list for guidance. It will remind you of your needs, what you're looking for, and what's important to you. It can help you shift your focus from doubts about being good enough to 'Will he make me happy?' Getting to know yourself and what you want, both in your life and with your partners, helps you to shed your anxieties. Go out there with a positive attitude, and both you and those around you will reap the benefits.

Being single can be fun, but it can be a pain in the ass sometimes too. Some people thrive on being single, while others find it frustrating. Certain singles don't date at all, others date all the time. You're not alone if dating gives you conflicting feelings – meeting new people is exciting, but it can also be draining, and rejection sucks as well. At the same time, each new date builds up hope. Is this the one? Feeling like the odd one out as the years slip by and it seems like everyone else has found someone can be intimidating, but we're all at different stages in our lives. One person's life might be bubbling with hope and confidence while another's might feel like a lifeless echo chamber. Sometimes you meet someone and feel infatuation blossom, only to find out that they're not ready to quit dating yet. Maybe – with your stomach all tied up in knots – you've had to end something really promising, only because it wasn't what you were looking for. Both situations might seem familiar to you or you might have seen all kinds of extremes. You might have felt like life was handed to you anew, and that it got ripped away from you as well. We fly through the highs and trudge through the lows, and it's all a part of the human experience. Sometimes you win, sometimes you lose, and your luck changes from one day to the next.

But you're not alone, and you're good enough the way you are. You don't need to completely reinvent yourself to live up to some imagined expectation. Stop fretting about the texts you could have phrased better, if you laughed too much, or if you spilled the beans too early. If you fake it, you'll just get stuck in that performance until the cows come home. No, it's much better to become the best version of yourself you can be.

If life seems like it's the way it's supposed to be right now, then enjoy what it has to offer. Avoid angst or self-criticism. If your life happens to feel empty and alone, remember not to kick yourself when you're down – if there was ever a time to be extra kind to yourself, this is it. Find the things that bring you joy and invest your energy in the right places and you'll feel your spirits lift.

I'd like to end this book by telling you that I'm delighted to think that my words, thoughts, and advice might aid you on your journey. But this is *your* journey, so I'm afraid I'll have to let you continue on your own. As I let go of your hand, from now on I hope that you always remind yourself that you're worthy of the best. Until the best comes along, keep that bar high: prioritize your own needs, recognize your worth, stay active, have a little fun, and let the quest take however long it needs.

Godspeed, my friend!

With warmth and kindness,
Angela Ahola

Acknowledgements

This book became the book it is thanks to so many of my nearest and dearest.

I would like to thank my mother Seija Karjalainen for proofreading, and for our invaluable discussions. My friend Johnathan Daily for his sharp eye and endless hours of rumination. During my writing process, he would send me exciting research discoveries he'd come across or get interesting ideas which he gladly shared. Thank you to Professor Åke Hellström at the Institute of Psychology at Stockholm University, who has been there for me as the true friend he is. It has been genuinely rewarding to discuss source material together.

Thank you to all of you who have contacted me with your questions and queries regarding dating and relationships. These conversations have helped me stay updated on the most pressing challenges facing the contemporary world of dating.

Last but not least, an enormous thanks to my family: my sister Mariana, my nieces and nephews, father Mauno, and my little golden nuggets Alexia and Antonia. Watching you grow and play everyday, focusing on your schoolwork and extra-curricular activities, puts everything around me into its proper perspective. Life is good the way it is.

Thank you ♡

About the author

Angela Ahola is a doctor of psychology, public speaker, and author. She writes about human behaviour, relationships, love, attraction, dating, our primal drives, and first impressions. Angela has been ranked as one of Sweden's best keynote speakers. Spotify, H&M, Samsung, Manpower, Bonnier, and the Swedish Parliament are among her many clients. She regularly gives expert advice on morning television shows.

In Sweden, Angela has previously published the books *Konsten att göra intryck* (*The Art of Making an Impression*; Natur & Kultur, 2016) and *Dina dolda drivkrafter – Hur tre psykologiska behov styr ditt liv* (*Your Hidden Motives – How Three Psychological Needs Control Your Life*; Roos & Tegner, 2020). Her books have also been published in the UK, Australia, Russia, China, Finland, Korea, Taiwan, Ukraine, and Lithuania.

Find out more about Angela and her work at:

www.angelaahola.com

Instagram: @angelaahola

YouTube: Angela Ahola

References

Why *one hundred* dates?

1 Brown, A, 'Nearly Half of US Adults Say Dating Has Gotten Harder for Most People in the Last 10 Years', *Pew Research Center* (2020). www.pewsocialtrends.org/2020/08/20/nearly-half-of-u-s-adults-say-dating-has-gotten-harder-for-most-people-in-the-last-10-years/

Introduction

1 Ahola, A. *Dina dolda drivkrafter* (*Your Hidden Motives*) (Roos & Tegner, 2020).
2 Eisenberger, N. I., & Lieberman, M. D., 'Why rejection hurts: a common neural alarm system for physical and social pain', *Trends in Cognitive Sciences* (2004) vol. 8(7), pp. 294–300.
3 Lambert, N. M., Stillman, T. F., Hicks, J. A., Kamble, S., Baumeister, R. F., & Fincham, F. D, 'To Belong Is to Matter: Sense of Belonging Enhances Meaning in Life', *Personality and Social Psychology Bulletin* (2013), vol. 39 (11), pp. 1418–27.
4 Leary, M. R. & Baumeister, R. F., 'The Need to Belong: Desire for Interpersonal Attachments as a Fundamental Human Motivation', *Psychological Bulletin* (1995), vol. 117, no. 3, pp. 497–529.
5 Leary, M. R. & Baumeister, R. F., 'The Need to Belong: Desire for Interpersonal Attachments as a Fundamental Human Motivation', *Psychological Bulletin* (1995), vol. 117, no. 3, pp. 497–529. Krebs, A., 'Zwischen Ich und Du', *Eine dialogische Philosophie der Liebe*

(Frankfurt: Suhrkamp, 2014). Lambert, N., Stillman, T. F., Hicks, J. A., Kamble, S., Baumeiter, R. F., Fincham, F. D., 'Belong is to matter: Sense of belonging enhances meaning in life', *Personality and Social Psychology Bulletin* (2013), vol. 39, pp. 1418–27.

6 Zoosk, 'Why do we look for love.' zoosk.com/date-mix/online-dating/why-do-we-look-for-love/

7 Cohen, S., Frank, E., Doyle, W. J., Skoner, D. P., Rabin, B. S., & Gwaltney, J. M., Jr., 'Types of stressors that increase susceptibility to the common cold in healthy adults', *Health Psychology* (1998), vol. 17, pp. 214–223.

8 Kiecolt-Glaser, J. K., Loving, T. J., Stowell, J. R., et al., 'Hostile Marital Interactions, Proinflammatory Cytokine Production, and Wound Healing', *Arch Gen Psychiatry* (2005), vol. 62(12), pp. 1377–84.

9 Gallo, L. C., Troxel, W. M., Matthews, K. A., & Kuller, L. H., 'Marital status and quality in middle-aged women: Associations with levels and trajectories of cardiovascular risk factors', *Health Psychology* (2003), vol. 22, pp. 453–63.

10 Diener, E., & Seligman, M. E. P., 'Very happy people', *Psychological Science* (2002), vol. 13, pp. 81–4. Myers, D. G., *The Pursuit of Happiness: What Makes a Person Happy – And Why* (William Morrow & Co, 1992).

11 Cacioppo, J. T., Hawkley, L. C., Crawford, L. E., Ernst, J. M., Burleson, M. H., Kowalewski, R. B., Malarkey, W.B., Van Cauter, E., Berntson, G. G., 'Loneliness and health: Potential mechanisms', *Psychosomatic Medicine* (2002), vol. 64(3), pp. 407–17.

12 Acevedo, B. P., & Aron, A. P., 'Romantic love, pair-bonding, and the dopaminergic reward system', M. Mikulincer & P. R. Shaver (eds.), *The Herzliya series on personality and social psychology. Mechanisms of social connection: From brain to group*, American Psychological Association (2014), pp. 55–69.

13 Xu, X., Aron, A., Brown, L., Cao, G., Feng, T., & Weng, X., 'Reward and motivation systems: A brain mapping study of early-stage intense romantic love in Chinese participants', *Human Brain Mapping* (2011), vol. 32, pp. 249–57.

   Xu, X., Brown, L., Aron, A., Acevedo, B., Cao, G., Feng, T., & Weng, X., 'Brain activations during early-stage intense romantic love associated with relationship outcomes 40 months later', Neuroscience Letters (2012), vol. 526, pp. 33–8.

14 Höjer, H, 'Living alone is increasing all over the world, and Sweden

is at the top', Forskning & Framsteg (2014). fof.se/tidning/2014/10/artikel/ensamboendet-okar-i-hela-varlden-och-sverige-ligger-i-topp

15 Eisenberger, N. I., & Lieberman, M. D., 'Why rejection hurts: a common neural alarm system for physical and social pain', *Trends in Cognitive Sciences* (2004), vol. 8(7), pp. 294–300.

16 Wilder, D. A., & Thompson, J. E., 'Intergroup contact with independent manipulations on in-group and out-group interaction', *Journal of Personality and Social Psychology* (1980), vol. 38(4), pp. 589–603.

17 Latané, B., Eckman, J., & Joy, V., 'Shared stress and interpersonal attraction', *Journal of Experimental Social Psychology* (1966), vol. 1, pp. 80–94

18 Kenrick, D. T., & Cialdini, R. B., 'Romantic attraction: Misattribution versus reinforcement explanations', *Journal of Personality and Social Psychology* (1977), vol. 35(6), pp. 381–91.

19 Anderson, R, 'The Ugly Truth About Online Dating', *Psychology Today* (2016). www.psychologytoday.com/us/blog/the-mating-game/2016 09/the-ugly-truth-about-online-dating

20 Survey: Svenskarna och internet, Internetstiftelsen. svenskarnaoc hinternet.se/amne/natdejting/

21 Smith, C., 'By the numbers: 41 impressive Tinder statistics', *DMR* (2016). Retrieved from http://expandedramblings.com/index.php/tinder-statistics/

22 Dredge, S., 'Research says 30% of tinder users are married', *Guardian* (2015).

23 Anderson, R, 'The Ugly Truth About Online Dating', *Psychology Today* (2016). www.psychologytoday.com/us/blog/the-mating-game/201609/the-ugly-truth-about-online-dating

24 Goffman, E., *The Presentation of Self in Everyday Life* (Garden City, NY: Doubleday, 1959).

25 Finkel, E. J., Eastwick, P. W., Karney, B. R., Reis, H. T., & Sprecher, S., 'Online Dating: A Critical Analysis From the Perspective of Psychological Science', *Psychological Science in the Public Interest* (2012), vol. 13(1), pp. 3–66.

26 Joel, S., Eastwick, P. W., Finkel, E. W., 'Is Romantic Desire Predictable? Machine Learning Applied to Initial Romantic Attraction', *Psychological Science* (2017), vol. 28(10), pp. 1478 –89.

27 Iyengar, S. S., & Lepper, M. R., 'When choice is demotivating: Can one desire too much of a good thing?' *Journal of Personality and Social Psychology* (2000), vol. 79 (6), pp. 995–1006.

28 Iyengar, S. S., Simonson, I., Fisman, R., & Mogilner, C., 'I know what I want but can I find it? Examining the dynamic relationship between stated and revealed preferences', *Society for Personality and Social Psychology Annual Meeting*, New Orleans, LA. (2005).

29 Toffler, A., *Future Shock* (New York: Random House, 1970).

30 Shah, A. M., & Wolford, G., 'Buying Behavior as a Function of Parametric Variation of Number of Choices', *Psychological Science* (2007), vol. 18 (5), pp. 369-70.

31 Ryan, R. M., & Deci, E. L., 'On happiness and human potentials: A review of research on hedonic and eudaimonic well-being', *Annual Review of Psychology* (2001), vol. 52, pp. 141-66.

32 Iyengar, S. S., & Lepper, M. R., 'When choice is demotivating: Can one desire too much of a good thing?' *Journal of Personality and Social Psychology* (2000), vol. 79 (6), pp. 995-1006.

33 Finkel, E. J., Eastwick, P. W., Karney, B. R., Reis, H. T., & Sprecher, S., 'Online dating: a critical analysis from the perspective of psychological science', *Psychological Science in the Public Interest* (2012), vol. 13 (1), pp. 3-66.

34 Kruglanski, A. W., Thompson, E. P., Higgins, E. T., Atash, M. N., Pierro, A., Shah, J. Y., & Spiegel, S., 'To "do the right thing" or to "just do it": Locomotion and assessment as distinct self-regulatory imperatives', *Journal of Personality and Social Psychology* (2000), vol. 79, pp. 793-815.

35 Gollwitzer, P. M., & Bayer, U., 'Deliberative versus implemental mind-sets in the control of action', S. Chaiken & Y. Trope (eds.), *Dual-process theories in social psychology* (pp. 403-22) (New York, NY: Guilford, 1999).

36 Heino, R., Ellison, N., & Gibbs, J., 'Relationshopping: Investigating the market metaphor in online dating', *Journal of Social and Personal Relationships* (2010), vol. 27, pp. 427-47. Lawson, H. M., & Leck, K., 'Dynamics of Internet dating', *Social Science Computer Review* (2006), vol. 24, pp. 189-208.

37 Sunnafrank, M., 'Predicted outcome value in initial conversations', *Communication Research Reports* (1988), vol. 5, pp. 169-72.

38 Lenton, A. P., Fasolo, B., & Todd, P. M., 'The relationship between number of potential mates and mating skew in humans', *Animal Behaviour* (2009), vol. 77, pp. 55-60. Lenton, A. P., & Francesconi, M., 'How humans cognitively manage an abundance of mate options', *Psychological Science* (2010), vol. 21, pp. 528-33.

39 Aron, A., 'Online Dating: The Current Status—and Beyond', *Psychological Science in the Public Interest* (2012), vol. 13(1), pp. 1–2.

40 Wu, P., & Chiou, W., 'More options leads to more searching and worse choices in finding partners for romantic relationships online: An experimental study', *CyberPsychology & Behavior* (2009), vol. 12, pp. 315–18.

41 Lenton, A. P., & Francesconi, M., 'Too much of a good thing? Variety is confusing in mate choice', *Biology Letters* (2011), vol. 7, pp. 528–31. Lenton, A. P., & Stewart, A., 'Changing her ways: Number of options and mate standard strength impact mate choice strategy and satisfaction', *Judgment and Decision Making* (2008), vol. 3, pp. 501–11.

42 Iyengar, S. S., & Lepper, M. R. (2000). 'When choice is demotivating: Can one desire too much of a good thing?', *Journal of Personality and Social Psychology* (2000), vol. 79, pp. 995–1006.

43 Botti, S., & Hsee, C. K., 'Dazed and confused by choice: How the temporal costs of choice freedom lead to undesirable outcomes', *Organizational Behavior and Human Decision Processes* (2010), vol. 112, pp. 161–71. Botti, S., & Iyengar, S. S., 'The psychological pleasure and pain of choosing: When people prefer choosing at the cost of subsequent satisfaction', *Journal of Personality and Social Psychology* (2004), vol. 87, pp. 312–26. Botti, S., Orfali, K., & Iyengar, S. S., 'Tragic choices: Autonomy and emotional responses to medical decisions', *Journal of Consumer Research* (2009), vol. 36, pp. 337–52.

44 Drigotas, S. M., & Rusbult, C. E., 'Should I stay or should I go? A dependence model of breakups', *Journal of Personality and Social Psychology* (1992), vol. 62, pp. 62–87. Miller, R. S., 'Inattentive and contented: Relationship commitment and attention to alternatives', *Journal of Personality and Social Psychology* (1997), vol. 73, pp. 758–66. Le, B., & Agnew, C. R., 'Commitment and its theorized determinants: A meta-analysis of the investment model', *Personal Relationships* (2003), vol. 10, pp. 37–57. Le, B., Dove, N. L., Agnew, C. R., Korn, M. S., & Mutso, A. A., 'Predicting non-marital romantic relationship dissolution: A meta-analytic synthesis', *Personal Relationships* (2010), vol. 17, pp. 377–90.

45 Gladue, B. A., & Delaney, H., 'Gender differences in perception of attractiveness of men and women in bars', *Personality and Social Psychology Bulletin* (1990), vol. 16, pp. 378–91.

46 Schwartz, B., Ward, A., Monterosso, J., Lyubomirsky, S., White, K., & Lehman, D. R., 'Maximizing versus satisficing: Happiness is a matter of choice', *Journal of Personality and Social Psychology* (2002), vol. 83(5), pp. 1178–97.

47 Wygant, D., 'The shocking truth about Tinder dating', *The Huffington Post* (June 2014). Retrieved from www.huffingtonpost.com/david-wygant/the-shocking-truth-about-_3_b_4967472.html

48 Cacioppo, J. T., Cacioppo, S., Gonzaga, G. C., Ogburn, E. L., & VanderWeele, T. J., 'Marital satisfaction and break-ups differ across on-line and off-line meeting venues', *Proceedings of the National Academy of Sciences* (2013), vol. 110, pp. 10135–40.

PART I: BEFORE YOU MEET

1: Mr Right or Mr Right Now?

1 Sumter, S. R., Vandenbosch, L., Ligtenberg, L., 'Love me Tinder: Untangling emerging adults' motivations for using the dating application Tinder', *Telematics and Informatics* (2017), vol. 34, pp. 67–78.

2 Timmermans, E., & De Caluwé, E. (2017) 'Development and Validation of the Tinder Motives Scale', Computers in Human Behavior. 70:341-350.

3 Carpenter, C. J., & McEwan, B., 'The players of micro-dating: Individual and gender differences in goal orientations toward micro-dating apps', *First Monday* (2016), 21.

4 Ando, R., & Sakamoto, A., 'The effect of cyber-friends on loneliness and social anxiety: differences between high and low self-evaluated physical attractiveness groups', *Computers in Human Behavior* (2008), vol. 24 (3), pp. 993–1009.

5 Lieberman, M. D., *Social – Why our brains are wired to connect* (New York: Crown Publishers, 2013).

6 Lieberman, M. D., *Social – Why our brains are wired to connect* (New York: Crown Publishers, 2013)/

7 Tyson, G., Perta, V. C., Haddadi, H., & Seto, M. C., 'A first look at user activity on Tinder', *ASONAM '16: Proceedings of the 2016 IEEE/ACM International Conference on Advances in Social Networks Analysis and Mining* (2016), pp. 461–6.

2: First impressions

1 Schupp, H. T., Öhman, A., Junghöfer, M., Weike, A. I., Stockburger, J., Hamm, A. O., 'The Facilitated Processing of Threatening Faces: An ERP Analysis', *Emotion* (2004), vol. 4(2), pp. 189-200. Winston, J.S., Strange, B.A., O'Doherty, J., & Dolan, R.J., 'Automatic and intentional brain responses during evaluation of trustworthiness of faces', *Nature Neuroscience* (2002), vol. 5, pp. 277-83.

2 Cacioppo, J. T., Gardner, W. L., & Berntson, G. G., 'Beyond bipolar conceptualizations and measures: the case of attitudes and evaluative space', *Personality and Social Psychological Review* (1997), vol. 1(1), pp. 3-25. Tsukiura, T., Shigemune, Y., Nouchi, R., Kambara, T. & Kawashima, R., 'Insular and hippocampal contributions to remembering people with an impression of bad personality', *Social Cognition and Affective Neuroscience* (2013), vol. 8(5), pp. 515-22.

3: Picking a good 'un

1 Polderman, T. J. C., Benyamin, B., de Leeuw, C. A., Sullivan, P. F., van Bochoven, A., Visscher, P. M., & Posthuma, D., 'Meta-analysis of the heritability of human traits based on fifty years of twin studies', *Nat Genet* (2015), vol. 47(7), pp. 702-9.

2 Pramodh, K.C., & Vijayalata, Y., 'Automatic personality recognition of authors using big five factor model', *2016 IEEE International Conference on Advances in Computer Applications (ICACA)* (2016), pp. 32-7.

3 Researchers James E. King and José Figueredo describe dominance or submissiveness as a person's 'will' in relation to others, in different social contexts. So dominance is not about being unsympathetic or unwilling to cooperate. It is instead about a will to win over others, sometimes at any cost.

4 Ben-Ari, A., & Lavee, Y., 'Dyadic Characteristics of Individual Attributes: Attachment, Neuroticism, and Their Relation to Marital Quality and Closeness', *American Journal of Orthopsychiatry* (2005), vol. 75(4), pp. 621-31.

5 Karney, B. R., Bradbury, T. N., Fincham, F. D., & Sullivan, K. T., 'The role of negative affectivity in the association between attributions

and marital satisfaction', *Journal of Personality and Social Psychology* (1994), vol. 66(2), pp. 413–24.

6 Blum, J. S., & Mehrabian, A., 'Personality and temperament correlates of marital satisfaction', *Journal of Personality* (1999), vol. 67(1), pp. 93–125.

7 Huston, T. L., 'What's love got to do with it? Why some marriages succeed and others fail', *Personal Relationships* (2009), vol. 16(3), pp. 301–27.

8 Berry, D. S., Pennebaker, J. W., Mueller, J. S., & Hiller, W. S., 'Linguistic bases of social perception', *Personality and Social Psychology Bulletin* (1997), vol. 23, pp. 526–37. Fast, L. A., & Funder, D. C., 'Personality as manifest in word use: Correlations with self-report, acquaintance report, and behavior', *Journal of Personality and Social Psychology* (2008a), vol. 94, pp. 334–6. Mehl, M. R., & Pennebaker, J. W., 'The sounds of social life: A psychometric analysis of students' daily social environments and conversations', *Journal of Personality and Social Psychology* (2003), vol. 84, pp. 857–70. Oberlander, J., & Gill, A. J., 'Language with character: A corpus-based study of individual differences in e-mail communication', *Discourse Processes* (2006), vol. 42, pp. 239–70. Pennebaker, J. W., & King, L. A., 'Linguistic styles: Language use as an individual difference', *Journal of Personality and Social Psychology* (1999), vol. 77, pp. 1296–1312.

9 Wall, H. J., Kaye, L. K., & Malone, S. A., 'An exploration of psychological factors on emoticon usage and implications for judgement accuracy', *Computers in Human Behavior* (2016), vol. 62, pp. 70–8.

10 Yarkoni, T., 'Personality in 100,000 Words: A large-scale analysis of personality and word use among bloggers', *Journal of Research in Personality* (2010), vol. 44(3), pp. 363–73.

11 Marengo, D., Giannotta, F., & Settanni, M., 'Assessing personality using emoji: An exploratory study', *Personality and Individual Differences* (2017), vol. 112, pp. 74–8.

12 Gill, A., Nowson, S., & Oberlander, J., 'What Are They Blogging About? Personality, Topic and Motivation in Blogs', conference paper (2009).

13 Pennebaker, J. W., & King, L. A., 'Linguistic styles: Language use as an individual difference', *Journal of Personality and Social Psychology* (1999), vol. 77, pp. 1296–1312.

14 Lim, A., 'The big five personality traits', *Simply Psychology* (15 June 2020). www.simplypsychology.org/big-five-personality.html.

15 Berry, D. S., Pennebaker, J. W., Mueller, J. S., & Hiller, W. S., 'Linguistic

bases of social perception', *Personality and Social Psychology Bulletin* (1997), vol. 23, pp. 526–37. Pennebaker, J. W., & King, L. A., 'Linguistic styles: Language use as an individual difference', *Journal of Personality and Social Psychology* (1999), vol. 77, pp. 1296–1312.

16 Marengo, D., Giannotta, F., & Settanni, M., 'Assessing personality using emoji: An exploratory study', *Personality and Individual Differences* (2017), vol. 112, pp. 74–8.

17 Mehl, M. R., Pennebaker, J, W., & Gosling, S. D., 'Personality in its natural habitat: Manifestations and implicit folk theories of personality in daily life', *Journal of Personality and Social Psychology* (2006), vol. 90(5), pp.862–77.

18 Lim, A., 'The big five personality traits', *Simply Psychology* (15 June 2020). www.simplypsychology.org/big-five-personality.html.

19 Berry, D. S., Pennebaker, J. W., Mueller, J. S., & Hiller, W. S., 'Linguistic bases of social perception', *Personality and Social Psychology Bulletin* (1997), vol. 23, pp. 526–37. Pennebaker, J. W., & King, L. A., 'Linguistic styles: Language use as an individual difference', *Journal of Personality and Social Psychology* (1999), vol. 77, pp. 1296–1312.

20 Marengo, D., Giannotta, F., & Settanni, M., 'Assessing personality using emoji: An exploratory study', *Personality and Individual Differences* (2017), vol. 112, pp. 74–8.

21 Berry, D. S., Pennebaker, J. W., Mueller, J. S., & Hiller, W. S., 'Linguistic bases of social perception', *Personality and Social Psychology Bulletin* (1997), vol. 23, pp. 526–37. Pennebaker, J. W., & King, L. A., 'Linguistic styles: Language use as an individual difference', *Journal of Personality and Social Psychology* (1999), vol. 77, pp. 1296–1312.

22 Ross, C., Orr, E. S., Sisic, M., Arseneault, J. M., Simmering, M. G., & Orr, R. R., 'Personality and motivations associated with Facebook use', *Computers in Human Behavior* (2009), vol. 25(2), pp. 578–86.

23 Ibid

24 Stepansky, P. E., & Goldberg, A. (eds.), *Kohut's Legacy: Contributions to Self Psychology* (Hillsdale, NJ: The Analytic Press, 1984).

25 Paulhus, D. L., & Williams, K. M., 'The Dark Triad of personality: Narcissism, Machiavellianism, and psychopathy', *Journal of Research in Personality* (2002), vol. 36(6), pp.556–63.

4: Catching their eye

1 Dion, K., Berscheid, E., & Walster, E., 'What is beautiful is good', *Journal of Personality and Social Psychology* (1972), vol. 24(3), pp. 285–90.

2 Hamermesh, D.S., & Biddle, J.E., 'Beauty and the Labor Market', *The American Economic Review* (1994), vol. 84(5), pp. 1174–94. Rhodes, G., 'The Evolutionary Psychology of Facial Beauty', *Annual Review of Psychology* (2006), vol. 57, pp. 199–226. Dipboye, R.L., Fromkin, H.L., & Wilback, K., 'Relative importance of applicant sex attractiveness and scholastic standing in job applicant resumés', *Journal of Applied Psychology* (1975), vol. 60(3), pp. 30–43.

3 Cherulnik, P.D., 'Physical Attractiveness and Judged Suitability for Leadership', Annual Meeting of the Midwestern Psychological Association (61st, Chicago, IL, 4–6 May 1989).

4 Feingold, A., 'Good-looking people are not what we think', *Psychological Bulletin* (1992), vol. 111(2), pp. 304–41. Raza, S.M., & Carpenter, B.N., 'A model of hiring decisions in real employment interviews', *Journal of Applied Psychology* (1987), vol. 72(4), pp. 596–603. Langlois & Roggman & Riesen-Danner, 'Attractive faces are only average. Family, consumers and human development', *Faculty Publications* (1990), vol. 1(2), pp. 115–21. Dion, K., Berscheid, E., & Walster, E., 'What is beautiful is good', *Journal of Personality and Social Psychology* (1972), vol. 24(3), pp. 285–90.

5 Monin, B., 'The Warm Glow Heuristic: When Liking Leads to Familiarity', *Journal of Personality and Social Psychology* (2003), vol. 85(6), pp. 1035–48.

6 Lewandowski, G., Aron, A., & Gee, J. (2007). 'Personality goes a long way: The malleability of opposite-sex physical attractiveness. Personal Relationships, vol. 14, pp. 571–85.

7 Corneille, O., Monin, B., & Pleyers, G., 'Is positivity a cue or a response option? Warm glow vs evaluative matching in the familiarity for attractive and not-so-attractive face', *Journal of Experimental Social Psychology* (2005), vol. 41, pp. 431–7.

8 McNulty, J. K., Neff, L. A., & Karney, B. R., 'Beyond initial attraction: Physical attractiveness in newlywed marriage', *Journal of Family Psychology* (2008), vol. 22, pp. 135–43.

9 Sangrador, J. L., & Yela, C., '"What is beautiful is loved": Physical

attractiveness in love relationships in a representative sample', Social Behavior and Personality (2000), vol. 28, pp. 207–18.

10 Ahola, A., *Konsten att göra intryck (The Art of Making an Impression)* (Natur & Kultur, 2016).

11 Harris, M.B., 'Sex Differences in Stereotypes of Spectacles', *Journal of Applied Social Psychology* (1991), vol. 21, pp. 1659–80.

12 Yamaguchi, Nobuyuki, Cooper, A., Werdelin, L., MacDonald, D. W., 'Evolution of the mane and group-living in the lion (Panthera leo): a review', *Journal of Zoology* (2004), vol. 263 (4), pp. 329–42. West, P. M., & Packer, C., 'Sexual Selection, Temperature, and the Lion's Mane', *Science* (2002), vol. 297 (5585), pp. 1339–1943.

13 Fiore, A. T., Taylor, L. S., Mendelsohn, G.A., Hearst, M., 'Assessing attractiveness in online dating profiles', *Proceedings of the SIGCHI Conference on Human Factors in Computing Systems* (2008), pp. 797–806.

5: Your profile bio

1 Tyson, G., Perta, V. C., Haddadi, H., Seto, M. C., 'A first look at user activity on Tinder', *ASONAM '16: Proceedings of the 2016 IEEE/ACM International Conference on Advances in Social Networks Analysis and Mining* (2016), pp. 461–6.

2 Rosen, L.D., Cheever, N.A., Cummings, C., & Felt, J., 'The impact of emotionality and self-disclosure on online dating versus traditional dating', *Computers in Human Behavior* (2008), vol. 24, pp. 2124–57.

3 Schellenberg, G. E., & Mankarious, M., 'Music training and emotion comprehension in childhood', *Emotion* (2012), vol. 12 (5), pp. 887–91. Schäfer, T., & Mehlhorn, C., 'Can personality traits predict musical style preferences? A meta-analysis', *Personality and Individual Differences* (2017), vol. 116, pp. 265–73. Brown, R.A., 'Music preferences and personality among Japanese university students', *International Journal of Psychology* (2012), vol. 47 (4), pp. 259–68. Langmeyer, A., Guglhör-Rudan, A., Tarnai, C., 'What do music preferences reveal about personality: a cross-cultural replication using self-ratings and ratings of music samples', *Journal of Individual Differences* (2012), vol. 33 (2), pp. 119–30. Chamorro-Premuzic, T., Gomà-i-Freixanet, M., Furnham, A., Muro, A., 'Personality, self-estimated intelligence, and uses of music: A Spanish replication and

extension using structural equation modeling', *Psychology of Aesthetics, Creativity, and the Arts* (2009), vol. 3(3), pp. 149–55.

4 Luo, S., & Klohnen, E. C., 'Assortative Mating and Marital Quality in Newlyweds: A Couple-Centered Approach', *Journal of Personality and Social Psychology* (2005), vol. 88(2), pp. 304–26.

6: Making a match

1 Suler, J., 'Hypotheses about online text relationships', *Psychology of Cyberspace* (2000). Retrieved 15 March 2004, from www.rider. edu/~suler/psycyber/emailrel.html. Levine, D., 'Virtual attraction: What rocks your boat', *CyberPsychology & Behavior* (2000), vol. 3, pp. 565–73. Shatfeld, R. & Barak, A., 'Factors Related to Initiating Interpersonal Contacts on Internet Dating Sites: A View From the Social Exchange Theory', *Interpersona: An International Journal on Personal Relationships*, [S.l.] (2009), vol. 3, pp. 19–37.

2 Rosen, L.D., Cheever, N.A., Cummings, C., & Felt, J., 'The impact of emotionality and self-disclosure on online dating versus traditional dating', *Computers in Human Behavior* (2008), vol. 24, pp. 2124–57.

3 Fiore, A., & Donath, J., 'Homophily in online dating: When do you like someone like yourself?', *Conference on Human Factors in Computing Systems Proceedings* (2005), pp. 1371–4.

4 Ghoshal, G., & Holme, P., 'Attractiveness and activity in Internet communities', Department of Physics, University of Michigan (2005). Retrieved 12 May 2006, from: http://arxiv.org/PS_cache/physics/pdf/0504/0504167.pdf.

5 Tyson, G., Perta, V. C., Haddadi, H., Seto, M. C., 'A first look at user activity on Tinder', *ASONAM '16: Proceedings of the 2016 IEEE/ACM International Conference on Advances in Social Networks Analysis and Mining* (2016), pp. 461–6.

6 Trivers, R., *Parental investment and sexual selection* (Harvard University, 1972).

7: Text, call, or 'Let's meet up'?

1 Seltzer, L. J., Prososki, A. R., Ziegler, T. E., & Pollak, S. D., 'Instant messages vs. speech: hormones and why we still need to hear each

other', *Evolution and Human Behavior: Official journal of the Human Behavior and Evolution Society* (2012), vol. 33(1), pp. 42–5.

PART II: ON THE DATE

8: Got chemistry?

1 Sharabi, L. L., & Caughlin, J. P., 'What predicts first date success? A longitudinal study of modality switching in online dating', *Personal Relationships* (2017), vol. 24, 2.

2 Ramirez, A., Jr., & Wang, Z., 'When online meets offline: An expectancy violations theory perspective on modality switching', *Journal of Communication* (2008), vol. 58, pp. 20–39. Ramirez, A., Jr., & Zhang, S., 'When online meets offline: The effect of modality switching on relational communication', *Communication Monographs* (2007), vol. 74, pp. 287–310.

3 Ramirez, A., Jr., & Wang, Z., 'When online meets offline: An expectancy violations theory perspective on modality switching', *Journal of Communication* (2008), vol. 58, pp. 20–39. Ramirez, A., Jr., & Zhang, S., 'When online meets offline: The effect of modality switching on relational communication', *Communication Monographs* (2007), vol. 74, pp. 287–310. Huston, T. L., Caughlin, J. P., Houts, R. M., Smith, S. E., & George, L. J., 'The connubial crucible: Newlywed years as predictors of marital delight, distress, and divorce', *Journal of Personality and Social Psychology* (2001), 80.

4 Atkins, C. P., 'Perceptions of speakers with minimal eye contact: Implications for stutterers', *Journal of Fluency Disorders* (1988), vol. 13(6), pp. 429–36.

5 Zsok, F., Haucke, M., De Wit, C. Y., & Barelds, D. P. H., 'What kind of love is love at first sight? An empirical investigation', *Personal Relationships* (2017), vol. 24(4), pp. 869–85.

6 Finkel, E. J., Eastwick, P. W., & Matthews, J., 'Speed-dating as an invaluable tool for studying romantic attraction: A methodological primer', *Personal Relationships* (2007), vol. 14, pp. 149–66. Ireland, M. E., Slatcher, R. B., Eastwick, P. W., Scissors, L. E., Finkel, E. J., & Pennebaker, J. W., 'Language Style Matching Predicts Relationship Initiation and Stability', *Psychological Science* (2010), 1–6. Gonzales, A. L., Hancock, J. T., & Pennebaker, J. W., 'Language style matching

as a predictor of social dynamics in small groups', *Communications Research*(2010), vol. 31, pp. 3-19. Lakin, J. L., Chartrand, T. L., & Arkin, R. M., 'I am too just like you: Nonconscious mimicry as an automatic behavioral response to social exclusion', *Psychological Science* (2008), vol. 19, pp. 816-22.

7   Senft, N., Chentsova-Dutton, Y., & Patten, G. A., 'All smiles perceived equally: Facial expressions trump target characteristics in impression formation', *Motivation and Emotion* (2016), vol. 40, pp. 577-87.

8   Tessler, R., & Sushelsky, L. (1978). 'Effects of eye contact and social status on the perception of a job applicant in an employment interviewing situation. Journal of Vocational Behavior, vol. 13(3), pp. 338-47.

9   Atkins, C. P., 'Perceptions of speakers with minimal eye contact: Implications for stutterers', *Journal of Fluency Disorders* (1988), vol. 13(6), pp. 429-36.

10 Aron, A., Melinat, E., Aron, E. N., Vallone, R. D., & Bator, R. J., 'The Experimental Generation of Interpersonal Closeness: A Procedure and Some Preliminary Findings', *Personality and Social Psychology Bulletin* (1997), vol. 23(4), pp. 363-77. Kreysa, H., Kessler, L., & Schweinberger, S. R., 'Direct Speaker Gaze Promotes Trust in Truth-Ambiguous Statements', *PLoS One* (2016), vol. 11(9): e0162291.

11 Seltzer, L. J., Prososki, A. R., Ziegler, T. E., & Pollak, S. D., 'Instant messages vs. speech: hormones and why we still need to hear each other', *Evolution and Human Behavior: Official Journal of the Human Behavior and Evolution Society* (2012), vol. 33(1), pp. 42-5.

12 Demattè, L., Österbauer, R., & Spence, C., 'Olfactory Cues Modulate Facial Attractiveness', *Chemical Senses* (2007), vol. 32(6), 603-310.

9: It's about finding things in common

1   Gaunt, R., 'Couple Similarity and Marital Satisfaction: Are Similar Spouses Happier?', *Journal of Personality* (2006), 74, 5.

Caspi, A., & Herbener, E. S., 'Continuity and change: Assortative marriage and the consistency of personality in adulthood', *Journal of Personality and Social Psychology* (1990), vol. 58, pp. 250-8. Gaunt, R., 'Couple similarity and marital satisfaction: Are similar spouses happier?', *Journal of Personality* (2006), 74:1401-20.

Luo, S., Chen, H., Yue, G., Zhang, G., Zhaoyang, R., & Xu, D.,

'Predicting Marital Satisfaction From Self, Partner, and Couple Characteristics: Is It Me, You, or Us?', Journal of Personality(2008), 76(5): 1231–66.

2 van Baren, R.B., Holland, R.W., & van Knippenberg, K., 'Mimicry and prosocial behaviour', *Psychological Science* (2004), vol. 15, pp. 71–4.

3 Finkel, E. J., Eastwick, P. W., & Matthews, J., 'Speed-dating as an invaluable tool for studying romantic attraction: A methodological primer', *Personal Relationships* (2007), vol. 14, pp. 149–66. Ireland, M. E., Slatcher, R. B., Eastwick, P. W., Scissors, L. E., Finkel, E. J., & Pennebaker, J. W., 'Language Style Matching Predicts Relationship Initiation and Stability', *Psychological Science* (2010), 1–6. Gonzales, A. L., Hancock, J. T., & Pennebaker, J. W., 'Language style matching as a predictor of social dynamics in small groups', *Communications Research* (2010), vol. 31, pp. 3–19. Lakin, J. L., Chartrand, T. L., & Arkin, R. M., 'I am too just like you: Nonconscious mimicry as an automatic behavioral response to social exclusion', *Psychological Science* (2008), vol. 19, pp. 816–22.

4 Berger, J., *Invisible Influence: The hidden forces that shape behavior* (Simon & Schuster, 2016).

5 Berger, J., *Invisible Influence: The hidden forces that shape behavior* (Simon & Schuster, 2016).

6 Rusbult, C. E., Kumashiro, M., Kubacka, K. E., & Finkel, E. J., '"The part of me that you bring out": Ideal similarity and the Michelangelo phenomenon', *Journal of Personality and Social Psychology* (2009), vol. 96(1), pp. 61–82.

7 Aronson, E., *The Social Animal* (New York: Freeman, 2003; first published 1969). Berscheid, E., & Hartfild-Walster, E., *Interpersonal Attraction* (New York: Random House, 1978).

8 Rusbult, C. E., Kumashiro, M., Kubacka, K. E., & Finkel, E. J., '"The part of me that you bring out": Ideal similarity and the Michelangelo phenomenon', *Journal of Personality and Social Psychology* (2009), vol. 96(1), pp. 61–82.

9 Jamieson, D. W., Lydon, J. E., & Zanna, M. P., 'Attitude and activity preference similarity: Differential bases of interpersonal attraction for low and high self-monitors', *Journal of Personality and Social Psychology* (1987), vol. 53(6), pp. 1052–60.

10 Lydon, J. E., Jamieson, D. W., & Zanna, M. P., 'Interpersonal similarity and the social and intellectual dimensions of first impressions', *Social Cognition* (1988), vol. 6(4), pp. 269–86.

11 Blau, P. M., 'Attitudes, values, and personality, Justice in Social Exchange', (1964), vol. 34(2), pp. 193–206.

12 Blau, P., *Exchange and Power in Social Life* (New York: Wiley, 1964). Homans, G. C., *Elementary Forms of Social Behavior* (New York: Harcourt, 1961).

13 Dijkstra, P., & Barelds, D. P. H., 'Do people know what they want: A similar or complementary partner?', *Evolutionary Psychology* (2008), vol. 6(4), pp. 595–602.

14 Gigy, L., & Kelly, J. B., 'Reasons for divorce: Perspectives of divorcing men and women', *Journal of Divorce & Remarriage* (1992), vol. 18(1–2), pp. 169–87.

15 Bouchard, T. J. & McGue, M., Jr., 'Familial studies of intelligence: a review', *Science* (1981), pp. 1055–9.

16 Luo, S., & Klohnen, E. C., 'Assortative Mating and Marital Quality in Newlyweds: A Couple-Centered Approach', *Journal of Personality and Social Psychology* (2005), vol. 88(2), pp. 304–26.

17 de Graaf, P. M., & Kalmijn, M., 'Change and Stability in the Social Determinants of Divorce: A Comparison of Marriage Cohorts in the Netherlands', *European Sociological Review* (2006), vol. 22(5), pp. 561–72.

18 Tamir, D. I., & Mitchell, J. P., 'Disclosing information about the self is intrinsically rewarding', *Proceedings National Academic Sciences USA* (2012), 109(21), pp. 8038–43.

19 Watson, D., Klohnen, E. C., Casillas, A., Nus Simms, E., Haig, J., & Berry, D. S., 'Match makers and deal breakers: Analyses of assortative mating in newlywed couples', *Journal of Personality* (2004), vol. 72, pp. 1029–68.

20 D'Onofrio, B. M., Eaves, L. J., Murrelle, L., Maes, H. H., & Spilka, B., 'Understanding biological and social influences on religious affiliation, attitudes, and behaviors: A behavior genetic perspective', *Journal of Personality* (1999), vol. 67, pp. 953–84.

21 Cuperman, R., & Ickes, W. 'Big Five predictors of behavior and perceptions in initial dyadic interactions: Personality similarity helps extraverts and introverts, but hurts "disagreeables"', *Journal of Personality and Social Psychology* (2009), vol. 97, pp. 667–84

22 Dijkstra, P., & Barelds, D. P. H., 'Do people know what they want: A similar or complementary partner?', *Evolutionary Psychology* (2008), vol. 6(4), pp. 595–602.

23 Eastwick, P. W., & Finkel, E. J., 'Sex differences in mate preferences

revisited: Do people know what they initially desire in a romantic partner?', *Journal of Personality and Social Psychology* (2008), vol. 94(2), pp. 245–64.

24 Mitnick, D. M., Heyman, R. E., Malik, J., & Slep, A. M. S., 'The differential association between change request qualities and resistance, problem resolution, and relationship satisfaction', *Journal of Family Psychology* (2009), vol. 23(4), pp. 464–73.

25 Condon, J. W., & Crano, W. D., 'Inferred evaluation and the relation between attitude similarity and interpersonal attraction', *Journal of Personality and Social Psychology* (1988), vol. 54(5), pp. 789–97.

26 Montoya, R. M., Horton, R. S., & Kirchner, J., 'Is actual similarity necessary for attraction? A meta-analysis of actual and perceived similarity', *Journal of Social and Personal Relationships* (2008), vol. 25, pp. 889–922.

27 Davis, J. L., & Rusbult, C. E., 'Attitude alignment in close relationships', *Journal of Personality and Social Psychology* (2001), vol. 81, pp. 65–84.

28 Botwin, M. D., Buss, D. M., & Shackelford, T., 'Personality and mate preferences: Five factors in mate selection and marital satisfaction', *Journal of Personality* (1997), vol. 65, pp. 107–36.

29 Buss, D. M., 'Human Mate Selection: Opposites are sometimes said to attract, but in fact we are likely to marry someone who is similar to us in almost every variable', *American Scientist* (1985), vol. 73(1), pp. 47–51.

10: Body language that attracts

1 Honzel, N. & Kelly, S., 'Emotional states influence the neural processing of affective language', *Social Neuroscience* (2008), vol. 3., pp. 434–42. 10.1080/17470910802188339

2 Reis, H. T., Mcdougal Wilson, I., Monestere, C., Bernstein, S., Clark, K., Seidl, E., Franco, M., Gioioso, E., Freeman, L., & Radoane, K., 'What is smiling is beautiful and good', *European Journal of Social Psychology* (1990), vol. 20(3), pp. 259–67.

3 Dipboye, R. L., & Wiley, J. W., 'Reactions of college recruiters to interviewee sex and self-presentation style', *Journal of Vocational Behavior* (1977), vol. 10(1), pp. 1–12.

4 Riggio, R. E., & Friedman, H. S., 'Impression formation: The role of expressive behavior', *Journal of Personality and Social Psychology* (1986), vol. 50(2), pp. 421–7.

5 Westen, D., *The Political Brain: The role of emotion in deciding the fate of the nation* (New York: PublicAffairs, 2007).

6 Ambady N., Laplante D., Nguyen T., Rosenthal R., Chaumeton N., Levinson W., 'Surgeons' tone of voice: a clue to malpractice history', *Surgery*, vol. 132(1), pp. 5-9. Barnes, S., Brown, K. W., Krusemark, E., Campbell, W. K., & Rogge, R. D., 'The role of mindfulness in romantic relationship satisfaction and responses to relationship stress', *Journal of Marital and Family Therapy* (2007), vol. 33(4), pp. 482-500.

7 Ambady N., Laplante D., Nguyen T., Rosenthal R., Chaumeton N., Levinson W., 'Surgeons' tone of voice: a clue to malpractice history', *Surgery*, vol. 132(1), pp. 5-9.

8 Janz, P., Pepping, C. A., & Halford, W. K., 'Individual differences in dispositional mindfulness and initial attraction: A speed dating experiment', *Personality and Individual Differences* (2015), vol. 82, pp. 14-19.

9 Donald, J., Atkins, P. W., Parker, P., Christie, A. M., Ryan, R. M., 'Daily stress and the benefits of mindfulness: Examining the daily and longitudinal relations between present-moment awareness and stress responses', *Journal of Research in Personality* (2016), p.65. Remmers, C., Topolinski, S., & Koole, S. L., 'Why being mindful may have more benefits than you realize: Mindfulness improves both explicit and implicit mood regulation', *Mindfulness* (2016), vol. 7(4), pp. 829-37.

11: Pumping up your charisma

1 Friedman, H. S., Riggio, R. E., & Casella, D. F., 'Nonverbal Skill, Personal Charisma, and Initial Attraction', *Personality and Social Psychology Bulletin* (1988), vol. 14(1), pp. 203-11.

2 Koppensteiner, M., & Grammer, M., 'Motion patterns in political speech and their influence on personality ratings', *Journal of Research in Personality* (2010), vol. 44, pp. 374-9.

12: In touch

1 Crusco, A. H., & Wetzel, C. G., 'The Midas Touch: The effects of interpersonal touch on restaurant tipping', *Personality and Social*

Psychology Bulletin (1984), vol. 10(4), pp. 512–17. Zak, P. J., Stanton, A. A., & Ahmadi, S., 'Oxytocin increases generosity in humans', *PloS one* (2007), vol. 2(11), e1128.

2   Linden, D. J., *Touch: The Science of Hand, Heart, and Mind* (Viking, 2015).

PART III: DATING

13: Booking the next date

1   Ahola, A. *Dina dolda drivkrafter* (*Your Hidden Motives*) (Roos & Tegner, 2020).
2   Moreland, R. L., & Zajonc, R., 'Exposure Effects in Person Perception: Familiarity, Similarity, and Attraction', *Journal of Experimental Social Psychology* (1982), vol. 18, pp. 395–415.

15: When words are not enough

1   North, A., *Text Chemistry*, independently published (2019).
2   Ibid

16: Communication in the early dating stage

1   Riordan, M. A., & Kreuz, R. J., 'Emotion encoding and interpretation in computer mediated communication: Reasons for use', *Computers in Human Behavior* (2010b), vol. 26, pp. 1667–73.
2   Kennedy, P., 'Who made that emoticon?', *The New York Times* (23 November 2012). Retrieved from www.nytimes.com/2012/11/25/magazine/who-made-that-emoticon.html.
3   Derks, D., Bos, A. E. R., & von Grumbkow, J., 'Emoticons and online message interpretation', *Social Science Computer Review* (2008), vol. 26, pp. 379–88. Skovholt, K., Gronning, A., & Kankaanranta, A., 'The communicative functions of emoticons in workplace e-mails::-)', *Journal of Computer-Mediated Communication* (2014), vol. 19, pp. 780–97.
4   Skovholt, K., Gronning, A., & Kankaanranta, A., 'The communicative

functions of emoticons in workplace e-mails::-)', *Journal of Computer-Mediated Communication* (2014), vol. 19, pp. 780–97.

5   Luor, T. T., Wu, L., Lu, H-P., & Tao, Y.-H., 'The effect of emoticons in simplex and complex task-oriented communication: An empirical study of instant messaging', *Computers in Human Behavior* (2010), vol. 26, 5, pp. 889–95.

6   Provine, R. R., Spencer, R. J., & Mandell, D. L., 'Emotional expression online: Emoticons punctuate website text messages', *Journal of Language and Social Psychology* (2007), vol. 26, pp. 299–307. Rezabek, L. L., & Cochenour, J. J., 'Visual cues in computer-mediated communication: Supplementing text with emoticons', *Journal of Visual Literacy* (1998), vol. 18, pp. 210–15.

7   Sarkar, T., Shetty, N., & Humstoe, M. K., 'Emoticons and emotions: Contextual interpretation in text messages and consensus of meaning', *Learning Curve* (2014), vol. 3, pp. 24–33.

8   Kelly, R., & Watts, L., 'Characterizing the inventive appropriation of emoji as relationally meaningful in mediated close personal relationships' (2015). Retrieved from https://projects. hci.sbg.ac.at/ ecscw2015/wp-content/uploads/sites/31/2015/08/Kelly_Watts.pdf.

9   Sugiyama, A., 'Kawaii meiru and Maroyaka neko: Mobile emoji for relationship maintenance and aesthetic expressions among Japanese teens', *First Monday* (2015), 20. Retrieved from http://firstmonday. org/ojs/index.php/fm/article/view/5826/4997.

10 Kelly, R., & Watts, L., 'Characterizing the inventive appropriation of emoji as relationally meaningful in mediated close personal relationships' (2015). Retrieved from https://projects.hci.sbg. ac.at/ecscw2015/wp-content/uploads/sites/31/2015/08/Kelly_ Watts.pdf.

11 Carey, J., 'Paralanguage in computer-mediated communication', N. K. Sondheimer (ed.), *The 18th annual meeting of the Association for Computational Linguistics and parasession on topics in interactive discourse: Proceedings of the conference* (Philadelphia: University of Pennsylvania, 1980, pp. 67–9). Harris, R. B., & Paradice, D., 'An investigation of the computer-mediated communication of emotion', *Journal of Applied Sciences Research* (2007), vol. 3, pp. 2081–90.

12 Yuasa, M., et al. 'Brain activity when reading sentences and emoticons: an fMRI study of verbal and nonverbal communication', *Electron. Commun. Jpn* (2011), vol. 94, pp. 17–24.

17: How *could* you!?

1 Novak, J. R., Sandberg, J. G., Jeffrey, A. J., & Young-Davis, S., 'The Impact of Texting on Perceptions of Face-to-Face Communication in Couples in Different Relationship Stages', *Journal of Couple & Relationship Therapy* (2016), vol. 15(4), pp. 274–94.

2 Schade, L. C., Sandberg, J., Bean, R., Busby, D., & Coyne, S., 'Using Technology to Connect in Romantic Relationships: Effects on Attachment, Relationship Satisfaction, and Stability in Emerging Adults', *Journal of Couple & Relationship Therapy* (2013), vol. 12(4), pp. 314–38.

3 Bowlby, J., *Attachment and loss: Vol. 2. Separation: Anxiety and anger* (New York, NY: Basic Books, 1973). Johnson, S. M., *The practice of emotionally focused couple therapy: Creating connection* (New York, NY: Brunner-Routledge, 2004, 2nd edn). Sandberg, J. G., Busby, D. M., Johnson, S. M., & Yoshida, K., 'The Brief Accessibility, Responsiveness, and Engagement (BARE) Scale: A tool for measuring attachment behavior in couple relationships', *Family Process* (2012), vol. 51(4), pp. 512–26.

4 Gottman, J., & Silver, N., *The Seven Principles for Making Marriage Work*. (Three Rivers Press, 1999).

5 Ahola, A. *Dina dolda drivkrafter* (*Your Hidden Motives*) (Roos & Tegner, 2020).

6 Hatfield, E., & Sprecher, S., 'Measuring passionate love in intimate relationships', *Journal of Adolescence* (1986), 9(4). Sternberg, R. J., 'Construct validation of a triangular love scale', European Journal of Social Psychology (1997), vol. 27(3), pp. 313–35.

19: Friend-zoned or ghosted – which sucks worse?

1 Pawlowski, B., & Sorokowski, P., 'Men's Attraction to Women's Bodies Changes Seasonally', *Perception* (2008), vol. 37(7), pp. 1079–85. Svartberg, J., Jorde, R., Sundsfjord, J., Bønaa, K. H., & Barrett-Connor, E. J., 'Seasonal variation of testosterone and waist to hip ratio in men: the Tromsø study', *Clinical Endocrinol Metab* (2003), vol. 88(7), pp. 3099–3104. REMOVED

2 Lambert, G. W., Reid, C., Kaye, D. M., Jennings, G. L., Esler, M. D., 'Effect of sunlight and season on serotonin turnover in the brain', *The Lancet* (2002), vol. 360, 9348(7), pp. 1840–42.

3 Hong, J., & Sun, Y., 'Warm It Up with Love: The Effect of Physical Coldness on Liking of Romance Movies', *Journal of Consumer Research* (2012), vol. 39(2), pp. 293–306.

4 Markowitz, D. M., Hancock, J. T., 'Deception in Mobile Dating Conversations', *Journal of Communication* (2018), vol. 68(3), pp. 547–69. Kristi Dosh, 'The 10 Most Common Lies in Online Dating Profiles', *Woman's Day* (2012). www.womansday.com/relationships/dating-marriage/advice/a6759/online-dating-profile-lies. Hancock, J. T., Toma, C., & Ellison, N., 'The truth about lying in online dating profiles', Proceedings of the SIGCHI Conference on Human Factors in Computing Systems (CHI 07) (2007). Association for Computing Machinery, New York, NY, pp. 449–52.

5 Lanquist, Lindsey. '4 In 5 Young Single People Have Been Ghosted' (2016). self.com/story/4-in-5-young-single-people-have-been-ghosted

6 Facebook newsroom, 'Messages Matter: Exploring the Evolution of Conversation' (2017). https://about.fb.com/news/2017/11/messages-matter-exploring-the-evolution-of-conversation/

7 Molloy, K., Griffiths, T. D., Chait, M., Lavie, N., 'Inattentional Deafness: Visual Load Leads to Time-Specific Suppression of Auditory Evoked Responses', *Journal of Neuroscience* (2015), vol. 35 (49), pp. 16046–54.

20: Wanting what we can't have

1 Ahola, A. *Dina dolda drivkrafter* (*Your Hidden Motives*) (Roos & Tegner, 2020).

PART IV: RELATIONSHIPS

21: Your relationship toolkit

1 Josefsson, D. & Linge, E., *Hemligheten. Från ögonkast till varaktig relation* (Natur & Kultur, 2008).

2 Josefsson, D. & Linge, E., *Hemligheten. Från ögonkast till varaktig relation* (Natur & Kultur, 2008).

3 Levine, A., Heller, R. S. F., *Attached: The new science of adult attachment*

and how it can help you find and keep love (New York: Jeremy P. Tarcher/Penguin, 2011).

4 Shaver, P. R., & Mikulincer, M., 'Attachment-related Psychodynamics', *Attachment and Human Development* (2000), vol. 4, pp. 133–61.

5 Shaver, P. R., & Mikulincer, M., 'Attachment-related Psychodynamics', *Attachment and Human Development* (2000), vol. 4, pp. 133–61.

6 Levine, A., Heller, R. S. F., *Attached: The new science of adult attachment and how it can help you find and keep love* (New York: Jeremy P. Tarcher/Penguin, 2011).

7 Levine, A., Heller, R. S. F., *Attached: The new science of adult attachment and how it can help you find and keep love* (New York: Jeremy P. Tarcher/Penguin, 2011).

8 Gilliath, O., Shaver, P. R., Baek, J. M., and Chun, S. D., 'Genetic Correlates of Adult Attachment Style', *Personality and Social Psychology Bulletin* (2008), vol. 34, pp. 1396–1405.

9 Levine, A., Heller, R. S. F., *Attached: The new science of adult attachment and how it can help you find and keep love* (New York: Jeremy P. Tarcher/Penguin, 2011).

10 Levine, A., Heller, R. S. F., *Attached: The new science of adult attachment and how it can help you find and keep love* (New York: Jeremy P. Tarcher/Penguin, 2011).

11 Pietromonaco, P. R., & Carnelley, K. B., (1994). Gender and working models of attachment: Consequences for perceptions of self and romantic relationships, vol. 1:1, pp. 63–82.

22: You and I – forever and ever

1 Sheets, V. L., 'Passion for life: Self-expansion and passionate love across the life span', *Journal of Social and Personal Relationships* (2014), vol. 31(7), pp. 958–74.

2 Lyubomirsky, S., *The Myths of Happiness: What Should Make You Happy, but Doesn't, What Shouldn't Make You Happy but Does* (New York: The Penguin Press, 2013).

3 Hatfield, E., & Rapson, R. L., *Love, sex, and intimacy: Their psychology, biology, and history.* (HarperCollins College Publishers, 1993).

4 Hatfield, E., & Rapson, R. L., *Love, sex, and intimacy: Their psychology, biology, and history.* (HarperCollins College Publishers, 1993).

5   Baumeister, R.F., Bratslavsky, E. (1999) Passion, Intimacy, and Time: Passionate Love as a Function of Change in Intimacy. *Personality and Social Psychology Review*. 3(1):49-67.

6   Hatfield, E., & Rapson, R. L., *Love, sex, and intimacy: Their psychology, biology, and history*. (HarperCollins College Publishers, 1993).

7   Grote, N. K., Hanson Frieze, I., 'The measurement of friendship-based love in intimate relationships', *Personal Relationships* (1994), vol. 1(3), pp. 275–300.

8   Hatfield, E., Bensman, L., & Rapson, R. L., 'A brief history of social scientists' attempts to measure passionate love', *Journal of Social and Personal Relationships* (2012), vol. 29(2), pp. 143–64. Hatfield, E., & Sprecher, S., 'Measuring passionate love in intimate relationships', *Journal of Adolescence* (1986), vol. 9(4), pp. 383–410. Sternberg, R. J., 'Construct validation of a triangular love scale', *European Journal of Social Psychology* (1997), vol. 27(3), pp. 313–35.

23: Passion: from tragic to magic

1   Sassler, S., Addo, F. R., & Lichter, D. T., 'The tempo of sexual activity and later relationship quality', *Journal of Marriage and Family* (2012), vol. 74(4), pp. 708–25.

2   Acevedo, B. P., & Aron, A., 'Does a Long-Term Relationship Kill Romantic Love?', *Review of General Psychology* (2009), vol. 13(1), pp. 59–65.

3   Lyubomirsky, S., *The Myths of Happiness: What Should Make You Happy, but Doesn't, What Shouldn't Make You Happy but Does* (New York: The Penguin Press, 2013). Aron, A., Norman, C., Aron, E., McKenna, C., & Heyman, R., 'Couples' shared participation in novel and arousing activities and experienced relationship quality', *Journal of Personality and Social Psychology* (2000), vol. 78, pp. 273–84.

4   Reissman, C., Aron, A., & Bergen, M. R., 'Shared Activities and Marital Satisfaction: Causal Direction and Self-Expansion versus Boredom', *Journal of Social and Personal Relationships* (1993), vol. 10(2), pp. 243–54.

5   Tsapelas, I., Aron, A., & Orbuch, T., 'Marital boredom now predicts less satisfaction 9 years later', *Psychological Science* (2009), vol. 20(5), pp. 543–5.

6   O'Leary, K. D., Acevedo, B., Aron, A., Huddy, L., & Mashek, D., 'Is Long-Term Love More than a Rare Phenomenon? If So, What are Its

Correlates?', *Social Psychological and Personality Science* (2012), vol. 3, pp. 241–9.

7   Acevedo, B., Aron, A., Fisher, H., & Brown, L., 'Neural correlates of marital satisfaction and well-being: Reward, empathy, and affect', *Clinical Neuropsychiatry* (2012), vol. 9.

8   Perel, E., *Lust* (Brombergs, (2018).

9   Paniccia, L.. (2011). Self-Expansion and Couple Possessions: The Representation of The Self and Other in Valued Possessions. Thesis. Indiana State University.

10 Graham, J. M., 'Self-expansion and flow in couples' momentary experiences: An experience sampling study', *Journal of Personality and Social Psychology* (2008), vol. 95(3), pp. 679–94.

11 Aron, A., Norman, C., Aron, E., McKenna, C., & Heyman, R., 'Couples' shared participation in novel and arousing activities and experienced relationship quality', *Journal of Personality and Social Psychology* (2000), vol. 78, pp. 273–84.

12 Jowett, S., Lafrenière, M.-A. K., & Vallerand, R. J. (2012). Passion for activities and relationship quality: A dyadic approach', *Journal of Social and Personal Relationships*, vol. 30(6), pp. 734–49.

13 Philippe, F., Vallerand, R., & Lavigne, G., 'Passion Does Make a Difference in People's Lives: A Look at Well-Being in Passionate and Non-Passionate Individuals', *Applied Psychology: Health and Well-Being* (2009).

14 Botton, A. (2016). *Why You Will Marry the Wrong Person*. The School of Life. London.

15 Boszormenyi-Nagy, I., & Spark, G. M., *Invisible Loyalties: Reciprocity in intergenerational family therapy* (Harper & Row, 1973).

16 Marist Poll survey '2/10: "It's Destiny!" Most Americans Believe in Soul Mates' (2011). maristpoll.marist.edu/polls/210-its-destiny-most-americans-believe-in-soul-mates/

17 Eidelson, R. J., & Epstein, N. (1981). 'Cognition and relationship maladjustment: Development of a measure of dysfunctional relationship beliefs', *Journal of Consulting and Clinical Psychology* (1982), vol. 50, pp. 15–20. Epstein, N., & Eidelson, R. J., 'Unrealistic beliefs of clinical couples: Their relationship to expectations, goals and satisfaction', *American Journal of Family Therapy*, vol. 9, pp. 13–22.

18 Franiuk, R., Cohen, D., & Pomerantz, E. M., 'Implicit theories of relationships: Implications for relationship satisfaction and longevity', *Personal Relationships* (2002), vol. 9, pp. 345–67. Franiuk, R., Pomerantz, E. M., & Cohen, D., 'The causal role of theories of relationships:

Consequences for satisfaction and cognitive strategies', *Personality and Social Psychology Bulletin* (2004), vol. 30, pp. 1494–1507.

19   Finkel, E. J., Burnette, J. L., & Scissors, L. E., 'Vengefully ever after: Destiny beliefs, state attachment anxiety, and forgiveness', *Journal of Personality and Social Psychology* (2007), vol. 92, pp. 871–86.

20   Blackburn, E., & Epel, E., *The Telomere Effect: A Revolutionary Approach to Living Younger, Healthier, Longer* (Orion Spring, 2018).

24:   Be an optimist – or at least find an optimist

1   Srivastava, S., Richards, J. M., McGonigal, K. M., & Butler, E.A., 'Optimism in Close Relationships: How Seeing Things in a Positive Light Makes Them So', *Journal of Personality and Social Psychology* (2006), vol. 91(1), pp. 143–53.

2   Murray, S. L., & Holmes, J. G., 'A Leap of Faith? Positive Illusions in Romantic Relationships', *Personality and Social Psychology Bulletin* (1997), vol. 23(6), pp. 586–604.

3   Scheier, M. F., Carver, C. S., & Bridges, M. W., 'Optimism, pessimism, and psychological well-being', E. C. Chang (ed.), *Optimism & pessimism: Implications for theory, research, and practice* (2001; pp. 189–216). American Psychological Association.

4   Scheier, M. F., & Carver, C. S., 'Optimism, coping, and health: Assessment and implications of generalized outcome expectancies', *Health Psychology* (1985), vol. 4(3), pp. 219–47.

5   Geers, A. L., Reilley, S. P., & Dember, W. N., 'Optimism, pessimism, and friendship', *Current Psychology: A Journal for Diverse Perspectives on Diverse Psychological Issues* (1998), vol. 17(1), pp. 3–19.

6   Carver, C. S., Kus, L. A., & Scheier, M. F., 'Effects of Good Versus Bad Mood and Optimistic Versus Pessimistic Outlook on Social Acceptance Versus Rejection', *Journal of Social and Clinical Psychology* (1994), vol. 13(2), pp. 138–51.

7   Scheier, M. F., & Carver, C. S., 'Optimism, coping, and health: Assessment and implications of generalized outcome expectancies', *Health Psychology* (1985), vol. 4(3), pp. 219–47.

8   Murray. S. L., & Holmes, J. G., 'A leap of faith? Positive illusions in romantic relationships', *PSPB* (1997), vol. 23(6), pp. 586–604.

9   Diener, E., & Biswas-Diener, R., *Happiness* (Blackwell Publishing, 2016).

10   Danner, D. D., Snowdon, D. A., Friesen W. V. 'Positive emotions in

early life and longevity: findings from the nun study', *Journal of Personality and Social Psychology* (2001), vol. 80(5), pp. 804–13.

11 Diener, E., & Biswas-Diener, R., *Happiness* (Blackwell Publishing, 2016).

12 Dolan, P., *Happiness by design* (2015).

13 Suss, J., 'Five minutes with Paul Dolan: "Happiness is experiences of pleasure and purpose over time"', *LSE blog* (2014). https://blogs.lse.ac.uk/europpblog/2014/08/30/five-minutes-with-paul-dolan-happiness-is-experiences-of-pleasure-and-purpose-over-time/

25: Compliments, criticism and saying *I'm sorry*

1 Doohan, E.-A. M., & Manusov, V., 'The Communication of Compliments in Romantic Relationships', *Western Journal of Communication* (2004), vol. 68(2), p. 170.

2 Dijkstra, P., Barelds, D. P. H., Groothof, H. A. K., & van Bruggen, M., 'Empathy in intimate relationships: The role of positive illusions', *Scandinavian Journal of Psychology* (2014), vol. 55, pp. 477–82.

3 Stocks, E. L., Lishner, D. A., Waits, B. L., & Downum, E. M., 'I'm embarrassed for you: The effect of valuing and perspective taking on empathic embarrassment and empathic concern', *Journal of Applied Social Psychology* (2011), vol. 41(1), pp. 1–26.

4 Stocks, E. L., Lishner, D. A., & Decker, S. K., 'Altruism or psychological escape: Why does empathy promote prosocial behavior?', *European Journal of Social Psychology* (2009), vol. 39(5), pp. 649–65.

5 Lishner, D. A., Batson, C. D., & Huss, E., 'Tenderness and Sympathy: Distinct Empathic Emotions Elicited by Different Forms of Need', *Personality and Social Psychology Bulletin* (2011), vol. 37(5), pp. 614–25.

6 McComb, K., Baker L., & Moss, C., 'African elephants show high levels of interest in the skulls and ivory of their own species', *The Royal Society Publishing* (2005). https://royalsocietypublishing.org/doi/10.1098/rsbl.2005.0400

7 Rostowski, J., 'Selected aspects of the neuropsychology of love', *Acta Neuropsychologica* (2009), vol. 7, pp. 225–48.

8 Rostowski, J., 'Selected aspects of the neuropsychology of love', *Acta Neuropsychologica* (2009), vol. 7, pp. 225–48.

9 Doohan, E.-A. M., & Manusov, V., 'The Communication of Compliments in Romantic Relationships', *Western Journal of Communication* (2004), vol. 68(2), p. 170.

10 'Benjamin Franklin and cognitive dissonance', Utforska Sinnet (2018) utforskasinnet.se/ben-franklin-effekten-dissonans

11 Flora, J., & Segrin, C., 'Affect and Behavioral Involvement in Spousal Complaints and Compliments', *Journal of Family Psychology* by the American Psychological Association (2000), vol. 14, no. 4, pp. 641–57.

12 Clements, M. L., Cordova, A. D., Markman, H. J., & Laurenceau, J.-P., 'The erosion of marital satisfaction over time and how to prevent it', R. J. Sternberg & M. Hojjat (eds.), *Satisfaction in close relationships* (Guilford Press, 1997), pp. 335–55.

13 Gottman J. M., Coan, J., Carrère, S., & Swanson, C., 'Predicting marital happiness and stability from newlywed interactions', *Journal of Marriage and the Family* (1998), vol. 60, pp. 5–22.

14 Gottman, J. M., & Krokoff, L. J., 'Marital interaction and satisfaction: A longitudinal view', *Journal of Consulting and Clinical Psychology* (1989), vol. 57(1), pp. 47–52.

15 Gottman J. M., Coan, J., Carrère, S., & Swanson, C., 'Predicting marital happiness and stability from newlywed interactions', *Journal of Marriage and the Family* (1998), vol. 60, pp. 5–22.

16 Stafford, L., & Canary, D. J., 'Maintenance strategies and romantic relationship type, gender and relational characteristics', *Journal of Social and Personal Relationships* (1991), vol. 8(2), pp. 217–42.

17 Beier, E. G., & Sternberg, D. P., 'Marital communication', *Journal of Communication* (1977), vol. 27(3), pp. 92–7.

18 Coker, D. A., & Burgoon, J. K., 'The nature of conversational involvement and nonverbal encoding patterns', *Human Communication Research* (1987), vol. 13(4), pp. 463–94.

19 Fehr, B. J., & Exline, R. V., 'Social visual interaction: A conceptual and literature review', in A. W. Siegman & S. Feldstein (eds.), *Nonverbal behavior and communication* (Lawrence Erlbaum Associates, Inc., 1987), pp. 225–325.

20 Lewandowski, G. W. Jr., Mattingly, B. M., & Pedeiro, A., 'Under Pressure: The Effects of Stress on Positive and Negative Relationship Behaviors', *The Journal of Social Psychology* (2014), vol. 154, pp. 463–73.

21 Buck, A., & Neff, L., 'Stress Spillover in Early Marriage: The Role of Self-Regulatory Depletion', *Journal of Family Psychology: JFP. Journal of the Division of Family Psychology of the American Psychological Association*, Division 43 (2012), vol. 26, pp. 698–708.

22 Ledermann, T., Bodenmann, G., Rudaz, M., & Bradbury, T., 'Stress, Communication, and Marital Quality in Couples', *Family Relations* (2010). 59.

23 Neff, L., & Karney, B., 'Stress and Reactivity to Daily Relationship Experiences: How Stress Hinders Adaptive Processes in Marriage', *Journal of Personality and Social Psychology* (2009), vol. 97, pp. 435–50.

24 Machia, L., & Lewandowski, G. Jr., & Agnew, C., 'Reduced self-expansion in current romance and interest in relationship alternatives', *Journal of Social and Personal Relationships* (2011), vol. 28, pp. 356–73. Machia, L., Lehmiller, J., & Kelly, J., 'Commitment in Friends with Benefits Relationships: Implications for relational and safe-sex outcomes', *Personal Relationships* (2012). 19.

25 Fenell, D., 'Characteristics of long-term first marriages', *Journal of Mental Health Counseling* (1993), vol. 15, pp. 446–60.

26 Risen, J. L., & Gilovich, T., 'Target and observer differences in the acceptance of questionable apologies', *Journal of Personality and Social Psychology* (2007), vol. 92(3), pp. 418–33. Tomlinson, E. C., Dineen, B. R., & Lewicki, R. J., 'The Road to Reconciliation: Antecedents of Victim Willingness to Reconcile Following a Broken Promise', *Journal of Management* (2004), vol. 30(2), pp. 165–87. Zechmeister, J. S., Garcia, S., Romero, C., Vas, S. N., 'Don't Apologize Unless You Mean It: A Laboratory Investigation of Forgiveness and Retaliation', *Journal of Social and Clinical Psychology* (2004), vol. 23(4), pp. 532–64.

27 Schumann, K., 'Does love mean never having to say you're sorry? Associations between relationship satisfaction, perceived apology sincerity, and forgiveness', *Journal of Social and Personal Relationships* (2012), vol. 29(7), pp. 997–1010.

28 Finkel, E. J., Rusbult, C. E., Kumashiro, M., & Hannon, P. A., 'Dealing with betrayal in close relationships: Does commitment promote forgiveness?', *Journal of Personality and Social Psychology* (2002), vol. 82(6), pp. 956–74.

29 Allemand, M., Zimprich, D., & Hendriks, J., 'Age Differences in Five Personality Domains Across the Life Span', *Developmental Psychology* (2008), vol. 44, pp. 758–70.

30 Struthers, C. W., Eaton, J., Santelli, A. G., Uchiyama, M., & Shirvani, N., 'The effects of attributions of intent and apology on forgiveness: When saying sorry may not help the story', *Journal of Experimental Social Psychology* (2008), vol. 44(4), pp. 983–92.

31 Zechmeister, J. S., Garcia, S., Romero, C., Vas, S. N., 'Don't Apologize Unless You Mean It: A Laboratory Investigation of Forgiveness and Retaliation', *Journal of Social and Clinical Psychology* (2004), vol. 23(4), pp. 532–64.

32 Scher, S. J., & Darley, J. M., 'How effective are the things people say to apologize? Effects of the realization of the apology speech act', *Journal of Psycholinguistic Research* (1997), vol. 26(1), pp. 127–40.

26: How to fight right

1 Gottman, J. M., *What Predicts Divorce? The relationship between marital processes and marital outcomes* (Hillsdale, NJ: Erlbaum, 1994).

2 Perel, E., *Mating in Captivity: Reconciling the erotic and the domestic* (New York: HarperCollins, 2006).

3 Gottman, J. M., & Levenson, M. W., 'The timing of divorce: Predicting when a couple will divorce over a 14-year period', *Journal of Marriage and Family* (2004), vol. 62:3.

4 Busby, D. M., Holman, T. B., & Taniguchi, N., 'RELATE: Relationship Evaluation of the Individual, Family, Cultural, and Couple Contexts', *Family Relations* (2001), vol. 50(4), pp. 308–16.

5 Holman, T. B., Busby, D. M., Doxey, C., Klein, D. M., & Loyer-Carlson, V., *The Relationship Evaluation (RELATE)* (Provo, UT: RELATE Institute, 1997).

6 Holman, T. B., Busby, D. M., Doxey, C., Klein, D. M., & Loyer-Carlson, V., *The Relationship Evaluation (RELATE)* (Provo, UT: RELATE Institute, 1997).

7 Holman, T. B., Busby, D. M., Doxey, C., Klein, D. M., & Loyer-Carlson, V., *The Relationship Evaluation (RELATE)* (Provo, UT: RELATE Institute, 1997).

8 Buehlman, K., Gottman, J., & Katz, L., 'How a Couple Views Their Past Predicts Their Future: Predicting Divorce from an Oral History Interview', *Journal of Family Psychology* (1970).

9 Holman, T. B., Busby, D. M., Doxey, C., Klein, D. M., & Loyer-Carlson, V., *The Relationship Evaluation (RELATE)* (Provo, UT: RELATE Institute, 1997).

10 Holman, T. B., Busby, D. M., Doxey, C., Klein, D. M., & Loyer-Carlson, V., *The Relationship Evaluation (RELATE)* (Provo, UT: RELATE Institute, 1997).

11 Buehlman, K., Gottman, J., & Katz, L., 'How a Couple Views Their Past Predicts Their Future: Predicting Divorce from an Oral History Interview', *Journal of Family Psychology* (1970).

12 Buehlman, K., Gottman, J., & Katz, L., 'How a Couple Views Their Past Predicts Their Future: Predicting Divorce from an Oral History Interview', *Journal of Family Psychology* (1992), vol. 5 (3 & 4), pp. 295–318.

13 Buehlman, K., Gottman, J., & Katz, L., 'How a Couple Views Their Past Predicts Their Future: Predicting Divorce from an Oral History Interview', *Journal of Family Psychology* (1970).

27: Love *should* be blind – at least a wee bit

1 Holmes, J. G., & Boon, S. D., 'Developments in the field of close relationships: Creating foundations for intervention strategies', *Personality and Social Psychology Bulletin* (1990), vol. 16(1), pp. 23–41.

2 Huston, T. L., & Houts, R. M., 'The psychological infrastructure of courtship and marriage: The role of personality and compatibility in romantic relationships', in T. N. Bradbury (ed.), *The developmental course of marital dysfunction* (Cambridge University Press, 1998), pp. 114–51.

3 Murray, S. L., & Holmes, J. G., 'A leap of faith? Positive illusions in romantic relationships', *Personality and Social Psychology Bulletin* (1997), vol. 23, pp. 586–604.

4 Murray, S. L., & Holmes, J. G., 'A leap of faith? Positive illusions in romantic relationships', *Personality and Social Psychology Bulletin* (1997), vol. 23, pp. 586–604.

5 Carrére, S., Buehlman, K., Gottman, J., Coan, J., & Ruckstuhl, L., 'Predicting marital stability and divorce in newlywed couples', *Journal of Family Psychology: JFP: Journal of the Division of Family Psychology of the American Psychological Association*, Division 43 (2000), vol. 14, pp. 42–58.

6 Swami, V., Furnham, A., Georgiades, C., & Pang, L., 'Evaluating self and partner physical attractiveness', *Body Image* (2007), vol. 4, pp. 97–101.

7 Barelds, D. P. H., & Dijkstra, P., 'Positive illusions about a partner's physical attractiveness and relationship quality', *Personal Relationships* (2009), vol. 16, pp. 263–83.

8 O'Leary, K. D., Acevedo, B. P., Aron, A., Huddy, L., & Mashek, D., 'Is

Long-Term Love More Than A Rare Phenomenon? If So, What Are Its Correlates?', *Social Psychological and Personality Science* (2012), vol. 3(2), pp. 241–9.

9 O'Leary, K. D., Acevedo, B. P., Aron, A., Huddy, L., & Mashek, D., 'Is Long-Term Love More Than A Rare Phenomenon? If So, What Are Its Correlates?', *Social Psychological and Personality Science* (2012), vol. 3(2), pp. 241–9. Krauss Whitbourne, S., 'Love from Afar: Staying Close While You Live Apart', *Psychology Today* (2012), www. psychologytoday.com/us/blog/fulfillment-any-age/201210/love-afar-staying-close-while-you-live-apart

10 Bazzini, D. G., Stack, E. R., Martincin, P. D., & Davis, C. P., 'The effect of reminiscing about laughter on relationship satisfaction', *Motivation and Emotion* (2007), vol. 31, pp. 25–34.

11 Lenger, K. A., & Gordon, C. L., 'To have and to savor: Examining the associations between savoring and relationship satisfaction', *Couple and Family Psychology: Research and Practice* (2019), 8(1), pp. 1–9.

12 O'Leary, K. D., Acevedo, B. P., Aron, A., Huddy, L., & Mashek, D., 'Is Long-Term Love More Than A Rare Phenomenon? If So, What Are Its Correlates?', *Social Psychological and Personality Science* (2012), vol. 3(2), pp. 241–9.

13 Ibid.

14 Gable, S. L., Reis, H. T., Impett, E. A., & Asher, E. R., 'What Do You Do When Things Go Right? The Intrapersonal and Interpersonal Benefits of Sharing Positive Events', *Journal of Personality and Social Psychology* (2004), vol. 87, pp. 228–45.

15 Edenfield, J. L., Adams, K. S., & Briihl, D. S., 'Relationship maintenance strategy use by romantic attachment style', *North American Journal of Psychology* (2012), vol. 14, pp. 149–62.

16 Flora, J., & Segrin, C., 'Affect and behavioral involvement in spousal complaints and compliments', *Journal of Family Psychology* (2000), vol. 14(4), pp. 641–57.

17 Ibid

18 Algoe, S. B., Gable, S. L., & Maisel, N. C., 'It's the little things: Everyday gratitude as a booster shot for romantic relationships', *Personal Relationships* (2010), vol. 17, pp. 217–33.

19 Gordon, A. M., Impett, E. A., Kogan, A., Oveis, C., & Keltner, D., 'To have and to hold: Gratitude promotes relationship maintenance in intimate bonds', *Journal of Personality and Social Psychology* (2012), vol. 103(2), pp. 257–74.

20 Balzarini, R. N., Muise, A., Zoppolat, G., Di Bartolomeo, A., Rodrigues, D. L., Alonso-Ferres, M., & Slatcher, R. B., 'Love in the Time of Covid: Perceived partner responsiveness buffers people from lower relationship quality associated with COVID-related stressors. PsyArXiv, 16 May 2020. Web. (2020).

21 Maisel, N. C., Gable, S. L., & Strachman, A., 'Responsive behaviors in good times and in bad', *Personal Relationships* (2008), vol. 15(3), pp. 317–38.

22 MacIntosh, H. B., & Johnson, S., 'Emotionally Focused Therapy for Couples and Childhood Sexual Abuse Survivors', *Journal of Marital and Family Therapy* (2008), vol. 34, 3.

23 Aron, A., Melinat, E., Aron, E. N., Vallone, R. D., & Bator, R. J., 'The experimental generation of interpersonal closeness: A procedure and some preliminary findings', *Personality and Social Psychology Bulletin* (1997), vol. 23, pp. 363–77.

24 Edenfield, J. L., Adams, K. S., & Briihl, D. S., 'Relationship maintenance strategy use by romantic attachment style', *North American Journal of Psychology* (2012), vol. 14, pp. 149–62.

25 Mattingly, B., Clark, E., & Cahill, M., 'Approach and avoidance motivation as predictors of pro-relationship behaviors', *Personality and Individual Differences* (2012), vol. 52, pp. 21–5.

26 Brandau-Brown, F. E., & Ragsdale, J. D., 'Personal, moral, and structural commitment and the repair of marital relationships', *Southern Communication Journal* (2008), vol. 7 3, pp. 68–83.

27 Baxter, L. A., & Simon, E. P., 'Relationship Maintenance Strategies and Dialectical Contradictions in Personal Relationships', *Journal of Social and Personal Relationships* (1993), vol. 10(2), pp. 225–42.

28 Brandau-Brown, F. E., & Ragsdale, J. D., 'Personal, moral, and structural commitment and the repair of marital relationships', *Southern Communication Journal* (2008), vol. 7 3, pp. 68–83.

29 MacIntosh, H. B., & Johnson, S., 'Emotionally Focused Therapy for Couples and Childhood Sexual Abuse Survivors', *Journal of Marital and Family Therapy* (2008), vol. 34, 3.

30 Weigel, D. J., & Ballard-Reisch, D. S., 'How couples maintain marriages: A closer look at self and spouse influences upon the use of maintenance behaviors in marriages', *Family Relations: An Interdisciplinary Journal of Applied Family Studies* (1999), vol. 48(3), pp. 263–69.

31 Brandau-Brown, F. E., & Ragsdale, J. D., 'Personal, moral, and structural commitment and the repair of marital relationships', *Southern*

Communication Journal (2008), vol. 73, pp. 68–83. Bello, R. S., Brandau-Brown, F. E., & Ragsdale, J. D., 'Attachment Style, Marital Satisfaction, Commitment, and Communal Strength Effects on Relational Repair Message Interpretation among Remarrieds', *Communication Quarterly* (2008), vol. 56:1, pp. 1–16. Canary, D., & Stafford, L., 'People Want – and Maintain – Fair Marriages: Reply to Ragsdale and Brandau-Brown', *The Journal of Family Communication* (2007), vol. 7:1, pp. 61–8.

32   Weigel, D. J., & Ballard-Reisch, D. S., 'How couples maintain marriages: A closer look at self and spouse influences upon the use of maintenance behaviors in marriages', *Family Relations: An Interdisciplinary Journal of Applied Family Studies* (1999), vol. 48(3), pp. 263–69.

33   Edenfield, J. L., Adams, K. S., & Briihl, D. S., 'Relationship maintenance strategy use by romantic attachment style', *North American Journal of Psychology* (2012), vol. 14, pp. 149–62.

34   Roberts, J. A., & David, M. E., 'My life has become a major distraction from my cell phone: Partner phubbing and relationship satisfaction among romantic partners', *Computers in Human Behavior* (2016), vol. 54, 1, pp. 34–41.

35   Luo, S., & Tuney, S., 'Can texting be used to improve romantic relationships? The effects of sending positive text messages on relationship satisfaction', *Computers in Human Behavior* (2015), vol. 49, pp. 670–8.

36   O'Leary, K. D., Acevedo, B. P., Aron, A., Huddy, L., & Mashek, D., 'Is Long-Term Love More Than A Rare Phenomenon? If So, What Are Its Correlates?', *Social Psychological and Personality Science* (2012), vol. 3(2), pp. 241–9.

37   Ibid

38   Ibid

39   Ibid. *This factor was primarily true for women, not men.*

40   Baumeister, R. F., Wotman, S. R., & Stillwell, A. M., 'Unrequited love: On heartbreak, anger, guilt, scriptlessness, and humiliation', *Journal of Personality and Social Psychology* (1993), vol. 64(3), pp. 377–94.